Democracy and Political Change in Sub-Saharan Africa

Since the end of the 1980s the most important political development in sub-Saharan Africa has been the move towards democracy, which has affected nearly all the countries in the region. Whilst changes in the global political environment have played a role, it has been the determination of peoples within the states concerned which has provided the main impetus for change.

This book will provide the student with a set of case studies, by an international group of contributors, covering a diverse range of African states in order to identify the major causes of recent change, the progress made so far and the prospects for the future. The case studies range from states like Nigeria and Uganda, where the transition to multi-partyism has not occurred, to those like Malawi, Mali and Zambia where a democratic change of government through the ballot has already taken place. Case studies of Côte d'Ivoire, Eritrea, Ethiopia and Ghana present a more ambivalent picture.

The development of democracy in sub-Saharan Africa has been extremely varied. This book will be an essential guide for those who wish to understand the nature and scope of the most recent changes.

John A. Wiseman is Senior Lecturer in Politics at the University of Newcastle upon Tyne.

Democracy and Political Change in Sub-Saharan Africa

WITHDRAWN

Edited by John A. Wiseman

London and New York

published 1995
Routledge
11 New Fetter Lane, London EC4P 4EE

Simultaneously published in the USA and Canada
by Routledge
29 West 35th Street, New York, NY 10001

© 1995 John A. Wiseman for the collection; the contributors for individual
chapters

Typeset in Times by LaserScript, Mitcham, Surrey
Printed and bound in Great Britain by
Biddles Ltd, Guildford and King's Lynn.

British Library Cataloguing in Publication Data
A catalogue record for this book is available from the British Library

Library of Congress Cataloging in Publication Data
A catalogue record for this book has been requested

ISBN 0–415–11301–6 (hbk)
ISBN 0–415–11302–4 (pbk)

This book is dedicated to the countless Africans who have struggled courageously, at all levels of society, to make democracy a reality on the continent.

Contents

Contributors

Christopher Clapham is Professor of Politics and International Relations, University of Lancaster.

Richard C. Crook is Senior Lecturer in Politics, University of Glasgow.

Holger Bernt Hansen is Director of the Centre for African Studies, University of Copenhagen.

Jeff Haynes is Senior Lecturer in Politics, London Guildhall University.

Julius Ihonvbere is Associate Professor of Politics, University of Texas at Austin.

Moctar Kone is Professor of Agricultural Extension, Institut Polytechnique Rural, Mali.

Michael Twaddle is Reader in Politics, Institute of Commonwealth Studies, University of London.

Jan Kees van Donge is Senior Lecturer in Public Administration, Chancellor College, University of Malawi.

Olufemi Vaughan is Assistant Professor of African Studies and History, State University of New York at Stony Brook.

Richard Vengroff is Dean of International Affairs, University of Connecticut.

Denis Venter is Executive Director of the Africa Institute of South Africa, Pretoria.

John A. Wiseman is Senior Lecturer in Politics, University of Newcastle upon Tyne.

Acknowledgements

Like many edited books this collection of essays had its point of origin at an academic conference; in this case the biennial conference of the African Studies Association of the UK (ASAUK) held at the University of Stirling in September 1992. I am grateful to John McCracken, the then President of ASAUK, for inviting me to organise a panel on the theme of 'The Road to Multi-party Democracy'. The interest in the panel was such that it proved necessary to extend it to two sessions and I am grateful to the conference organiser (and ASAUK Hon. Sec.) Nici Nelson who made all the arrangements in her customary cheerful and efficient manner. Those of us who have been connected with ASAUK for a lengthy period know well just how much we are all indebted to Nici for the contribution she has made to our efforts over many years.

Although the conference sessions provided the point of origin, the format of the book has changed considerably since then. In order to expand the range of the case studies it was necessary to recruit additional specialist scholars, and the final list of contributors contains only a minority who were involved with the original conference sessions. It goes without saying that I am grateful to all my contributors, and especially to those who were punctual in sending me their essays. Many of the contributors have been willing to undertake considerable revision of their essays, both to incorporate editorial suggestions and to reflect the rapidly changing situation in Africa. I think both Denis Venter and myself have now lost track of the number of times his contribution has been revised to take into account the developments which have taken place in Malawian politics over the past couple of years. Amongst my contributors I am especially indebted to Christopher Clapham, who not only provided his own essay on Ethiopia and Eritrea and co-authored the concluding essay, but also provided me with the benefits of his own experience of editing books. As a novice book editor I probably made less mistakes than I might otherwise have done because of his advice.

At Routledge Caroline Wintersgill has exemplified cheerful and rigorous competence at each stage in the development of the book.

As usual my wife and my four children have helped in ways that are not always easy to define.

John A. Wiseman
Newcastle upon Tyne

1 Introduction: the movement towards democracy

Global, continental and state perspectives

John A. Wiseman

Since the end of the 1980s the political systems of African states have undergone a quite remarkable and unprecedented transformation. At the beginning of 1989 there were just a handful of African states that were operating relatively democratic, competitive multi-party systems, whilst the majority were ruled by the authoritarianism of single-party and military regimes. In South Africa Nelson Mandela was still a political prisoner and anti-apartheid groups, such as the African National Congress (ANC), existed either underground or in exile. By the beginning of 1995 the political situation had changed dramatically. Multi-party systems, admittedly embodying varying levels of democratic credibility, were in place in the vast majority of African states. Military regimes remained in power in a handful of states but the fully fledged single-party state, a form which had dominated the post-independence period, was totally absent from the political map of Africa. In South Africa President Mandela presided over a government in which ANC members held a majority of ministerial portfolios following a democratic election which even the most cynical observers had found emotionally moving. Certainly, more negative examples of African politics were still observable in some states. In 1994 Rwanda had been the setting for the greatest human and political catastrophe of the post-independence period as genocidal conflict claimed perhaps as many as a million lives and left even greater numbers living in appalling conditions as refugees in neighbouring states. In a few other states, such as Angola, Somalia and Liberia, civil war prevented the formation of any semblance of national government.

However, although the picture was mixed nobody could deny that Africa as a whole had made substantial strides in the direction of democracy during this period. By 1995 the vast majority of African states had held genuinely competitive elections. In most cases these elections were the first for a very long time to involve opposition parties competing for the support of the voters: in a few states these were the first competitive elections ever to be held. Although it would be a mistake to take seriously only those elections in which the opposition defeat an incumbent regime and political succession occurs through the ballot box, it is important to note that these elections produced a significant number of cases where this is precisely what took place, Prior to the recent period the island state of Mauritius, in 1982 and 1983, had provided the only African example of this phenomenon. In the past some observers of Africa's handful of multi-party democracies, for example Botswana, had raised doubts regarding the authenticity of democracy because of the continued electoral success of ruling parties. In the period since 1989 the number of African states with experience of change of government through elections rose from one to fourteen (or fifteen if one includes the 1989 pre-independence elections in Namibia). Interestingly, some observers have now decided that it is necessary for this to happen twice to authenticate democracy! In most of those states where regime change through elections had not taken place, newly legalised opposition parties nevertheless had begun to play important roles within what had previously been, at least in a formal sense, monolithic political systems. Political liberalisation in many states extended far beyond the phenomena of parties and elections. Media freedom expanded very significantly, producing and reinforcing a far more vibrant public discussion of political issues. Civil society groups, such as trade unions and professional associations, along with groups formed specifically to promote democracy and human rights, grew afresh, or delinked themselves from incumbent regimes, and became active participants in the political process.

The changes in African political systems summarised above resulted from the conjunction of a wide range of factors which combined to influence the external and internal conditions shaping political life. The political environment in which a struggle for and against democracy in Africa has taken place has been subjected to a number of important changes.

AFRICA IN A CHANGING GLOBAL ENVIRONMENT

Africa is not a major actor on the world stage: in both military and economic terms it is extremely weak by global standards. However, during the period of the cold war, when bi-polar competition between the USA and the USSR was the major structuring factor in global politics, Africa was perceived by both superpowers as having strategic importance. These perceptions created a situation in which both the USA and the USSR sought to establish spheres of influence within Africa and, perhaps more importantly, to prevent their opponents from doing so. In pursuit of this aim both superpowers were willing to reward compliant regimes with economic support and military hardware even if those regimes chose to act in an oppressive manner towards their domestic populations. Many of Africa's more authoritarian leaders were happy to exploit this situation to the full and to market their strategic importance in exchange for foreign support for regime survival. The end of the cold war in the 1980s transformed the external environment in which African political systems operated. In a sense, the ending of the cold war began with the succession of the reformist Mikhail Gorbachev to the post of CPSU General Secretary in 1985 but, once underway, the process of change within the Soviet Union progressed with great rapidity, producing not a reformed system but the demise of the Soviet state which occurred in a manner which was sometimes peaceful (e.g. independence for Estonia and Latvia) and sometimes violent (e.g. the secession struggle in Chechnya). For Russia and the other Soviet successor states Africa became an area of negligible concern and the end of its strategic importance only served to underline its global economic marginality. The end of Soviet interest in Africa removed at a stroke the major rationale behind American strategic interest in the continent.

Change in the Soviet Union also had a profound effect on the smaller states of Eastern Europe as, one after another, popular uprisings overthrew the communist governments which had survived only on the basis of Soviet support. The movement away from authoritarianism and towards democracy in Eastern Europe could be seen from a different perspective as mirroring similar changes in other parts of the world which had seen the demise of undemocratic rule in some thirty countries of Asia, Latin America and Southern Europe in the period from 1974 to 1990. By the end of the 1980s Africa's military regimes and single-party states were looking increasingly anachronistic in the light of changes elsewhere in the world and the international environment provided a less supportive context for authoritarianism. Freed from the perceived need to turn a blind eye to the domestic excesses of cold war allies, and increasingly convinced that the absence of democratic government and political accountability in Africa was a significant contributory factor in economic malaise, a number of Western governments and international financial agencies such as the World Bank (WB) and the International Monetary Fund (IMF) began to insist that aid and investment had to be linked to political reform in Africa. Thus, around the end of the 1980s political conditionality was added to the economic conditionality which had emerged around a decade earlier. The fundamental concept of political conditionality was that aid and investment should be withheld from African governments which abused human rights and denied political freedoms to their citizens until such time as these abuses were removed. In some cases political conditionality was specifically linked to democratisation but in others the more nebulous notion of 'good governance' was used. This is not the place to enter into a debate on the morality of imposing political conditionality, but the point needs to be made that in no single case in Africa (that I am aware of) was external conditionality imposed without there already being strong domstic pressure for democracy from within the African state concerned.

Changes in the global political environment produced an external situation by the late 1980s which was more supportive of African democratisation, or at least less obstructive to it, than had previously been the case. This made things marginally less difficult for those in Africa seeking to democratise their political systems and marginally more difficult for those (mainly incumbent authoritarian elites) who sought to prevent them from doing so.

AFRICAN CONTINENTAL TRENDS

Although the changed external environment was more conducive to political reform, the major pressures for democratisation were those being exerted in Africa by Africans. In trying to assess the relative importance of internal and external pressures a very large majority of academic observers, particularly those who are African, have concluded that it has been the internal pressures which have played the major role and that external developments have, at most, contributed relatively modestly. For once I find myself in agreement with the majority of analysts. In passing it can be noted that these conclusions regarding the primacy of domestic factors replicate the main conclusions arrived at by scholars analysing democratisation in Latin America and Southern Europe. Right across Africa in virtually every state one has been able to witness a broad-based movement for political reform demanding a return to democracy which has ubiquitously been defined as requiring a multi-party political system. The uniformity of this demand in so many different states at more or less the same time has been very striking. Although democratic reform movements in Africa have been influenced by developments in other parts of the world, the major contributory factors have been concerned with African experience. Although large numbers of Africans have long cherished the idea of democratic government, the goal received fresh impetus from the twin problems of economic decline and the crisis of legitimacy faced by the rulers of authoritarian states.

The chronic failure of economic development in most African states is too well known to rehearse here, but the more pertinent factor is that during the 1980s most states suffered serious economic decline. For most people things not only failed to improve, they actually got worse as per capita income levels fell. Because the justification for the various types of authoritarian rule in Africa had usually been their supposed contribution to economic development, it is hardly surprising that negative development undermined the legitimacy of this type of rule. The situation was exacerbated by soundly based popular perceptions that those closely associated with government did not personally share the effects of economic decline and, through the massive corruption of public office, actually prospered whilst the majority suffered. An important aspect of the demand for democracy was the popular desire to make the political elites accountable for their actions.

The pro-democracy movements of most African states in the late 1980s and early 1990s represented a remarkable coalescence of political participation by all levels of society from elite to mass level. At the elite level, pressure came from educated groups who had managed to retain, or were able to assert, some degree of autonomy from state control. Church leaders were especially prominent in a good number of cases. Enjoying a high level of popular respect in highly religious African societies, church leaders also had the organisational advantages of belonging to well-established institutions. In the more highly authoritarian of African states, church congregations often represented one of the few legal ways of bringing people together in large numbers: the 'political sermon' became common in this period. Professional associations, especially those organised by lawyers, medical staff and academics, played an important role in the pressure for political reform. Members of these associations, along with students and journalists, were often prominent in the large numbers of groups established to promote the linked causes of democracy and human rights.

The activities of these educated elites were effectively complemented by the growth of mass-based political action in support of democratic reform. Mass action was in some cases organised by the trade union movement but in other cases it was of a more spontaneous character. The ability of the trade unions to use the strike weapon was often important: in many states the pattern that emerged was one of strikes being used initially to support economic demands, such as those for better wages and conditions, and then being widened in focus to include a political reform agenda. In many states there were mass demonstrations in favour of democratisation. Although it is impossible to be precise on the numbers participating, there were several cases which involved hundreds of thousands of demonstrators out on the streets demanding democracy. This often involved considerable risk to physical safety as regimes under threat ordered state security forces to attack demonstrators. This also illustrates a widespread feature of recent developments, the sheer bravery shown by pro-democracy activists in confronting authoritarian regimes.

In broad macro-level terms it is plausible to identify common patterns of political change taking place in almost all the states of sub-Saharan Africa in the period since 1989. Partly, but not predominantly, influenced by the restructuring of the global political system, there has been massive opposition mounted against the authoritarian state, both single-party and military versions, in Africa by a wide range of political forces. Almost ubiquitously this has taken the form of demands for democracy which have been understood to include the establishment of multi-partyism. In most, but not all, states this has forced incumbent ruling elites to make concessions in the form of fundamental adjustments to the formal rules of public life, most especially the legislation of opposition parties and the holding of competitive elections. However, the question needs to be asked as to how much this uniformity of experience is more apparent than it is real. To what extent do seemingly parallel political trends mask a diversity of practice?

THE SPECIFICITY OF AFRICAN STATES

The questions posed at the end of the previous section are essentially empirical questions which can only be answered through an empirical examination of the experiences of a range of individual African states. One would certainly expect such an examination to reveal important differences between different African states: although it may be a banal truism it still has to be stressed that all previous evidence has indicated that the political systems of African states are very different from each other in spite of some partially shared characteristics. These differences arise from a range of causal factors including levels of development and underdevelopment; the social composition of the population, including the relative balance or imbalance between different ethnic, racial, religious or linguistic groups; the styles of political leadership which have operated and the distinctive historical experiences over the *longue durée* combined with the memories of those experiences which exist in often conflicting forms within the population.

The major aim of this edited collection is to present precisely this form of empirical examination of the experiences of a range of African states. Each essay has been written, or co-written, by a specialist, or specialists, on the politics of the state they are examining and seeks to place recent political experience in the context of the past political experience of the state concerned. The only exception to this is the concluding essay by Christopher Clapham and myself which attempts to assess the prospects for democratic consolidation in Africa from a wider perspective. To what extent can the nine states covered in this volume be regarded as 'representative' of recent African experience? Perhaps in an ideal world one might have included essays on all of the forty-eight states of sub-Saharan Africa, but to have done so, whilst at the same time retaining the depth of analysis which is presented here, would have required a multi-volume series rather than a single book and, to be honest, sounds like one of those overambitious projects from which nothing ever materialises. Of course, any editor is dependent on being able to recruit specialist contributors who are willing and able to write individual essays. In spite of these problems it does seem to me that the states covered here can be regarded collectively as broadly representative of the range of recent African experience. Certainly, there has been no attempt to select only the 'most successful' or 'least successful' examples of democratisation, either of which would have undoubtedly produced an unbalanced picture. Both of the major Anglophone and Francophone traditions are represented along with Ethiopia and Eritrea which fit into neither category. In regional terms we have four West African cases, three from Eastern Africa and two from South Central Africa. Although all the states covered have a past record of political authoritarianism, the types of authoritarianism experienced until recently have varied considerably. Côte d'Ivoire, Malawi and Zambia were classic examples of relatively stable single-party states in which one individual national leader had dominated the post-independence period. Whilst the treatment of opposition was far more brutal in Malawi than in the other two (in January 1995 ex-President Hastings Kamuzu Banda of Malawi was legally charged with the murder of several political opponents including three Cabinet Ministers over a decade earlier), the three shared a range of common characteristics. All of the other states had experienced fairly lengthy periods of military rule, although in Ghana and Nigeria (and to some extent Uganda) these had been interspersed with periods of multi-party politics. Even the common categorisation of military rule hides further important differences: for sheer awfulness Amin's Uganda has little competition. In the Nkrumah period Ghana had also experienced single-party rule. Nigeria, Uganda and Ethiopia/Eritrea had all been subjected to the horrors of civil war at some time in the past thirty years.

More recent experience exhibits equal diversity. At the time of writing neither Uganda nor Nigeria have made the transition to multi-party rule. As Holger Bernt Hansen and Michael Twaddle explain, the Ugandan President Yoweri Museveni remains committed to some form of 'no-party democracy', a form of politics which seems closely to resemble that advocated in the past by Jerry Rawlings in Ghana, before the latter agreed to a restoration of multi-partyism.   In Uganda political parties are legally permitted to exist but are banned from campaigning. A further fascinating aspect of Uganda politics which receives attention is the restoration of the monarchy in Buganda and the questions that raises regarding other traditional polities in the country. The Nigerian case, as described by Julius Ihonvbere and Olufemi Vaughan, is very different. Here we see a military regime deciding to cling to power after completing the final stages (in terms of the presidential election) of a demilitarisation process which the regime itself had largely controlled and directed throughout. There seems little doubt that, had the transition gone ahead, Nigerian democracy in the Third Republic would have been deeply flawed, but in the event the military were unwilling to allow Nigerians even a flawed democracy. However, as Ihonvbere and Vaughan make clear, it would be unwise to write off the prospects for democratic rule in Nigeria. Paradoxically, the actions of the military have given considerable impetus to the development of a 'vibrant democratic movement' with a firm base in civil society which transcends class and communal divisions. Ironically, the likes of Ibrahim Babangida and Sanni Abacha may have unwittingly made a significant contribution to the longer-term development of Nigerian democracy.

Clearly Uganda and Nigeria have exhibited the least movement in the direction of multi-party democracy. With the exception of Eritrea, which might be regarded as being in a transitional phase, all of the other states covered in this volume have had some form of competitive multi-party election during the recent period. These elections have varied significantly both in terms of how fairly they were conducted and the sort of outcomes they produced. In terms of being marked by fair competition, Clapham's essay makes clear that the elections in Ethiopia were the least successful. The 1992 regional council elections were marred by serious malpractice and in some areas were not even held. The 1994 elections to the Constituent Assembly were boycotted by almost all of the opposition parties on grounds of harassment, which left only the EPRDF and its ethnically based affiliated parties to take part. As analysed here by Richard Crook and Jeff Haynes, the elections in Côte d'Ivoire and in Ghana exhibited similarities. In both cases the elections were won by incumbent rulers, Felix Houphouet-Boigny and the PDCI and Jerry Rawlings and the (newly created) NDC respectively, amidst accusations of cheating from the opposition. On the basis of the evidence presented here, electoral malpractice appears to have been ~~~ erious in Côte d'Ivoire than it was in Ghana. In the latter the n concerned the inadequacy of registers of voters. However, nd Haynes argue that the victory of incumbent rulers cannot explained by electoral malpractice, although this probably influenced the scale of their victories. It is clearly suggested that in both of these states the candidates with the greatest popular support won the elections, although the explanations of support levels are not the same in each case. In a very detailed and nuanced analysis Crook also demolishes the argument put forward elsewhere that electoral competitiveness between political parties has the effect of reducing voter participation in Côte d'Ivoire and instead suggests that it is the urban–rural distinction which is the most persuasive explanation for differences in turnout.

In the other three states covered in this volume democratic elections produced new governments. In Mali, as Richard Vengroff and Moctar Kone explain, the elections were also connected with demilitarisation. In marked contrast to the Nigerian case, the Malian military permitted the free formation of political parties and after the elections unreservedly handed over power to the winners of what was perceived to be a free and fair contest. Vengroff and Kone examine the extreme proliferation of political parties in Mali but also show how the effects of this were mitigated by the fact that only a minority of them could be considered as significant contenders and also by the fact that the use of a non-proportional electoral system in the national elections concentrated gains, so reducing the potential for fragmentation. The neighbouring states of Zambia and Malawi, analysed here by Jan Kees van Donge and Denis Venter respectively, provide examples of cases of opposition parties triumphing over established ruling parties in what had hitherto been single-party states and coming to power through competitive elections. In Zambia the opposition was relatively united within the MMD, which had previously led the struggle for a return to multi-party democracy, and achieved a very convincing victory over Kenneth Kaunda and UNIP. Although Kaunda was not averse to using his control of the state to try to create electoral advantages for UNIP, the very strength of the opposition resulted in this having limited effects and was clearly insufficient in preventing an electoral defeat of considerable magnitude which produced the first peaceful transfer of power through the ballot box of any mainland Anglophone African state. In his essay van Donge makes clear that opposition to Kaunda and the single-party state was longstanding but that the return to multi-partyism made possible the replacement of both. In many ways the case of Malawi is the most remarkable of all those covered in this volume. For nearly three decades Malawi had been dominated by the highly personalised authoritarianism of the Banda State which had produced one of the most tightly controlled political systems in Africa. With Banda apparently securely installed as 'president for life' and all potential opposition crushed, the one question which exercised observers of Malawi was the problem of political succession, which, it was assumed, would occur when the nonagenarian personal ruler finally died: the general consensus appeared to be that Malawi would collapse into chaos. In the event, political succession took place through peaceful change in a democratic election. If one were trying to identify a single event to encapsulate the change which has taken place in African politics it would be difficult to match the ousting through the ballot box of this most dictatorial of dictators. In the past the tightly controlled system presented a major barrier to scholarly political research in the country with the result that Malawian politics has been significantly underrepresented in the academic literature; Venter's detailed essay provides a very useful corrective to this lacuna.

The final essay in this collection represents a move away from the case-study format, which provides the dominant approach in the rest of the book, by returning to a wider canvas in an examination of the likely effects of recent redemocratisation on the future political life of Africa. Over recent years it has become something of an academic convention to characterise scholars writing on this topic as either 'demo-optimists' or 'demo-pessimists' depending on how highly they rate the chances of recent moves towards democracy producing a more sustained form of democratic rule in at least a significant number of African states. Because I had clearly been identified by others as belonging to the 'demo-optimist' school of thought, it seemed an interesting idea to invite a scholar more identified with 'demo-pessimism' to collaborate with me over the writing of the concluding essay. With this in mind I approached Christopher Clapham and suggested that if we worked on this together he could 'dampen down my cheery optimism' and I might be able to 'perk up his dreary pessimism'. Although I was delighted when he agreed to this proposal neither of us was very sure as to the best way to proceed: I was quickly persuaded that my original idea of having separately written 'grounds for optimism' and 'grounds for pessimism' sections which could be tacked together with a couple of linking paragraphs was unacceptably cumbersome. We decided that we ought at least to attempt to write a genuinely collaborative essay which was not schizophrenic. In the event we found virtually nothing seriously to disagree on. Even in relation to our, undoubtedly over-ambitious, attempt to place all of sub-Saharan Africa's states into one of four categories relating to the prospects for democratic consolidation, we experienced only mild disagreement over a couple of marginal cases and, even then, in one of them it was the supposed 'demo-pessimist' who was arguing for the promotion of one particular state into the higher category. Whilst neither of us would claim that the future of African politics is really predictable, an analysis of the past and present may well provide some clue as to the possibilities and probabilities of the future.

2 Côte d'Ivoire: multi-party democracy and political change

Surviving the crisis

Richard C. Crook

INTRODUCTION

On 7 December 1993, the thirty-third anniversary of Côte d'Ivoire's independence from France, the death was announced of President Houphouet-Boigny. He died peacefully in office, halfway through his seventh term as Côte d'Ivoire's elected executive President. He was thought to be at least eighty-seven years old in 1993, and had been too infirm in his final term to exercise more than a general direction over the government of his newly appointed Prime Minister, Allasane Ouattara. On 9 December Ouattara resigned and a new government took office under President Henri Konan Bédié, former Speaker of the National Assembly, in accordance with Article 11 of the Constitution. The new President holds office until the next general and presidential elections due at the end of 1995.

This simple sequence of events vividly symbolises the situation of stable continuity underlying real but erratic change which has characterised the Ivorian political system since the early 1980s. On the one hand, the succession of Bédié perpetuated the uninterrupted thirty-three-year regime of the *Parti démocratique de la Côte d'Ivoire* (PDCI), a political elite which had formed around Houphouet-Boigny in the late 1940s and early 1950s and which had continued to be dominated by the President and the original core group until the late 1980s.

Even more significantly, the peaceful and constitutional nature of the succession confirmed what most informed observers of the Ivorian system had long predicted, namely, that not even the intra-elite factional conflicts which had preceded the President's long-anticipated demise by some years would upset the fundamental stability of the ruling group and its attachment to the system which Houphouet-Boigny had built.

On the other hand, the events of 1993 revealed important changes and uncertainties in the political system, given a new impetus by the President's illness in the period leading up to his death. In 1990 Houphouet-Boigny had won his seventh term as President in an election which, for the first time in over thirty years, had been contested. Although the opposition candidate, Laurent Gbagbo, had been convincingly defeated, the move towards competitive multi-party politics had had a profound effect on the ruling party, which had already been shaken by the President's own 1980s programme for political reform and renewal. Further uncertainties had been added by the President's delegation of power to the Prime Minister, endowed with a 'doctor's mandate' to impose an economic austerity programme and a purge of corrupt state and parastatal institutions which, as much as the economic crisis itself, threatened the very core of the PDCI patronage system (see Crook 1991a). True to form, the aged President had attempted to balance the inevitable conflict by accepting a revised Article 11 of the Constitution which made Bédié the effective President-in-waiting. It was this situation of change and upheaval within the ruling elite combined with a deep and apparently insoluble economic crisis which Bédié inherited in 1993.

THE PDCI REGIME

The origins of the PDCI, founded in 1946, lay in the *Syndicat africain agricole* (SAA), an organisation of large commercial coffee planters formed by Houphouet-Boigny and a group of fellow Ecole William Ponty graduates in 1944 (see Zolberg 1964: 67). The membership (although not the leadership) of the SAA was predominantly farmers from the central (Baoulé) areas of the country, but it failed to gain the support of cocoa and coffee farmers from what was then the main centre of export crop cultivation in the country, the south east. By the time of the 1957 Territorial Assembly elections the PDCI had gained almost complete electoral dominance, having coopted most of its former opponents in the *Parti progressiste de la Côte d'Ivoire* and developed an electoral machine based on local notables and the ethnic associations of Abidjan. By this date too the character and long-term policy outlook of the regime had also been formed.

Both because of its original association with export crop farmers and its close ties with the French (Houphouet-Boigny served as a minister in several French governments in the 1950s), the PDCI had sought a special deal for coffee and cocoa prices within the French market in the immediate pre-independence period. The regime was committed both to a policy of expanding export crop production and to a marketing system which benefited the buying companies, which now included major Ivorian enterprises formed by the new elite as well as foreigners. After independence these policies led naturally into a development orientation which emphasised cooperation with foreign capital, extensive use of expatriate (French) man-power in the civil service, teaching and private management sectors, and an open door to foreign African migrants in order to guarantee labour supplies to the booming cocoa industry.

By 1960 a pattern of executive or presidential dominance and of weakly developed mechanisms for popular participation and party democracy had also set in. From 1960 onwards, the National Assembly was 'elected' on a single list drawn up by the President without contest. In the next two decades of economic boom, fuelled in particular by the successful expansion of the export crop economy, the Ivorian political elite built a much-expanded state which, to a degree unusual in Africa, was controlled by and highly integrated with its political masters. The elite had itself recruited from the expanded civil service and parastatal sectors to such an extent that it was also one of the most technocratic in Africa (Crook 1989 and 1991b). The monopoly of wealth and power which this elite possessed, through its control over access to public sector jobs, political careers, participation in the export crop marketing system and joint ventures with foreign companies, seemed virtually unchallengeable. Whatever its original connection with a farmers' organisation and its obvious dependence on the health of the cocoa/coffee export trade, this was clearly a *'bourgeoisie d'état'* (Fauré and Médard 1982), but one distinguished by its effectiveness, by its ability to attract the support of major social interests and by the inclusive political strategies of its supreme patron, the President himself. In many ways similar to the PRI regime of Mexico, the sheer longevity of the political elite had created a hegemonic group united not just by its power and wealth but also by ties of marriage, education and culture (Crook 1991b; Bakary 1984).

Unlike in many other African single-party states, the PDCI and the National Assembly had not withered away, although it could hardly be said that they performed any popular democratic functions. They functioned more as administrative adjuncts and channels of recruitment. Membership of the PDCI National Steering Committee (*Comité Directeur*) was the equivalent of a *nomenklatura*, coinciding with high office in government, the party/National Assembly and the civil service. Success was impossible without good standing in the party and, of course, loyalty to the President.

THE MOVE TOWARDS DEMOCRATISATION

Between 1978 and 1980 President Houphouet-Boigny decided to launch an Ivorian equivalent of Mao's Cultural Revolution, designed to shake out the corrupt ministers and barons, to revitalise the moribund and undemocratic party structures both locally and nationally and to renew the cadres of the regime with younger generations of political aspirants. In the process, he intended to reestablish presidential control over the economy and the political system (Fauré 1989). By showing that he could still command a following and renew the system with younger generations whom he judged to be more loyal, Houphouet-Boigny also hoped to head off pressures from potential successors for him to step aside.

The reforms, which proceeded throughout the 1980s, were targeted on the party, the civil service and local government system, and the parastatal corporations. The latter in particular had become notorious for their inflated salaries, corruption and incompetence and by 1980 employed almost as many staff as the civil service itself. They were the base of the so-called 'barons', a section of the post-independence elite which represented a real threat to the presidential monopoly of power (Contamin and Fauré 1990: 223). The parastatals were attacked through a radical programme of privatisation, liquidation or, most importantly, reintegration into the state administrative and financial systems. The President entrusted the civil service, itself undergoing a severe rationalisation, with this crucial task.[1]

The party was thrown into turmoil by the simple expedient of ending the single list for the National Assembly and throwing open constituency nominations to competing PDCI candidates in the 1980 and 1985 elections. At the same time, secretaries of local PDCI branches throughout the country were forced to stand for election.[2] The creation of 135 elected communes (local government authorities) in the main cities and most of the small towns of the interior provided new incentives for political aspirants to establish local political bases.[3]

Although the 'President's Revolution' was conceived before the full impact of the 1970s debt repayments and the collapse of commodity prices in 1979/80 were felt, the reforms quickly became associated with the consequences of that economic crisis and in particular with the public spending cuts and privatisation policies linked with the first IMF loan of 1981. As Fauré and Contamin have so persuasively argued, however, there was in fact a convenient coincidence between the need to reduce the scope of state patronage and a political agenda aimed at redistributing the opportunities which remained whilst renewing presidential power. This did not mean that the President was slavishly following a World Bank agenda; on the contrary, as a close analysis of the fate of the reforms during the 1980s shows, the President in fact spent the decade evading or circumventing the logic of the structural adjustment programmes.

Through agencies such as the DCGTx (*Direction et Contrôle des Grands Travaux*) and the CSSPPA (*Caisse de stabilisation et de soutien des prix des produits agricoles*) – the parastatal which ran the export crop marketing system – the government was able to sustain presidential spending programmes and defy World Bank pressure to cut cocoa producer prices (Fauré 1989: 72).[4] Many of the parastatals which were supposed to have been abolished under the restructuring programme in fact survived through reintegration into the public service as EPN (*Etablissements publics nationaux*) (Fauré and Contamin 1990: 37). It was President Houphouet-Boigny's attempts to use the reform programme to retain presidential control over the declining resources of the state which led him eventually, therefore, to a humiliating confrontation with the country's creditors in 1989. And it was the measures forced upon the government by the crisis of 1989 which led directly to the change to multi-partyism and the uncertainties of his final three years in office, rather than the carefully graduated 'democratisation' process of the 1980s.

That the reforms of the preceding decade in some senses 'prepared the way' for the competitive democracy of the 1990s is no doubt true. But the official gloss which presents the move to multi-partyism in 1990 as nothing more than a fully anticipated, logical next step, is little more than convenient hindsight. Throughout the 1980s Houphouet-Boigny had consistently and repeatedly voiced his total opposition to the notion of multi-party democracy.[5] Bakary, however, argues that the government's decision in May 1990 to permit opposition parties to contest the October elections was presented 'without drama', as simply the recognition of Article 7 of the Constitution and part of the government's continuing 'evolutionary' progress towards full democracy. The timing of the announcement was no more than a way of keeping the initiative in the government's hands and wrongfooting the opposition (Bakary 1991). In this view, the democratisation process was no more than a clever elite-inspired scheme, initiated and controlled at all times by the regime.

A close analysis of the events of 1989–90 shows, however, that both external pressures and domestic social and political forces had a decisive or 'triggering' effect on the government's change of heart (see Crook 1990 and 1991a). As a consequence of the CSSPPA's cumulating deficits the government faced both a liquidity crisis and an inability to meet its debt obligations. When Houphouet-Boigny's attempts to force up cocoa prices by withholding the 1988/9 Ivorian cocoa crop from the world market failed, the government had to bow to the inevitable and seek assistance from the international donors.

The conditions for the grant of immediate new loans from the World Bank and the French CCCE (*Caisse centrale de coopération économique*), together with the reopening of negotiations with the IMF for a fourth SAP included a halving of the producer price for cocoa and a radical restructuring of the machinery of government. This involved not merely reducing the number of ministries and the size of the Cabinet; a key aim of the international donors was to break the financial power of the DCGTx, to which end a new 'super' Ministry of Finance and the Budget had to be created to take over management of the debt and the implementation of the new SAP. This was effected in the October 1989 government restructuring. The donors further wanted the budget deficit to be tackled by real cuts of up to 20 per cent in the public salary bill and improvements in revenue performance. It was the implementation of the latter provisions rather than the attack on farmers' incomes which triggered the political crisis.

Whilst the new loans quickly enabled the export crop marketing system to begin operating again and ensured the survival of the CSSPPA (at the expense of the farmers), the already demoralised and suspicious public service workers and the urban middle classes were not prepared to accept the measures announced with such uncharacteristic lack of political finesse in February 1990. These included a general cut in public sector wages of 'up to' 40 per cent and rises of 11 per cent in private sector income tax. Strikes by public utility workers precipitated student riots and further strikes by educational and professional associations.

The newly emerged opposition led by Laurent Gbagbo and his *Front populaire ivoirien* (FPI) was quick to associate itself with the teachers and students and call for the resignation of the government. The teachers' union (*Syndicat des enseignants du secondaire de Côte d'Ivoire* – SYNESCI), and the lecturers' union (*Syndicat national de la récherche et de l'enseignement supérieur* – SYNARES) had already had numerous confrontations with the government in the 1980s, which were partly political in that their leaders had frequently called for multi-party democracy (*West Africa* 9–15 October 1989). (Gbagbo himself was a university history professor who had been forced into exile in 1982 and was strongly supported in 'intellectual' and student circles. He had returned to the country in 1989 and the FPI had been openly organising in the face of constant government harassment since then.) The period of upheaval culminated in May 1990 with police and customs service strikes and a brief takeover of the airport by young army conscripts. It was at this point that panic set in amongst the business community, precipitating further outflows of currency through the fixed rate franc-zone system and once again threatening the viability of the banks.

Houphouet-Boigny's reaction to the crisis came in two stages: first, in late April, the new Finance Minister's programme was scrapped in favour of an amended package put forward by the 'Ouattara committee' – an inter-ministerial committee chaired, not by a government minister but by the Governor of the *Banque centrale des Etats de l'Afrique de l'Ouest* (as he then was), a technocrat called in from outside the political elite. Ouattara had until 1988 been Director of the IMF's Africa Department and his appointment was no doubt intended to reassure the international community. Ouattara's plan to replace salary cuts with job losses, further reductions in civil service costs (e.g. the sale of official cars) and privatisations, together with a new range of taxes, did little, however, to calm the situation.

Then, in May, came the announcement of a range of political measures, including the opening up of the end-of-year general elections to opposition or non-PDCI candidates. Houphouet-Boigny also promised that he would settle the question of his successor at the forthcoming PDCI conference in October. Between May and October, therefore, the opposition was allowed to 'run with the ball'. The excitement created by the possibility of a contested presidential election in which Houphouet-Boigny might not stand, coupled with constant rallies and demonstrations, focused all attention on the opposition and temporarily diverted attention from the government's difficulties. The opposition, spurred perhaps by the unaccustomed attention in the press, euphorically called for a 'transitional government' to be formed to oversee the end of the PDCI regime (*Le Monde* 6/7 May 1990).

Whilst it is true that the timing allowed the opposition only five months to prepare itself, the May decisions can hardly be seen as merely a clever plan to outmanoeuvre the opposition. The FPI and its supporters were not regarded in themselves as that serious or significant a threat and, as has been shown, pressure from the opposition cannot plausibly be regarded as the determining factor in the government's decision to move to multi-party elections. The measures announced in May 1990 were in fact a way of buying time for Houphouet-Boigny to prepare his survival plan, and were clearly forced on the government by the seriousness of the crisis caused by the government's financial collapse and the demands of its creditors. The regime had to demonstrate that it was serious about reforming the structure of government – and provide a 'safety valve' for public anger and discontent. In allowing the opposition to surface on the back of a wave of anti-government protests in the public services and the urban middle classes it was taking a calculated risk. There were even some indications that the long-repressed disillusion and anger of cocoa farmers were beginning to emerge in parts of the countryside (Crook 1990: 657; Widner 1993 and 1994).[6] Houphouet-Boigny and the inner core of the PDCI leadership were, however, using the period between May and October 1990 to plan seriously for the President's seventh term and a PDCI victory at the polls.

THE MULTI-PARTY ELECTIONS OF 1990

In early October 1990, to the surprise and consternation of both the opposi- tion and many in the PDCI itself, Houphouet-Boigny emerged from the Ninth Congress of the PDCI as the party's unanimous choice for its presidential candidate. In spite of the impact of the ever-worsening economic situation, he remained the PDCI's greatest electoral asset, still genuinely respected and admired amongst large sections of the population. In this sense, his 1980s reforms had paid a very important dividend: successful shifting of the blame for the economic crisis away from the President and onto the shoulders of the 'corrupt' ministers and party barons. Houphouet-Boigny's chances were further strengthened by his decision, communicated to the opposition only at the end of September, to hold the presidential election separately (on 28 October), with the legislative and commune elections following in November and December respectively.

The opposition, on the other hand, was not only ill-prepared but exces- sively fragmented. By October as many as twenty-six new parties had emerged, many of them, of course, the vehicles of disgruntled PDCI losers in nomination contests, or no-hope, one-man bands. Only four were of any significance: the FPI, already the oldest and most credible challenger, followed by the *Parti ivoirien des travailleurs* (PIT) led by another univer- sity lecturer, the lawyer Francis Wodié and the former leader of the teachers' union, Laurent Akoun. The other two were the *Union des sociaux démocrates* (USD) led by Bernard Zadi Zaourou, and the *Parti socialiste ivoirien* (PSI) led by Bamba Moriféré. The FPI was the only one with the resources and the capability to fight a nation-wide campaign and to put up a presidential candidate.[7] In the legislative elections the FPI was able to field candidates in 114 constituencies out of 157, and would have fought more had the PDCI not used the local administrative machinery in some areas to prevent opposition candidates from being nominated. In spite, however, of the implications of the first-past-the-post electoral system which had been adopted, even the weakest of the opposition parties showed absolutely no willingness to cooperate. Thus, in Cocody, a wealthy middle- class suburb of Abidjan, the PIT leader Wodié was opposed by the FPI's number two, Sangare Drahamane, as well as the PDCI, three other opposi- tion parties and a PDCI independent.

The chances of this fragmented opposition beating the PDCI were further reduced by the formidable array of advantages in the hands of the governing party. The government administration (loyal to the President) controlled the electoral process at local level: nominations, party cam- paigning, voters' registers, giving out of polling cards, voting stations. The law enforcement agencies could be used if necessary to repress opposition activities deemed to be unruly, whilst at the same time the opposition complained bitterly about intimidation and provocations emanating from hooligans ('*loubards*') allegedly paid by the PDCI. The latter had vast resources – important not just for publicity but for paying out 'incentives' for voters, particularly in the rural areas, to come to the polls – and control of the mass media.

As part of the move to multi-partyism, an opposition press had, it is true, been allowed to emerge. Many of the new papers were very poor quality 'scandal sheets' with a limited distribution, but popular in Abidjan because of the contrast they offered to the pious tone of the government's national daily, *Fraternité Matin*.[8] The FPI managed to sustain both a respectable daily (*L'Evénement*, later replaced by *La Voie*) and a high-quality weekly (*Le Nouvel Horizon*), but even these had to struggle against frequent banning orders by government, and did not reach much beyond the main regional capitals and larger towns in the south. Coverage of the opposition on television and radio was only granted late on in the campaign and was brief and grudging. The FPI adopted the tactic of distributing cassettes of its message (Widner 1991).

Even had they had full opportunity to get their message across, it was not entirely clear what alternative was being proposed by some of the parties, other than a change of political leadership which would end PDCI corruption and 'dictatorship'. All presented themselves as 'Leftist' democrats and both the FPI and PIT had a well worked-out argument that indebtedness and economic failure were functionally linked with the corruption of one-party rule – a position reminiscent of Western donors' linking of 'transparency' in government with economic restructuring. Such arguments resonated with those excluded from patronage networks but were not necessarily vote-winners.

The FPI's economic and social policies, on the other hand, could not be described as either consistently Leftist or necessarily popular. In the opposition press, the attack on the PDCI elite in fact often had an ethnic overtone in so far as it attacked Houphouet-Boigny's 'Baoulé clan' dominance and whipped up memories of past PDCI repression of the opposition in particular localities of the centre-west and the south-east. These messages were inevitably stronger at the constituency level and, as the election results showed (see below), the opposition were extremely vulnerable to the PDCI counter-charge that *they* were the ones playing 'tribal' politics.

The FPI's main economic argument was that Côte d'Ivoire should reduce its dependence on France by leaving the CFA franc-zone and letting the currency float, whilst at the same time pursuing regional and African integration. Even Ivorians who did not appreciate the technical significance of devaluation valued the guaranteed exchangeability of the currency, and the idea of greater regional cooperation was in fact contradicted by the opposition's grassroots encouragement of native Ivorian resentment against the huge number of foreign African migrants in the country.[9] On the issue which dwarfed all others – how to resolve the impact of indebtedness and falling government revenues – the FPI appeared 'ill informed' on the true depth of the crisis and had little to offer except vague hopes of 'renegotiating' terms with the foreign donors whom it was busy attacking (*West Africa* 30 October 1989; Fauré 1991).

Given that the odds were stacked heavily in favour of the governing party, Houphouet-Boigny's overwhelming victory in the presidential election and the PDCI's similar victories in the legislative and commune elections were not unexpected. In fact, the opposition could be said to have done quite well in the circumstances especially when the figures are looked at in more detail.

Houphouet-Boigny's total number of votes in 1990 had in fact dropped by 30 per cent compared to his 1985 total of 3,512,882 out of a much smaller electorate (see Table 2.1).[10] This in itself, as much as Gbagbo's actual total in 1990, must be counted as one of the effects of the competitive elections. The opposition also did slightly better in the legislative elections, although their combined 28 per cent of the total vote only gained them 7 per cent of the seats. Nevertheless, the sharp successive drops in the participation rates in the legislative and commune elections showed quite clearly the 'bandwagon effect' of Houphouet-Boigny's presidential victory (see Tables 2.2 and 2.3). For large numbers of Ivorian voters, the presidency was seen (quite correctly) as the decisive contest.

Table 2.1 Results of the presidential election

Registered voters	Valid votes	F. Houphouet-Boigny	L. Gbagbo
4,408,808	2,993,806	2,445,365	548,441
% of vote	68%	82%	18%

Table 2.2 Results of the legislative elections

	No. of valid votes	%	No. of seats
PDCI	1,324,549	72	163
FPI	365,999	20	9
Others	157,264	8	3*
Total valid vote	1,847,812		
Registered voters	4,408,808		
Turnout		42	
Total seats			175

*One PIT seat and two Independents

Table 2.3 Results of the commune elections

	No. of communes
PDCI	123
FPI	6
Independents	3
(Suspended)	3
Total valid vote	806,561
Registered voters	2,364,484
Turnout	34%

More significant perhaps was the pattern and overall strength of opposition support underlying the rather meagre totals of National Assembly seats and commune councils actually won. In the presidential elections (see Map 1) Gbagbo obtained over 50 per cent of the vote in only three prefectures: Adzope, Bangolo and Gagnoa (his home area). In a further six, however, he obtained between 30 and 50 per cent and significant support of between 20 and 30 per cent in another eight prefectures. The spread of opposition support was therefore greater than the overall figures might at first have suggested. But it was undeniably concentrated in certain zones of the country: the south-east including Abidjan, the centre-west and west, with further pockets in the south-west. The appearance of some limited opposition support in the heartland of the far north around Korhogo did not

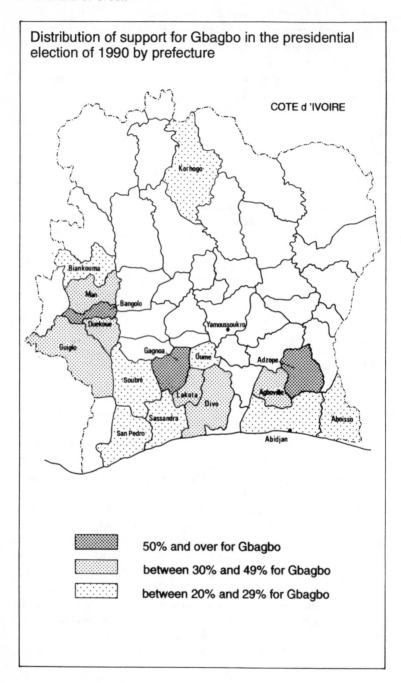

Distribution of support for Gbagbo in the presidential election of 1990 by prefecture

COTE d 'IVOIRE

50% and over for Gbagbo

between 30% and 49% for Gbagbo

between 20% and 29% for Gbagbo

survive into the November and December elections. The pattern of voting in National Assembly constituencies was concentrated in mostly the same areas as the presidential elections, except for the north (see Map 2). The FPI's nine seats were won in the eight constituencies of Adzope, Affery, Akoupé, Divo, Duékoué, Gagnoa (sub-prefecture), Guiberoua and Ouragahio (Gbagbo's home town). In another forty-three constituencies, an opposition party won between 30 and 50 per cent of the vote, including six constituencies in Abidjan. The only major differences from the presidential pattern were the strong showing of the PSI in the Koun-Fao (south-central Ghanaian border) and Daloa areas, and the PIT in Abengourou. The FPI also performed better in the Daloa and Issia prefectures.

By the time of the commune elections, the FPI was hard put to hang onto its core areas, but gained a 'surprise' victory in Bongouanou. Voting in Ouragahio itself was suspended because of violent protests over a fault on the ballot papers. As the FPI only put up thirty lists (compared to twenty-nine independents) and the PDCI, 235, the main interest of the commune elections was in the intra-PDCI conflicts at local level.

The most notable feature of anti-PDCI voting in the 1990 elections was, therefore, its extremely localised and regionally specific character. Any analysis of Côte d'Ivoire's first multi-party elections since independence must confront this fact.

Bakary has pointed out that the pattern of opposition support in 1990 closely resembled the divisions established during the struggle between the PDCI and its rivals in the 1940s and 1950s. It is as if, he comments, the loyalties of that period had been preserved frozen for forty years, to re-emerge in the thaw of 1990 (Bakary 1991). It is true that some of the strongest areas of opposition support in 1990 – Gagnoa, Divo and Lakota, Adzope – were also the last remaining pockets of resistance to the PDCI in the 1957 Territorial Assembly elections, when the PDCI (through a process of cooptation of most rivals) gained 89 per cent of the vote and fifty-eight of the sixty seats (Zolberg 1964: 211). On the other hand, the FPI attracted only weak support in Aboisso, heartland of the old Sanwi State movement.[11] Abidjan had also emerged as a centre of urban discontent with the government. Another new factor in 1990 was the emergence of much stronger opposition in the far west and in the newly opened-up forest areas of the south-west, such as Soubré, San Pedro and Sassandra.

To suggest that opposition in 1990 can be explained purely in terms of a revival of 1950s divisions is, of course, patently insufficient, given the changes that have taken place in the country over thirty-five years. Bakary himself emphasises the persistence of the 'local loyalties' factor in electoral behaviour, arguing that communities seek always to be represented by their

Distribution of support for the FPI, PSI and PIT in the
National Assembly elections by sub-prefecture and
commune constituencies

COTE d 'IVOIRE

Yamoussoukro

Abidjan

FPI: 6 constituencies 30-50%;
PIT: 1 victory; PSI: 1 @ 30-50%

Sub-Prefecture		Commune Constituencies
▓	FPI victory	....
▒	FPI loses with 30-50% of vote	1 San Pedro 2 Divo 3 Gagnoa
░	PIT loses with 30-50% of vote	4 Abengourou
░	PSI loses with 30-50% of vote	5 Daloa

own successful 'favourite sons' (or daughters). Such an explanation, however, begs two crucial questions: why did these particular areas refuse to join the PDCI national front in the 1950s and, even more importantly, why did this refusal persist and deepen over the next thirty years? (The most rational strategy for those seeking to advance local interests is to join the winning side – precisely the logic which underpinned the growth of a dominant- and then single-party system.)

In the south-east, support for the old *Progressiste* Party had come mainly from the Agni, Akan-style kingdoms of Moronou, Ndenié, Sanwi (and others) and the Abé and Attié-speaking chiefdoms of the Agboville and Adzope districts. Underlying the crystallisation of a *Progressiste* loyalty was a phenomenon very common in African late-colonial politics; a form of ethnic stratification resulting from uneven development. These areas were the earliest locations of African commercial cocoa-growing in the country, the core of what was still a fairly small industry in the 1930s. The Attié canton of Ketté is for instance the oldest area of cocoa cultivation in Côte d'Ivoire and it was here and in the surrounding areas that a 'rich peasant' class of cocoa farmers developed (Gastellu and Affou 1982). Both commercialisation of agriculture and the early impact of colonisation also meant that the first generation of Ivorian educated elites or *évolués* tended to come from this area, as did one of the earliest political associations for African advancement, the *Association pour la Défense des Intérêts des Autochthones de la Côte d'Ivoire*, founded in 1934. As in the eastern region of Ghana, elites from these areas saw themselves as the rightful or natural leaders of any struggle for African progress.

At the popular level, a politicised ethnicity or cultural awareness was forged, as elsewhere in Côte d'Ivoire, through the impact of rural migration. In the late 1940s and early 1950s at the same time as the boom in coffee-growing in the Baoulé central region, Dioula (northern) and Baoulé migrants began moving into the south-east seeking to establish themselves in the cocoa industry initially as labourers and sharecroppers with a view to obtaining land. The indigenous populations attempted to maintain control over both the land and their relations with the migrants by invoking the customary land rights common in Akan cultures. Although relations between migrants and indigenes were at first mutually beneficial, when large amounts of land began to be alienated the chiefs and intellectuals began to elaborate a culturally based defence against land sales which consolidated local ethnic identities. Unlike in Ghana, such claims were not strongly supported by colonial state enforcement of customary law (see Crook 1991b). Hence, the leaders of these areas did not join Houphouet-

Boigny's farmers' association (the SAA), which was seen as 'Baoülé coffee farmer' dominated, and created their own association instead.

This sense of separate identity and interest, established early on, was reinforced after the PDCI became a close ally and heir-apparent of the colonial government, thereby ousting the *Progressistes* from their position as 'sweethearts' of the administration. The *Progressiste* leadership was finally persuaded to join the PDCI camp in 1957; but popular opposition then rallied behind 'radical' (i.e. more nationalistic, anti-French) student leaders (Zolberg 1964: 210). The Sanwi State bid for separate independence from Côte d'Ivoire was perhaps the high point of this kind of local resistance.

After independence, the problems of the area changed. During the 1960s and 1970s, as the coffee and cocoa boom took off in the central and then south-western regions, the area began to experience a relative and then absolute decline, caused by falling productivity in the older plantations and the inevitable limits posed by a policy of expansion through extension of cultivation. This was coupled with continuing resentment at what was perceived as government neglect of the region in developmental allocations (most of the big projects in this period went to the north or centre, and to opening up the south-west). By the 1980s, the main local concerns were with the issue of land 'exhaustion' (in fact, the shortage of new or virgin forest) and the consequent problems of shortage of land for local youth together with the need for capital investment to improve or rehabilitate the old farms.[12] In this situation, regrets about past land alienations and resentment of migrants produced a feeling of 'loss of birthright' for which the government could also be blamed. For even more than their colonial predecessors, the PDCI's official support for a 'free-for-all' in the land market, coupled with its open-door policy on African immigration was seen, rightly, as hostile to 'traditional' assertions of restrictive land rights (cf., Crook 1991b). Even more importantly such policies were perceived as being pursued *because* they were in the interests of Baoülé migrant farmers, although such perceptions were probably stronger in the west and south-west than in the Agni and Attié areas.

The centre-west and south-western regions of Côte d'Ivoire were originally inhabited – very sparsely – by a multiplicity of acephalous peoples collectively labelled 'Kru' by ethnographers but with no common political structures or identities. In the 1950s the peoples of the Gagnoa and Daloa areas, loosely known as Bété, had already come into conflict with Baoülé and northern migrants pushing the cocoa frontier westwards. Weaker than the Agni, 'backward' educationally and without the political and social self-defence mechanisms which can be found in the structures of an Akan kingdom, these conflicts created a Bété ethnic identity which was politicised through the organisation of the *Mouvement socialiste africaine* (MSA), formed to oppose the PDCI in the 1956 and 1957 elections. Unlike the Agni and the Attié, however, the Bété and other western groups were quite unable to resist the veritable onslaught of rural migrations coming from the centre, the north and outside Côte d'Ivoire which hit them in the 1960s and 1970s. Much more sharply than the south-eastern groups, their efforts to assert indigenous rights clashed directly with state policy on expansion of cocoa and coffee cultivation (as well as timber exploitation) into the virgin forests of the west. For them, the state was seen as acting directly as an 'instrument of Baoulé domination', particularly when its agents supported migrants against indigenes in local conflicts (Chauveau and Dozon 1987; Crook 1991b: 220). Bété resistance took a violent form in 1970 when, after contested PDCI elections the clandestine *Parti nationaliste* seized control of Gagnoa with a ragged peasant army and declared a '*République d'Eburnie*' in the west. The whole revolt was crushed with considerable bloodshed by the Ivorian army. Its longer-term political legacy was to create an official paranoia around the idea of a 'Bété plot', confirmed by every new incident of student unrest or union protest – and dealt with in Houphouet-Boigny's time-honoured fashion both by self-conscious co-optation of Bété 'loyalists', and by attacking all opposition as 'tribalist'.

The politics of elite ethnic balancing could not alter the situation on the ground, however, as the multi-ethnic communities created by the cocoa boom in places such as Daloa, Duékoué, Issia and Soubré came up against the cocoa crisis of the 1980s. Without detailed case studies it is impossible to disentangle the various forces behind the expansion of the anti-PDCI vote beyond the core Bété areas into the far west and south-west. It is clear that the opposition in 1990 tapped much of the local hostility to foreign African migrants, a factor exacerbated by the government's official encouragement of foreigners to vote under the law amended specially for the occasion, coupled with popular perception that the PDCI, aided by government officials, deliberately rounded up the 'immigrant vote'.[13] Undoubtedly, the resentment of western indigenes reduced to a minority in their own areas played a part. In addition, one cannot discount the impact of the cocoa marketing crisis and the price cut of 1989 in such a region – the very heart of the cocoa industry – as indicated by the emergence during the presidential elections of significant anti-Houphouet-Boigny votes in the forest prefectures of Soubré and San Pedro. More surprising perhaps was the fact that these economic issues were reflected in such a limited way in the voting patterns – a result attributed by most observers to the government's ability to control the electoral process in many rural areas.

In Abidjan the anti-foreigner factor was undoubtedly a strong opposition card, since it was the new teeming populations of urban underemployed who were most savagely affected by the economic crisis. If to this factor is added the wave of anger amongst white-collar and public sector employees which exploded in 1989–90 – a movement which, as argued above, was the actual trigger for the move to multi-partyism – the opposition should have been on very strong ground in the big cities. In fact, the elections in the urban areas were vitiated by very low turnouts and the opposition, although it did record votes of between 30 and 50 per cent in six Abidjan constituencies, failed to gain its expected successes. The low participation rates had a number of organisational and political causes, discussed below.

The fact that the pattern of opposition support in 1990 reflected very specific regional and local grievances against the PDCI can therefore be accounted for by a variety of factors: the impact of large-scale, internal and external migrations on access to land, employment opportunities and other social relations; regional 'relative deprivation'; and the differential impact of the economic crisis in both urban and cocoa-growing areas. Although these factors affected all parts of the country to varying degrees, they had developed a particular salience in these areas through a process of ethnic and communal identity formation which had been politicised over a period of thirty-five years. These identities had been formed in relation to groups which were perceived – in spite of its constant efforts to construct an all-inclusive 'balanced ticket' – as specifically favoured by the PDCI regime: Baoulé migrants, northerners and foreigners, both at the popular level and in the business sector.

Some scholars have argued that the 1990 elections did not encourage or even depend upon the mobilisation of ethnic divisions (Widner 1991). Such a perspective depends upon one's definition of ethnic politics. Largely because of the highly fragmented and heterogeneous character of the language and cultural groups which make up the population of Côte d'Ivoire, the country has never been threatened by 'ethnic nationalism' – attempts by one group or another to achieve dominance or make special claims based on an historic political territory. But this has not necessarily produced an ethnically blind politics.

From its very inception, the PDCI was organised, particularly in the urban areas, through ethnic and 'home-district' committees, a mode of organisation formally abandoned only in the 1960s and then not always in practice. The process by which the PDCI built a national single party was through cooptation, based on a logic of ethnic coalition-building which recognised that no one group should appear to be dominant. Hence Houphouet-Boigny's constant concern to balance party and government positions. The changing composition of this balance has always provided one of the staple topics of political gossip in Côte d'Ivoire, as have ethnic stereotypes in social life. The politics of ethnic coalition-building, in so far as it manipulates already established group loyalties, is just as much a form of ethnic politics as any other, even if it is not 'system threatening'. Indeed, the Nigerians have long sought formally to construct such a system. Thus, in 1990 both the PDCI and the FPI were engaged in the same game of attempting to construct a winning coalition. Both stressed their 'national' character whilst accusing the other of 'tribalism'. The difference between them was that the PDCI, given its resources and experience, was much more effective than the FPI at that particular game.

The PDCI spared no effort, for instance, in persuading notables with a regional following who had joined the opposition camp to rejoin the party. The day before the presidential elections the former Mayor of Abidjan (E. Dioulo) who had been disgraced in a corruption scandal but still retained a following in his native Abidjan, announced that he was leaving the USD to rejoin the PDCI. The Deputy and former Mayor of Korhogo, who had also fallen out with Houphouet-Boigny in the 1980s, rejoined after the presidential elections (*West Africa* 26 November 1990; Fauré 1991). As a member of the Gbon Coulibaly chiefly family of Korhogo, historic allies of the SAA in the 1950s, he was a powerful vote-broker for the Senoufo vote of the north whose influence was amply demonstrated in the legislative and commune elections.

The FPI, on the other hand, was increasingly pushed back into its historic strongholds, reinforcing the PDCI's tribalist label even though Gbagbo did not, at the level of high politics or official manifestos, fight an ethnic campaign. But the language of the opposition press told a different story; it consistently attacked Houphouet-Boigny for running a nepotistic Baoulé regime, and ran stories on the history of the 1950s and the 1970 massacres in Gagnoa. Even two and a half years after the elections, *L'Oeil du Peuple* (7 June 1993) could run a headline on Gbagbo's visit to Gagnoa saying: 'Le peuple Bété est toujours derrière son fils', and during the period just before Houphouet-Boigny's death, *La Voie* (10 June 1993) referred to Bédié as 'le prince du pré-carré Baoulé'. Another story on the attempt by the Prefect of Gagnoa to continue imposing fees for sixth grade entry exams was presented as an attack on the future of the Bété people following the 'ethnicide' of 1970.[14] In stressing its identification with Bété and Agni or Attié grievances the FPI severely reduced its chances of constructing a majority coalition.

The limited success achieved by the opposition parties in 1990 raises the question of whether the elections were genuinely competitive. This has been linked by some observers with the issue of the 'low' participation rates in 1990, which, in spite of the apparent strength of popular demands for multi-partyism in the 1989/90 crisis, were either lower than or no better than those of the 1985 single party elections (Fauré 1991; Bakary 1991).[15] Such apparent lack of enthusiasm could be the product of a number of causes: the lack of a strong challenge from the opposition, rigging and pressure on opposition sympathisers not to vote, or general political apathy and alienation.[16] Fauré, however, suggests that the main explanation lies in a cultural preference for unanimity which derives from a distaste for the social consequences of openly expressed divisions and conflicts at local level; and, like Bakary, maintains that there is a systematic link between increased competitiveness and reduced propensity to participate (Fauré 1991: 147; Bakary 1991: 183). In other words, the divisive effects of party competition produce not greater mobilisation but greater alienation.

Looking first at the relationship between the introduction of multi-party competition and participation, it must be remembered that all turnout figures relate to the registered electorate; the size of the register, in a society without reliable means of drawing up lists by residence, has always been very much under the control of the administration and in the pre-1990 period could easily be made to correspond with actual voters on the day – particularly when there was political pressure to maximise the vote. The register for the 1990 elections, drawn up in 1987 with the help of a World Bank team, was 26 per cent larger than the 1985 register and represented approximately 86 per cent of the eligible population in 1990 – a relatively high proportion for any country.[17] On the basis of this register, a turnout of nearly 70 per cent for the presidential elections would seem perfectly respectable. The turnout in the legislative and commune elections was in fact little different from that in 1985, and, as indicated earlier, the large drop from the presidential election can at least partially be attributed to realism on the part of the electorate regarding their political significance, rather than a distaste for conflict.

The idea that the lower rate of participation in the legislative elections was due to a lack of real challenge from the opposition can easily be dismissed. There were 490 candidates put up for the 175 National Assembly seats; of these, 234 were PDCI, and 217 opposing parties or independents. The PDCI was challenged in 73 per cent of all constituencies; and out of the forty-three constituencies where there were only PDCI candidates, only fourteen were uncontested or single-candidate elections.[18] The renewal rate for Deputies (changes in the incumbency of seats) in 1990 was 65 per cent – slightly better than 1985, and certainly an indication of the continuing upheavals within the PDCI itself.

In the commune elections, although the opposition did not mount an effective challenge except in its regional strongholds, there was still considerable competition between PDCI lists and between the PDCI and independents. The number of uncontested elections went down from fifty-three in 1985 to only twenty-five (18.5 per cent of all communes) in 1990; and 50 per cent of all incumbent mayors lost office (Côte d'Ivoire 1991).

The hypothesis that participation varied systematically according to the degree of competitiveness requires first of all a definition of competitiveness. Fauré's main comparison is between single-party and multi-party contests; but he also suggests in addition the criterion of number of candidates or lists, arguing that where there were more than four candidates or, in the commune elections, larger numbers of competing lists, participation was lower than in constituencies or communes with lower numbers of contestants or single candidates/lists. A more precise definition of degree of competitiveness would, however, incorporate the idea of the 'strength of challenge' to the governing party; that is, the extent to which in any particular constituency the PDCI had a real fight on its hands as opposed to a walkover. In the following analysis, therefore, a category of 'highly competitive' constituency will be added to the categories defined by numbers of candidates and parties. The 'highly competititive' constituencies are defined not merely by the presence of opposition candidates but also by an opposition score of at least 30 per cent of the total vote (see Table 2.5).[19]

Table 2.4 Competitiveness and turnout by number of candidates (legislative elections)

Type of constituency	No. of constituencies (157)	Turnout (% average) [1]
Uncontested	14	70*
2 candidates	55	42
3 candidates	56	42
4+ candidates	32	40

*63% overall

1 In Tables 4, 5 and 6 the differences between average and overall turnouts are only shown if they exceed 1 per cent.

Table 2.5 Competitiveness and turnout by degree of party competition (legislative elections)

Type of constituency	No. of constituencies 157	Turnout (% overall)
PDCI only, uncontested	14	63
PDCI only, contested	29	45
PDCI only, 2 candidates	13	43
PDCI only, 4+ candidates	6	46**
Multi-party, contested	114	40
multi-party, 2 candidates	42	42
multi-party, 4+ candidates	26	34***
'highly competitive' multi-party*	52	40

*defined as constituencies where opposition vote more than 30% of total valid vote
**51% average; if exclude one constituency with 99%, average = 41%
***37% average

As Table 2.4 shows, it is undeniable that turnout in uncontested legislative constituencies was higher than in any other category. The same was true for the uncontested commune elections which had an average turnout of 71 per cent. It may well be asked, however, whether the results of uncontested elections can be treated as meaningful indicators of propensity to participate. In 50 per cent of the uncontested legislative constituencies and in 36 per cent of the uncontested communes, turnout was in the 80–100 per cent range – figures which not only distort the average but also indicate the persistence of electoral practices dating from the 'bad old days' of single-party unanimity.[20] Such figures, even in the most sophisticated of democracies, are so unusual as not to be credible. The figures for the other categories of constituency, classified purely by number of candidates, show a very slight (2 per cent) drop in the average turnout where there were more than four candidates.

A more instructive comparison would be between contested PDCI-only constituencies and multi-party constituencies. If the Fauré/Bakary hypothesis were correct, participation in PDCI-only constituencies would be generally higher than in multi-party constituencies, and in both categories there would also be a decline in participation relative to the number of candidates. As Table 5 shows, there was a small difference of 5 per cent in the overall turnout in PDCI as compared with multi-party contested constituencies: the former slightly above the national average, the latter slightly below. Participation in the PDCI group *increased*, however, with the number of candidates, whilst it dropped in the multi-party constituencies. In the case of the 'highly competitive' constituencies, however, turnout was no different from that of all multi-party contested constituencies, showing that such competition had little impact on mobilisation of the electorate, either way.

The difference between the PDCI and multi-party constituencies with four or more candidates does invite explanation, as does the rather smaller difference between the two categories generally. In the latter case, a much simpler and more practical explanation than the hypothesis of a 'cultural preference for avoiding conflict' may be offered: the PDCI had the resources and the machinery to get out its vote. Particularly in the rural areas of Côte d'Ivoire, successful candidates have always known that a scattered peasant electorate requires material 'incentives' to persuade them to come to the polls. This is not to dismiss Ivorian elections as 'bought' elections, but merely to emphasise the continuing importance of clientelistic power structures in such communities. The other important characteristic of the PDCI constituencies is that they were all rural and 69 per cent of them (twenty out of twenty-nine) were situated in the far north. In fact, it is the rural–urban distinction that proves to be the most powerful explanation of differences in turnout.

If the urban multi-party constituencies are removed from the multi-party category, the difference between the PDCI and multi-party categories virtually disappears: 45 per cent as opposed to 43 per cent turnouts (see Table 2.6). Such was the overall national contrast between rural and urban participation that to compare a group of all rural, mainly far northern constituencies with a group containing a significant number of urban contests is simply not a fair or meaningful exercise. In the case of the multi-party contests with the lowest turnout – those with more than four candidates – the turnout reverts to 40 per cent (near the national average) if the urban constituencies are removed. With the 'highly competitive' group, the rural–urban distinction is even more telling: the rural turnout is the same as the national average of 42 per cent. The commune elections reinforce the point; even though most contests were intra-PDCI, they were characterised by the same order of difference between rural and urban turnout. In Abidjan for instance, the turnout was only 22 per cent, whilst in Abidjan and the seven biggest towns (Urban 2 category) it was 31 per cent, compared to 51 per cent in all other communes, and 46 per cent in all other contested communes.[21]

Table 2.6 Competitiveness and turnout: the urban/rural dimension

Type of constituency	No. of constituencies (157)	Turnout (% overall)
Urban 1 (Abidj. + towns over 100,000*)	13	31
Urban 2 (Abidj. + towns over 50,000**)	17	34
Rural (all minus urban 2)	140	45
Rural contested	128	43
PDCI only, contested, rural	29	45
Multi-party contested, rural	99	43
Multi-party contested, urban	15	31***
Multi-party contested 4+ rural	19	40
Multi-party contested 4+ urban	7	30****
'Highly competitive' multi-party, rural	43	42
'Highly competitive' multi-party, urban	9	34

*Bouaké, Daloa and Gagnoa
**first three plus Korhogo, Abengourou, Man, Yamoussoukro
***27% average
****28% average

The competitiveness of the 1990 elections was, therefore, high as measured by the number of competing candidates, the spread of multi-party contests throughout the country and the strength of the opposition challenge in at least one-third of the constituencies in the legislative elections. It was also high within the PDCI itself, as the number of PDCI candidates and the turnover of sitting Deputies indicates. Nor can it be argued that the competitiveness of the elections had a demobilising effect on the electorate. Apart from the difference between the presidential and the other elections, the poorest participation rates were those in the big cities and large towns as compared with the rest of the country.

Explaining the contrast between urban and rural electoral behaviour does raise questions not just about the sociology of urban areas but also about the organisation of the elections themselves. In large cities like Abidjan (population two million) or Bouaké (370,000) it is clearly more difficult to organise the vote of multi-ethnic (and multi-national) shifting populations, large numbers of whom inhabit the sprawling shanty towns on the outskirts of the city and make a precarious living in the 'informal sector'. They are simply not so amenable to the 'hierarchical, personalised, communal forms of political domination' cited by Fauré as the underlying reality of Ivorian electoral behaviour. There is also evidence that large numbers of urban migrants prefer to return to their home towns to vote, or do not like to vote for candidates in the urban area who still tend to be 'sons of the soil', even when, as in Abidjan, the original inhabitants are now in the minority (Bakary 1985 and 1991). The urban environment also, however, has more demonstrable and practical effects on the organisation of elections: attempts to rig are more visible (particularly to the media), suppression of the opposition more likely to be resisted and violent confrontations between rival groups thus are more likely to occur.

The opposition alleged that the whole electoral process was fraudulent and preceded by general intimidation and interference with the opposition campaign. Opposition rallies were banned or broken up, particularly in Abidjan, and opposition supporters arrested after the ensuing confrontations. Government control of the electoral administration was used, in some areas, to prevent opposition candidates being nominated; but the most significant aspect of electoral administration lay in the drawing up of the register, and the issuing of identity cards and polling cards, without which voters could not (technically) be permitted to vote. Official sources admitted after the elections that there were problems with the register which was frequently incomplete or faulty, and with the issuing of polling cards (*Fraternité Matin* 28 November 1990; *Fraternité Hebdo* 20 December 1990). Linked to this problem was the controversy over the 'foreigner vote'. According to the law, especially updated for the 1990 elections, non-Ivorians could vote if they were already registered and had an ID card and polling card. The opposition accused the PDCI of using the foreigner vote as their 'secret weapon', and there is considerable evidence that prefects and mayors facilitated the rounding up of foreigners by the PDCI through the liberal issue of polling cards. Accounting for 28 per cent of the total population in 1988 (and a larger proportion of the adult labour force particularly in the cocoa areas and the southern cities), the potential of the foreign vote was highly significant, and was as important in the rural as in the urban areas (Crook 1991b; Fauré 1991).

It was from Abidjan, however, that reports of the most chaotic mismanagement and alleged rigging incidents emerged. During the presidential elections these led to violent incidents and the closure of polling stations by troops and police in several constituencies, including the opposition stronghold of Yopougon (*Le Monde* 29 and 30 October 1990; *Jeune Afrique* 7–13 November 1990). It was this atmosphere of intimidation and the sheer difficulty of voting which produced the noticeable apathy of Abidjan opposition supporters in the legislative elections a month later.[22]

In so far as there was rigging and mismanagement of the elections they therefore had their most visible and deleterious effect in Abidjan and the main urban areas, by reducing turnout particularly of opposition supporters. In the rural areas, by contrast, factors such as control of the register and the foreigner vote no doubt helped to swell the PDCI turnout.

Overall, however, it may be concluded that these aspects of the elections, although they may have accounted for differential turnouts, did not rob the opposition of victory. Even if the FPI had won in all areas where it had some kind of support, it would not have got more than around 30 per cent of the presidential vote, and perhaps a similar number of Assembly seats, subject to the vicissitudes of a first-past-the-post electoral system and a split opposition. In addition, as the FPI has itself pointed out, the structure and distribution of Assembly constituencies was stacked against the opposition in so far as the centre and north of the country were 'overrepresented' with larger numbers of smaller constituencies, meaning that for instance the average constituency in the southern region was twice the size of an average constituency in the centre-Yamoussoukro region (*Nouvel Horizon* 14 May 1993). An unknowable factor is what might have happened had all the localised conflicts of the north been translated into party terms instead of remaining strictly intra-PDCI. (The PDCI leadership has always been, and remains, acutely sensitive to the import- ance – and fragility – of its northern bastion.)

THE POLITICAL CONSEQUENCES OF THE 1990 ELECTIONS

It would be unrealistic to expect that the legacy of more than thirty years of single-party and single-presidential rule could have been wiped out in one single electoral contest. Indeed, opposition impotence combined with the unremitting economic crisis at first suggested that a deepening of popular alienation and the perpetuation of old patterns and habits of domination would be the most likely outcome in the 1990s. The first two years of multi-party democracy in Côte d'Ivoire were little short of disastrous for the opposition.

One part of the Ouattara government's austerity programme involved bringing into line with the rest of the public sector the relatively lavish salaries and working conditions of secondary and tertiary education teachers. (These benefits dated from the period when the majority of teachers were French expatriates.) Politically, this was a tactic designed to help sustain Ouattara's defence of standard civil service salaries against donor pressure for salary cuts, and to bolster his attempt to maintain morale in a severely rationalised public service (see Crook 1991a). The opposition, however, partly because of the nature of its leadership, chose strongly to support the series of strikes and confrontations launched by the teachers' unions in 1991 – a cause which attracted little popular sympathy.

In addition, the opposition associated itself with a series of student protests sparked off by an incident in which students, allegedly organised by the student union (*Fédération étudiante et scolaire de Côte d'Ivoire –* FESCI), lynched another student accused of being a 'government informer'. The unnecessarily brutal crackdown by police and troops in May 1991 led to a self-perpetuating cycle of protest and repression, culminating in an FPI-organised march in February 1992. The students and the FPI were demanding that the President take action against the Army Chief of Staff, General Robert Guei, who had been named in an enquiry as responsible for the repressive behaviour of troops on the campus. The demonstration degenerated into widespread violence on the streets of the capital, during which Gbagbo himself, the leader of the PIT, other opposition-elected Deputies and the leader of the Ivorian League for Human Rights were arrested. The government was clearly in no mood to tolerate dissent, and particularly not criticism of the Army commanders, who had had to put down another attempted revolt in August 1991. Within the next month, Gbagbo, his son and forty-five other opposition leaders were given one- or two-year jail sentences, joining the FPI Secretary General, editor of *Nouvel Horizon*, who had already been given six months for allegedly defaming Ouattara. Other opposition papers, *Le Jeune Démocrate* and *L'Oeil du Peuple*, were banned for insulting the Head of State.

What was particularly shocking about the government's actions, from the point of view of civil liberties and the building of a multi-party democracy, was that the elected Deputies had been jailed under a public order ordinance signed by the President himself in Paris only the night before the demonstration. The new law (which was not debated by the Assembly) purported to hold the organisers of any public demonstration automatically liable for any acts carried out by demonstrators.[23] As a direct result of this attack on the opposition, the remaining FPI Deputies in the National Assembly withdrew from the 1992 session in protest – although they were not joined by the PIT leader, who had been released soon after the demonstration.

In spite of this inauspicious beginning, relations between the government and the opposition entered a new phase in late 1992 after the release of
Gbagbo and other detainees under a presidential amnesty announced in July
1992. Gbagbo himself angrily rejected the amnesty as robbing him of his
chance to prove his innocence and was in no way humbled by the experience. But the FPI had been weakened, a fact demonstrated by the growing
number of splits and defections which began to plague the party, not least
over the issue of what tactics to pursue. Gbagbo clearly wanted to move
away from 'street politics' and confrontations which the opposition could
not win, whereas a 'radical' faction wanted to continue with direct action in
alliance with the students. In Gbagbo's view the increasingly public and
acrimonious conflict between the Ouattara government and Bédié's faction
grouped around the 'heir apparent', as well as other divisions within the
PDCI, offered excellent opportunities for the opposition to exploit. One
sign of this was Ouattara's offer to the opposition to form a government of
national unity by accepting ministerial posts, an offer repeated many times
throughout 1992 and 1993, but consistently refused by Gbagbo.

The appointment of Ouattara to the newly created office of Prime
Minister in November 1990 had been one of the concessions forced on
Houphouet-Boigny by the 1989 debt crisis. Ouattara's task was to do what
was necessary to restore control of public spending, increase revenue and
restructure the Ivorian economy. This involved taking control of the bud-
gets of the parastatal agencies including the CSSPPA hitherto protected by
the President, purging parastatal directors and senior civil servants
including those in charge of the Customs and the Revenue Services, and
implementing a radical new privatisation programme which included the
electricity and water corporations and state shares in agri-business and oil
companies. On the revenue side, a campaign was launched against tax
evasion, with new laws to force companies which received government
business to pay their taxes. Taken together, the Ouattara programme was
nothing less than an attack on the very heart of the state patronage system
which had sustained the core of the political elite for so long.

Once it had become clear that Ouattara intended to stay on and to
position himself for a bid for the presidency, Bédié formed the natural focus
for a range of disgruntled groups: both the old guard who had suffered
during the 1980s and ambitious younger generations in the new Assembly
intake and in the renewed 400-member *Bureau Politique* of the PDCI.
Some of the new PDCI cadres and Deputies, led by Djeni Kobena, formed
a 'reformist' faction which approved of the anti-corruption drive and urged
a more liberal treatment of the opposition. But when it came to the privatisation issue, it was the younger careerists in the National Assembly who

joined in the open revolt against government policy associated with the Bédié camp (*Jeune Afrique Economique* 166, April 1993).

The FPI, naturally enough, attempted to maintain a studied ambiguity on the question of which faction it favoured, and thus appeared to switch from one to the other as it suited them (see *Jeune Afrique* 29 April 1993). Although Gbagbo found it hard to forgive Ouattara for the 1992 repression, he seemed to support the anti-corruption and economic restructuring policies, blaming Ouattara only for having been compromised by his acceptance into the inner PDCI establishment. But when it came to the privatisation row, the FPI joined in with the rest of the National Assembly and the Bédié camp, attacking the lack of consultation and the 'sell-out' to French big business. Such was the virulence of the PDCI Deputies, however, that the FPI did not even have to speak in the debates; it simply sat back and watched the fight. It was left to Houphouet-Boigny himself to come to the support of his Prime Minister (*Jeune Afrique* 22 April 1993).

Thus, by 1993 Gbagbo and the FPI in the Assembly had begun to play a more orthodox political game at the elite level, and combined this with a new campaign in the rural areas and towns of the interior, designed to rebuild its organisation and to revive public awareness and support in the lead-up to the 1995 elections.[24]

By late 1993, as news of the serious deterioration in the President's health began to filter through from Paris to Abidjan, strong rumours developed of a more favourable FPI response to Ouattara's overtures. The reason was simple: the FPI's refusal to accept Ouattara's offer of a coalition government had been based on the demand that Article 11 of the Constitution must first be suspended so that, in the event of the President's death, elections would follow almost immediately. With the President's death imminent, this position began to look more attractive to Ouattara himself, who was now engaged in constructing a power bid based on support from the technocracy, northern elements (Ouattara is a Burkinabé by origin), PDCI reformers and what the Ivorian press call the PDCI 'dinosaurs': the old men of Houphouet-Boigny's original inner group, who, close to the President himself, had always supported his attempt to renew the party in the 1980s. He also had the support of Phillipe Yacé, the former Secretary General of the party and original 'heir apparent' who, although one of the first victims of the 1980s reforms, had become an elder statesman and, as President of the Economic and Social Council, had lent his weight to the undeclared campaign against Article 11.

These ploys, and in particular the idea of amending the Constitution again, never had time to come to fruition before Houphouet-Boigny's death in December 1993. Bédié ruthlessly pre-empted Ouattara's attempt to follow legal niceties (and thus delay the handover) by marching into the national TV station surrounded by gendarmes on the evening of Houphouet-Boigny's death, and proclaiming himself President on the TV news.[25] In the event, neither Ouattara nor the security forces were willing to force a constitutional crisis (*Jeune Afrique* 16 December 1993).

Bédié's position in relation both to the FPI and to the other PDCI factions was clearly demonstrated in his first Cabinet. The FPI refused absolutely to recognise the validity of the Bédié presidency, castigating it as a form of monarchical succession, and even when approached some weeks after the announcement of the new government, refused to accept any posts. The leader of the USD, Bernard Zaourou (which had no representation in the Assembly) did, however, accept the post of Minister of Culture, showing once again the PDCI's ability to pick off a disunited opposition.

The main body of ministers was a Houphouet-Boigny-style balancing act, which sought simultaneously to ensure continuity, satisfy regional interests and reward followers. No doubt with an eye to reassuring the international community, nine ministers from the Ouattara government were retained, including Daniel K. Duncan, Ouattara's Minister of Finance, a former BCEAO and IMF technocrat who became Prime Minister. Less reassuringly, a group of old-guard ministers and officials, casualties of the 1980s purges, were brought back into political life, including the former Director of Customs and the ex-Director of Air Afrique (*Jeune Afrique* 16 December 1993). A few of the 'dinosaurs' were also included.

Bédié's most significant move, however, was to recognise the importance of the growing 'northern' consciousness amongst northern PDCI politicians, many of whom had become increasingly dissatisfied with what they perceived as a lack of recognition of the north's loyalty in the 1990 upheavals. Three leading northerners were appointed to the Cabinet: the Secretary General of the PDCI (Laurent Fologo), Lanciné Coulibaly and Lamine Fadika, the former Minister of the Navy who had been sacked in the 1980s after rumours of his involvement in a coup plot. This was aimed at undermining the possibility of the opposition forming a broader coalition with a break-away PDCI faction of dissatisfied northerners, who might have been mobilised under Ouattara's banner.

After a shaky start the opposition in Côte d'Ivoire has, therefore, survived and still has a chance to challenge the PDCI in the 1995 elections. The situation with regard to freedom of expression had improved by 1993, to the extent that repression of the opposition press had moderated, with four main dailies and 19 weeklies on sale, and the emergence of at least two independent non-state radio stations.[26] The opposition's political position was considerably weakened, however, by the accession to power of

President Bédié at the end of 1993, not least because it lost the opportunity to exploit a major source of division and uncertainty within the political elite. It is unclear as yet whether the ex-Prime Minister Ouattara has the political base – or the inclination – to pose a real threat in 1995, either with or without an agreement with the FPI. On its own, the FPI faces an uphill task in breaking out of its regional strongholds and living down the PDCI's 'tribalist' label; but the continuation of the country's economic difficulties, magnified in the short term by the devaluation of the CFA franc in January 1994, will no doubt continue to provoke divisions within the ruling party, and offer the FPI opportunities to build a broader coalition.

NOTES

1 See Crook (1991a) for an extended analysis of the crisis within the civil service in this period.
2 The resulting renewal rates for National Assembly Deputies were 82 per cent (1980) and 61 per cent (1985) (Bakary 1991; Fauré 1991).
3 This was official policy – see the comments of the Head of the Local Government Department of the Ministry of the Interior in 1988 (*Fraternité Matin* 1988).
4 The CSSPPA was at the heart of the Ivorian state in that it allocated quotas to a selected group of export companies (which included the President's) and then guaranteed their profit margins, as well as those of the licensed up-country buyers. The DCGTx, created in 1977, was a public works and planning agency under the direct and exclusive control of the President. It recruited large numbers of expatriate and Ivorian technocrats during the 1980s and expanded its functions to include most of the capital budget, the management of the overseas debt and the SAPs; see Galy (1993) for a detailed account.
5 See for instance the report in *West Africa* (1–7 May 1989).
6 Houphouet-Boigny had to some extent recognised this danger when he agreed to meet a delegation of farmers' representatives at Yamoussoukro in 1989 (*Africa Confidential* 20 October 1989).
7 An amendment to the law passed hastily on 10 October required presidential candidates to make a deposit of twenty million CFA francs (a sum of around £44,000) which would be forfeited if the candidate gained less than 10 per cent of the vote (*Fraternité Hebdo* 18 October 1990).
8 See for instance *L'Oeil du peuple*, *Le Réformateur* and an independent weekly, *Notre Temps*.
9 The opposition press specialised in stories about the responsibility of 'foreigners' (usually Ghanaians) for the rise in crime and prostitution, a theme especially popular with the PIT and its urban/Abidjan supporters (cf. Widner 1991). When the CFA franc was eventually devalued in January 1994, Gbagbo, to give him due credit, remained consistent, and argued that in the long run it was better for Côte d'Ivoire to stand on its own feet in the international money markets. Other opposition politicians might have been tempted to capitalise on the deep shock and anger which this measure aroused amongst the population.

10 Election data drawn from the following sources: *Fraternité Matin* (28 November 1990); Côte d'Ivoire (1990 and 1991); Fauré (1991).

11 In 1959 traditional and educated leaders of the Sanwi State – a small Agni kingdom (population c. 40,000) had demanded a separate independence from Côte d'Ivoire, invoking (as did the Buganda kingdom in Uganda) a colonial Protectorate Treaty of 1843. All the leaders were promptly arrested and the movement ruthlessly crushed (Zolberg 1964: 294).

12 It was no coincidence, therefore, that this was a major plank of FPI agricultural policy (see *Front populaire ivoirien* 1987). In 1986, yields on cocoa farms in the south-west were 1000kg per hectare compared to 300kg per hectare in the south-east (Côte d'Ivoire 1987).

13 Indeed, scholars such as Médard argue that the main political cleavage in Côte d'Ivoire is between Ivorians and foreign Africans (Médard 1991:196).

14 *Le Jeune Démocrate* 7 June 1993. The report continued that the Prefect 'had been sent specially into the area by the PDCI to destroy the Bété people by attacking their nurseries for the future – their youth'.

15 The turnout in the presidential elections dropped from 99 per cent to 68 per cent; in the legislative elections from 46 to 42 per cent; and in the commune elections from 35 to 34 per cent.

16 Because of the pressures imposed on party and government officials to produce plebiscitary-style turnouts during the long period of single-party rule, abstention has long been regarded in Côte d'Ivoire as a form of positive hostility or refusal to cooperate; this was publicly stated by J.B. Mockey as long ago as 1959 (Zolberg 1964: 268).

17 Figure calculated from the *Recensement Générale de la Population* (Côte d'Ivoire 1988) by adding the population aged over 20 (4,683,195) to those aged 18 and 19 in 1988, making a total of 5,125,015.

18 Calculated from results published in *Fraternité Matin* (28 November 1990).

19 Figures in Tables 4, 5 and 6 calculated from raw results published in *Fraternité Matin* (28 November 1990) and Côte d'Ivoire (1990). Urban populations from Côte d'Ivoire (1992).

20 In some of the communes, the number of registered electors exceeded the estimated adult population (Côte d'Ivoire 1991).

21 Figures calculated from Côte d'Ivoire (1991).

22 See Chris Simpson's report in *West Africa* 3–9 December 1990.

23 The government's actions were condemned in the European Parliament and by Amnesty International, and criticised by the US Under-Secretary of State for African Affairs (*West Africa* 23–29 March 1992; *Africa Report* May/June 1992).

24 The campaign was called 'La Fête de la Liberté' and was designed to provide copy for the newspapers. The PDCI responded with its 'Caravane de la Paix', lavishly sponsored by 'Fine Music' which provided funky sounds for the rallies.

25 Ouattara had submitted the matter, as required, to the President of the Supreme Court knowing that the Court was technically inquorate because a new president had not been appointed to replace the one recently sacked for corruption (*Jeune Afrique* 9 December 1993).

26 The Catholic *Radio Espoir* and a commercial station, *Radio Nostalgie* (*Africa Research Bulletin* November 1993).

REFERENCES

Bakary, T. (1984) 'Elite transformation and political succession', in I. William Zartman and C. Delgado (eds) *The Political Economy of Ivory Coast*, New York: Praeger.

—— (1985) 'Les elections legislatives ivoiriennes de novembre 1980 et le système politique', Bordeaux: Travaux et Documents No. 8, CEAN.

—— (1991) 'Le retour au pluralisme politique en Côte d'Ivoire', *L'Année Africaine 1990–1991*, Bordeaux: CEAN.

Chauveau, J.P. and Dozon, J.P. (1987) 'Au coeur des ethnies ivoiriennes . . . l'Etat', in E. Terray (ed.) *L'Etat contemporain en Afrique*, Paris: L'Harmattan.

Contamin, B. and Fauré, Y. (1990) *La bataille des entreprises publiques en Côte d'Ivoire*, Paris: Karthala.

Côte d'Ivoire, République de (1987) *Annuaire de statistiques agricoles, 1986* (Ministère de l'agriculture).

—— (1988) *Recensement général de la population et de l'habitat, 1988* (Direction de la statistique).

—— (1990) *Elections à la présidence de la république: enregistrement des résultats communiqués au Ministère* (Ministère de l'interieur).

—— (1991) *Résultats des elections municipales en 1985 et 1990* (Ministère de l'interieur, DGCL).

—— (1992) Direction et contrôle des grands travaux, *Guide Municipale de la Côte d'Ivoire*.

Crook, R. (1989) 'Patrimonialism, administrative effectiveness and economic development in Côte d'Ivoire', *African Affairs*, 88, 351.

—— (1990) 'Politics, the cocoa crisis and administration in Côte d'Ivoire', *Journal of Modern African Studies*, 28, 4.

—— (1991a) 'Les changements politiques en Côte d'Ivoire: une approche institutionelle', *L'Année Africaine 1990–1991*, Bordeaux: CEAN.

—— (1991b) 'State, society and political institutions in Côte d'Ivoire and Ghana', in J. Manor (ed.) *Rethinking Third World Politics*, London: Longman.

Fauré, Y. (1989) 'Ivory Coast: analysing a crisis', in J. Dunn, R. Rathbone and D.C. O'Brien (eds) *Contemporary West African States*, Cambridge: Cambridge University Press.

—— (1991) 'Sur la démocratisation en Côte d'Ivoire: passé et présent', *L'Année Africaine 1990–1991*, Bordeaux: CEAN.

Fauré, Y. and Médard, J. F. (1982) *Etat et bourgeoisie en Côte d'Ivoire*, Paris: Karthala.

Fraternité Matin (1988) 'Communes: un pari sur l'avenir' (Spéciale Indépendence, dec.).

Front populaire ivoirien (1987) *Propositions pour gouverner la Côte d'Ivoire*, Paris: L'Harmattan.

Galy, M. (1993) 'Les avatars de la DCGTx en Côte d'Ivoire', *Politique Africaine* 52, December.

Gastellu, J.M. and Affou, Y. (1982) 'Un mythe à décomposer: la bourgeoisie de planteurs', in Fauré and Médard (1982).

Médard, J.F. (1991) 'The historical trajectories of the Ivorian and Kenyan states', in J. Manor (ed.) *Rethinking Third World Politics*, London: Longman.

Widner, J. (1991) 'The 1990 elections in Côte d'Ivoire', *Issue XX*, 1.

—— (1993) 'The discovery of politics: smallholder reactions to the cocoa crisis of 1987–1990 in Côte d'Ivoire', in T.Callaghy and J. Ravenhill (eds) *Hemmed In: Responses to Africa's Economic Decline*, New York: Columbia University Press.

—— (1994) 'Single party states and agricultural policies: the cases of Côte d'Ivoire and Kenya', *Comparative Politics* 26, 2.

Zolberg, A. (1964) *One Party Government in the Ivory Coast*, Princeton: Princeton University Press.

Newspapers and periodicals

Africa Confidential (London)
Africa Report (Washington DC)
Africa Research Bulletin (Oxford)
Fraternité Hebdo (Abidjan) (weekly)
Fraternité Matin (Abidjan) (daily)
Jeune Afrique (Paris)
Jeune Afrique Economique (Paris)
Le Jeune Démocrate (Abidjan) (weekly)
Le Monde (Paris)
Le Réformateur (Abidjan) (daily)
La Voie (Abidjan) (daily)
L'Oeil du Peuple (Abidjan) (daily)
Notre Temps (Abidjan) (weekly)
Nouvel Horizon (Abidjan) (monthly)

3 Mali: democracy and political change

Richard Vengroff and Moctar Kone

INTRODUCTION

Although many African countries have had to address pressures for demo-cratisation and are undergoing some form of transition (Decalo 1992), Mali is an especially interesting case which could provide useful insights into the durability of democracy on the African continent and elsewhere. Mali has experienced extraordinary changes in the past three years leading to the almost total transformation of the political system from a highly authori-tarian regime to one which has all of the trappings of a liberal democracy. Unlike many other nations, Mali was fortunate in being able to write a new constitution and hold elections without the burden of continued partici-pation in the process by a ruling party and head of state (Vengroff *et al.* 1992; Clark 1992; Nzrankeu 1993). Therefore, the more open procedure offers a better indication of the degree to which, given the opportunity, a modern democratic system can take root in the African milieu.

BACKGROUND

Mali, known under French colonial rule as the Soudan, gained its full legal independence in 1960 after an abortive effort to set up a union with Senegal (the Mali Federation). By that time, a single political party, the US-RDA (Union Soudanaise – Rassemblement Démocratique Africain), under the leadership of Modibo Keita, had already swept away or absorbed all semblance of an opposition. Keita's efforts to turn Mali into a thoroughly socialist one-party state, coupled with his alienation from France, left the country even more isolated than its landlocked geography would dictate.

The left-wing faction of the US-RDA emerged as the dominant force in the government. The more moderate wing of the party was swept along in the euphoria of the socialist transformation and for all intents and purposes was silenced. Early on Mali asserted its economic independence by leaving the French monetary union and creating the Malian franc. It paid the price in terms of convertibility of its currency and foreign trade. Open opposition to these measures took the form of demonstrations and protests by local business leaders imprisoned and later summarily executed. Rural development policies were promulgated which centred around state-run marketing boards and efforts to collectivise agriculture. Both led to a decline in the production of cash crops and an increase in smuggling.

The regime was able to sustain itself with strong support from the urban areas, particularly the large number of government functionaries and students. Both of these groups were favoured with a variety of benefits, including relatively high scholarship support and guaranteed life-long employment. Having eliminated opposition and taken control of most associational groups, only the Army remained as a potential threat to the regime. Modelling his efforts after those of the cultural revolution in China, Keita began to build a party-controlled militia as an alternative to the Army. Fear of an anti-corruption campaign which threatened to touch the leaders of the Army and encouraged by the successful wave of coups d'état sweeping the continent, the military decided to act. Perceiving Keita's actions as a direct threat to its corporate interests the military stepped in, seizing power in a bloodless coup in 1968.

After the coup, Traoré spent several years suppressing all opposition and consolidating his power within the military. He felt that to maintain control in the long term he had to legitimise his regime. His efforts included writing a new constitution, organising a single party, the UDPM (Union Démocratique du Peuple Malien), and generally insulating himself from dislocations occurring in the economy and Malian society as a whole. Competing candidates were allowed to contest elections within the context of the one-party state and considerable turnover did take place. The economy, already in difficulty because of Keita's socialist policies, suffered consecutively from the Sahelian droughts, the oil crisis and, in its final stages, the general downturn in the world economy which led to a long-term recession from which Mali has yet to recover.

Unable by the mid-1980s to raise sufficient revenue, the government could no longer guarantee employment for all high school and university graduates, and was unable on several occasions even to meet its own payroll. The IMF and the World Bank insisted that parastatals be closed or privatised, further increasing unemployment. The size of the public service sector became yet another issue for which serious reforms were demanded as part of the imposed structural adjustment package. As conflict with the urban elites proliferated the regime became increasingly dependent on the international donor community.

At the same time that the Traoré government faced pressures from the urban elites, the unions, students and other dissatisfied groups, its ability to hold the opposition in check declined. The donors pressured the regime to ensure that basic human rights were at least minimally respected. France, the USA and other Western countries funnelled support to associational groups, including many which were to become opposition parties. The general provision of foreign aid to Mali was linked to democratisation by several key donors.

Under intense pressure, Traoré moved to 'democratise' the system but, hoping to maintain control over the process, he refused to do so outside the context of the one-party state. An old and obscure provision of Malian law made it possible for opposition groups to operate openly as non-political associations. Because of international scrutiny Traoré had little choice but to let these groups organise and go about their business. In early 1991, encouraged by events elsewhere in Africa and in Eastern Europe, the opposition associations united in a common front with the principal labour union (UNTM) and the leading student association. As the Traoré regime found itself pushed to the wall, it increasingly defended itself with violent repression of opposition marches and protests, thus sealing its own fate. The deaths of hundreds of students turned even the bureaucracy against Traoré. The refusal of the Air Force to bomb UNTM headquarters, where the opposition groups gathered to launch a national strike on 24 March 1991 marked the critical precipitating event. Some elements of the Army, appalled by the role of the military in firing upon its own people, arrested President Traoré and seized power.

The leader of the coup, Lt Colonel Amadou Toumani Touré (affectionately known as ATT), promised a return to civilian rule within one year. The transition council, the Comité de Transition Pour le Salut du Peuple (CTSP), composed of both civilians and the military, proceeded to set up a transitional government and organised a national conference to write the new constitution, the new electoral code and a legal framework for establishing political parties (La Charte des partis). The military, which felt that its legitimacy had been severely compromised as a result of its complicity in the murder of unarmed civilians during the anti-government demonstrations, was eager to return to its self-defined role as defender of the nation.

Overseeing the transition to democracy made it possible for the Army, in the face of a sceptical opposition, to take the high ground while protecting itself from retribution for its past sins. ATT's commitment to a return to the barracks remained firm. In the interim period his government, in its effort to assure a smooth, peaceful transition, signed the 'Pacte du Nord', theoretically ending the Tuareg revolt in the northern regions, and the

'Pacte social' with the unions, establishing basic conditions for restoring labour's confidence in the government.

After thirty years of one-party and military rule, the legal basis for a multi-party competitive system was established for the new Third Republic by the transitional (CTSP) government in September of 1991. A broad-based National Constitutional Conference was held from 29 July to 12 August 1991, the charter of parties was promulgated in September and the new constitution was approved by referendum on 12 January 1992. Subsequently elections were held at the municipal level (19 January 1992), in two rounds for the National Assembly (24 February and 9 March) and in two rounds for the presidency (13 and 27 April). Much of this was possible because the entrenched economic and political interests identified with the Traoré regime were effectively out of power and thus unable to skew the process as has happened in some other African countries.

Mali's Constitution is closely 'patterned after the French Constitution of 1958' (Tessery 1992: 6). The system is 'semi-presidential', with a relatively powerful President elected by universal suffrage exercising an important leadership role, and a Prime Minister (named by the President) and government responsible to the National Assembly. The judiciary is constitutionally independent of political authorities (Ngom 1992) and is overseen by both a Supreme Court and a Constitutional Court. Adherence to the Universal Declaration of Human Rights is included as a fundamental principle in the Constitution itself.

While these many changes seem to provide the basis for development of a democratic polity, the rapidity with which they occurred leaves many questions to be answered. To what extent are they merely cosmetic as opposed to representative of a more profound commitment to democratic governance in the long term by both the Malian people and their leaders?

The successful legitimisation of institutions and the application of values associated with democratic governance are linked to important contingencies, including culture. Therefore, it is possible for a state to establish a facade that has all of the outward appearances of a democratic system without necessarily developing the 'participatory, democratic political culture' necessary to sustain it (Inglehart 1988, Eckstein 1988). This set of orientations may not have had sufficient time to be nurtured in the Malian context (Diamond 1988). As noted by Decalo, 'whatever demo-cratic advances have been attained in Africa at this stage are still structural and/or constitutional; certainly a breath of fresh air, but likely to end up in some countries as only cosmetic and/or temporary' (Decalo 1992). To assume that democratic institutions could be established in one or two years after decades of authoritarian rule, government mismanagement and difficult economic conditions would be naive.

There is considerable disagreement as to whether economic development is a necessary condition for legitimisation of a democratic government (Diamond, Linz and Lipset 1990; Inglehart 1988) or whether effective democratic governance is a co-requisite for economic development (Landell-Mills and Seregeldin 1991). For purposes of analysis, providing a means for operationalising the transition is critical.

Charlick argues that 'governance is conceived of as the effective management of public affairs through the generation of a regime (set of rules) accepted as legitimate, for the purpose of promoting and enhancing societal values sought by individuals and groups' (Charlick 1992). He further states that democratisation is

> a particular set of governance relationships or ways of achieving governance objectives. Democratization emphasizes accountability through open competition for authority (usually through electoral choice among alternatives), responsiveness and policy pluralism through participation, particularly by non-state actors, and respect for human rights, needed to assure the viability of these other democratic traits.
>
> (Charlick 1992; Diamond *et al.* 1990)

In this paper, analysis will be guided by this working definition.

The process of democratisation in Mali will be assessed in relation to the issues of accountability through open competition, responsiveness *vis à vis* the population and associational groups and on the development of and opportunities for policy pluralism. The basic assumption being made in this study is that parties and the party system have a key role to play in democratic governance. Hence, the key hypothesis for examination is: The greater the extent to which the party system functions in a manner consistent with democratic governance, the greater the level of system legitimacy. Furthermore, as legitimacy increases, the chances for the survival and institutionalisation of a democratic system increase.

THE NATURE OF THE PARTY SYSTEM IN MALI

The opening up of the Malian political system to democratic participation following the '*événements*' (the popular term associated with the anti-Traoré demonstrations) and the subsequent legalisation of political activities resulted initially in an extremely complex playing field which included some forty-seven different political parties (Vengroff 1992). Some trends have emerged from the series of five elections (municipal, two rounds of National Assembly, two rounds of presidential) having produced a clear shakeout in the system. It should be underlined, however, that the current party system in Mali was not born in a void, but evolved. The roots and ongoing organisational base of today's competitive parties are closely linked to Mali's historical development, especially in the period following the Second World War (Campmas 1978; Imperato 1989).

The number of organisations in Mali which can lay claim to being 'serious' political parties is significantly smaller than the total number of parties actually registered. The discussion here will be limited to those which were successful in winning seats in either the municipal councils or in the National Assembly. It is quite clear from analysis of the parties' organisational bases and the election returns that even among 'successful parties' only a few are likely to survive until the next national elections in 1997.

Surprisingly, the factors which seem to be of importance to the long-term survival and staying power of the various parties are the same as those which came into play in the 1960s when most African countries gained independence (Hodgkin 1961; Morgenthau 1964; Coleman and Rosberg 1966; Zolberg 1966; LaPalombara and Weiner 1966; McKown and Kauffman 1973; Vengroff 1977; 1979):

1   the development and maintenance of a strong party organisation, with the depth and breadth necessary to reach out to and penetrate the rural areas, recruit members and raise funds;
2   the degree of institutionalisation of the party as indicated by its historical roots, longevity, survival and continuing support;
3   the existence of a core home area, ethnic and/or regional base;
4   the perception that the role of party officials, including elected deputies and councillors, is that of providing constituent services, especially in matters relating to representation before administrative authorities (e.g. territorial administration);
5   the level and nature of communication between the population, party supporters and the party organisation and elected officials, including the degree of personal contact, both in the course of electoral campaigns and in the execution of day-to-day activities.

Consistent with the concept of democratic governance, these five factors reflect the ability of the parties to perform the representative function and to present policy alternatives either as a governing or opposition group. The degree to which the political parties currently on the scene in Mali meet these criteria is indicative of their current strength, their future survival and success and their potential contribution to the institutionalisation of democratic governance.

Here the parties have been grouped into three tiers based on the degree to which they satisfy the five criteria. Of the numerous parties participating in the electoral process in Third Republic Mali, only three, ADEMA, US-RDA (now split into the US-RDA and BDIA) and, to a lesser extent CNID, which will be labelled here the first-tier parties, meet most of the criteria. Among the first-tier national parties, the ADEMA and the US-RDA both have strong historical roots and important organisational resources and strengths throughout the country. Second-tier parties, the RDP and PSP, meet some of the criteria and at least have the potential to become national parties. Just below them is a group of very much regionally oriented parties, the RDT, UFDP, PDP, PMD and UDD, all of which, despite some electoral success in the National Assembly and the municipal councils, are likely to either merge, or at least go into coalition, either in the government, or in one of the opposition parliamentary groups with one of the larger parties, and/or continue to exert a strictly local/ regional influence.

ADEMA-PASJ (Alliance pour la Démocratie au Mali) has it origins in several parties which became clandestine organisations after the seizure of power by Moussa Traoré in 1968. These groups eventually merged into a broad-based coalition which was to become ADEMA. In 1990 it was allowed to exist openly as an association because of a legal technicality and international pressure for democratisation. ADEMA participated actively with student groups and the unions in the demonstrations which were to topple the government on 26 March 1991. The association formally transformed itself into a political party, ADEMA-PASJ (Parti Africain pour la Solidarité et la Justice) at a special congress two months after Traoré's fall.

Rather than starting from scratch, ADEMA-PASJ had, at the time of its official transformation into a party, an established organisation in every 'cercle', 'arrondissement' and in many rural villages and urban neighbour-hoods. Its supporters include a core of middle-aged teachers and health professionals, many of whom proved to be very influential organisers at the local level. The party was able to use this well-elaborated organisation, its many relatively well-educated local opinion leaders, the past persecution of many of its supporters and its association with the '*événements*' to build a strong communication network. Combined with a strategy that brought the maximum number of candidates, including its presidential candidate, Alpha Konaré, down to the base of the system for face-to-face contact with the rural voters, the well-articulated organisation became an unbeatable electoral machine. As a result the party was able to show its strength in every region in Mali, finishing first in the municipal elections and in both rounds of the National Assembly and in the presidential elections.

The US-RDA (Union Soudanaise-Rassemblement Démocratique Africain) is, overall, the second largest political party in Mali. It is the party which most directly competes with ADEMA for the 'core' Malian voter. Founded in 1946, making it one of the oldest political parties in West Africa (Campmas 1978; Morgenthau 1964), it emerged from its urban intellectual roots to become a serious force in pre-independence Mali. Its leaders built a core of support in Mopti and Toumbouctou in the early 1950s which was still in evidence forty years later in the 1992 elections. Coming to power in 1957, the socialist-oriented US-RDA became, for all intents and purposes, the sole party in Mali at the time of independence in 1960. Under President Modibo Keita, it enjoyed nearly a decade of leadership running the country, an experience abruptly ended by the coup of 1968.

The US-RDA party organisation, which included fifty-two sections, has split along lines which replicate its past internal ideological and personal disagreements. The smaller Haidara wing represents the older hardliners from the days of the Keita government. The now dominant historically more moderate Konaté wing retains a strong base in the rural areas as well as in some of the towns. Internal factional disputes led to an open breach which was contested in the courts. The Court of Appeals decision awarded the name and facilities of the party to the Haidara faction. The Konaté wing has been reconstituted first as the PRDA (*Le Miroir* 1993), then renamed the Bloc Démocratique pour l'Integration Africaine (BDIA). In spite of the split, it is still the most likely of all the parties to provide a serious opposition, an opposition with a chance of becoming a majority at some future date.

The third and youngest of the 'major' parties in Third Republic Mali, the CNID (Congrès National d'Initiative Démocratique), was founded as an association in October 1990, becoming a party in May 1991. CNID supporters were very active in the events leading up to the fall of the Traoré government. The party's core of 'militants' are relatively young, urban, include many who have studied abroad and, unlike their ADEMA counterparts, by and large are not part of the group of Malians who remained in the country and/or spent time in prison under Traoré's so-called Second Republic. The party's key strength rests with its ability to mobilise the politically relevant urban student population against the government.

The CNID has a dynamic, articulate spokesman in Mountaga Tall, who traces his ancestry in a direct line to a historically important Toucouleur traditional religious leader (El Hadj Oumar Tall). Its success in penetrating the countryside and generating support among the rural majority has thus far been limited. Tall's ethnicity tends to work against him (only about 5 per cent of the population is Toucouleur) even though he is a fluent

Bambara speaker. In spite of a very respectable third-place finish in the first-round presidential elections, the party showed little real strength outside the cities and Tall's home area, Ségou. Survival of the party, in spite of its relative success, including the election of nine deputies and a number of mayors and municipal councillors, will require extensive organisational work at the base if it is to develop into a serious challenger for power at some future date. Its agreement to join the government coalition after the April anti-government demonstrations placed it, albeit temporarily, in a very different role than it played from the other side of the aisle.

The second tier of parties includes the centrist RDP (Rassemblement pour la Démocratie et la Progrès), the only other party in the country whose national organisation and preliminary electoral success give it even a remote possibility of attaining national importance. The party organisation is well elaborated nationally, but probably could have done better if it had concentrated its limited resources in the three regions where it has the greatest strength. Party finance, partly underwritten by its leader during the elections, is now a critical problem.

Also in the second tier of parties, the PSP (Parti Progressiste Soudanais) is notable because of its historical role as the first African party to experience electoral success (Campmas 1978) under the colonial regime. The PSP, which failed to become a mass party, partially because of its association with the traditional authorities and the French colonial regime, was defeated definitively by the RDA in the territorial elections of 1957 (Campmas 1978). In 1962, as a result of participation in anti-government demonstrations associated with Mali's leaving the Franc-zone, it lost its founders to arrest and imprisonment (Verité 1991; Imperato 1989). After their martyrdom, allegedly executed on the orders of President Modibo Keita in 1964, the party all but disappeared.

After years in exile, the PSP's current leader, Professor Sékéné Sissoko, a widely respected Africanist historian, returned to Mali after the overthrow of Traoré. In 1992, thirty years after the arrest of its leaders and its disappearance from the scene, the PSP was remarkably still able to run a reasonably successful race in its old stronghold, Bafoulabé (the birthplace of its founder, Fily Dabo Sissoko), an area in which it has done well electorally since 1945. However, due to financial and organisational constraints, the future of the PSP is rather tenuous.

As noted in an independent Malian newspaper, *Aurore*, only the top few parties really merit the label political party. 'En dehors de ces formations, le reste dans une forte majorité n'est qu'un regroupement a base clanique, un lobby d'intérêt ou d'un regroupment regionaliste même' (*Aurore* 22 August 1991: 2). The third tier includes six or seven parties with significant electoral strength and organisation but which operate in limited regional, ethnic or local enclaves, rather than nationally.

The RDT (Rassemblement pour la Démocratie et le Travail), small and very localised, is indicative of some of the ways in which support in this third group of parties is generated in Mali. The RDT is composed principally of a core of former Mopti residents, the 'Association de Ressortissants de Mopti', living in Bamako (RDT 1992). Like some of the larger parties, ADEMA and CNID, it existed first as an association in opposition to Moussa Traoré, only becoming a party later on.

In the three-seat National Assembly constituency of Mopti, the RDT managed to assure itself of victory by bringing together a coalition including the three most important families of local notables. The RDT's carefully balanced local ticket had a positive effect in building on and reinforcing the tradition of compromise and coalition formation in the local traditional political system. It is currently part of the ruling 'Pacte Républicain' coalition with ADEMA in the National Assembly. As a result, it has been able to secure for itself the Ministry of Tourism (a post it retained even under the new government formed in April 1993) and the presidency of the National Assembly's Public Works Committee, both of vital interest to the economy of the north in general and Mopti in particular.

THE 1992 ELECTIONS

The results of the 1992 elections to select the first government under the Third Republic provide some evidence of the degree to which the party system is able to meet the critical conditions for democratic governance: accountability through open competition, responsiveness and opportunities for policy pluralism. Although the majority system of voting (party list by circumscription in two rounds) in the National Assembly elections (Ordinance No. 91-074/P/CTSP, 18 September 1991) does not appear to have been the first choice of any of the parties which participated in the National Conference, the spectre of an ungovernable system (Fourth Republic France being the most common reference cited) paralysed by an unstable legislative majority led to acceptance of a majority system (ADEMA (meeting with party officials, 1992)). As a compromise, proportionality was retained for the municipal elections.

THE MUNICIPAL ELECTIONS

The first partisan elections under the new Constitution, approved by referendum in late 1991, were for the municipal councils in January 1992.

The municipal elections, based on a system of proportional representation, are designed to accommodate the greatest diversity of interests and parties possible on the nineteen councils. Since the councils are relatively large (thirty-one to fifty-five members) and the proportional electoral system in use only requires an extremely small portion of the vote (between 1 and 2 per cent) to win a seat on a municipal council, all organisations with any possibility of legitimately claiming the title of political party were able to gain some seats. Although there were charges of fraud raised against the leading party, ADEMA, especially in Bamako, and in spite of the fact that a number of parties seem to have employed questionable methods, neither the international election monitors nor an analysis of the results lend much credence to accusations of broad-based irregularities (DNAT 1992).

The municipal elections provided the first opportunity and perhaps the easiest mechanism for many of the new parties to test their strength, at least in the urban areas. Voter participation (33.7 per cent, varying from 21.5–43.9 per cent per municipality) was somewhat disappointing, given the fact that these represented the first free multi-party elections held in Mali in over thirty years.

Twenty-four parties, on average more than nine per municipality, contested the elections. Of these, nineteen actually won municipal council seats. Only three parties, ADEMA, US-RDA and CNID, put up candidates in all the communes. These highly fractionalised elections produced results in which these three parties together captured well over half (59 per cent) of the 751 council posts. However, none of the three strongest parties were able to win the majority of seats on any councils, a majority of councillors being necessary to elect a mayor. Sixteen other parties, an average of about eight per commune, gained one or more seats in at least one of the nineteen municipal councils.

ADEMA captured, on average, 28.7 per cent of the vote per commune (ranging from 15-47 per cent), and led all other parties with 251 seats. The historically important US-RDA which, at the time of the municipal elections had not yet divided itself publicly in a factional, fratricidal struggle, finished second nationally with 130 municipal council seats, winning, on average, 17.6 per cent of the vote per commune (range 5-42 per cent). The third of the three parties with national ambitions, CNID, building on a relatively youthful urban base, averaged 12 per cent of the vote per municipality (range 3-28 per cent), for a total of ninety-six seats. Among the remaining sixteen parties obtaining municipal council seats, the RDP (sixty-four seats), the UDD (sixty-three seats) and the UFD (fifty seats) are the most important. The only other notable performance was by the small, very localised UFDP in San. This is the only municipal council in the country in which a single party (the UFDP) won a majority of the votes (52 per cent) and seats.

Table 3.1 Mali municipal election results – distribution of seats by party

	ADEMA	USRDA	CNID	PSP	UDD	PDJ	PDP	RDP	UDS	UFD	PUDP	PEI	PMPS	UFDP	PMD	RDT	PUPM	PPS	RJP	TOTAL
NIORO	11	2	8	5	11															37
KAYES	12	8	3	2		2	1	8	1											37
KITA	8	5	3	1			1	5		7	1									31
KATI	11	4	2	1	1		6	7		2	2	1								37
KOULIKORO	11	9	2					1		7			1							31
KOUTIALA	5	2	2	1	16		1	8			1			1						37
BOUGOUNI	6	7	2	1	5		3	6		1										31
SIKASSO	14	7	3				1	3							9					37
SEGOU	6	7	11	1	3		1	4		1		1				4				39
SAN	6	5	2				2	1		2				19						37
MOPTI	8	10	2	3			5	1		1				1		6				37
TOMBOUCTOU	18	2	1	1						14							1			37
GAO	13	16	6					2												37
COMMUNE I	18	8	9	2	6	1	3	2		3	1	1		1						55
COMMUNE II	12	8	7	3	5		3	2		2		1								43
COMMUNE III	11	8	9	2	3		3	1		3		1								41
COMMUNE IV	16	8	6	3	2	1	4	3		2		1		1		1		1		49
COMMUNE V	14	10	11	3	4		1	2		3									1	49
COMMUNE VI	14	4	7		7		5	8		2				1					1	49
TOTAL	214	130	96	29	63	4	40	64	1	50	5	6	1	24	9	11	1	1	2	751
% OF SEATS	28%	17%	13%	4%	8%	1%	5%	9%	0%	7%	1%	1%	0%	3%	1%	1%	0%	0%	0%	100%

With an average of eight (range four to thirteen) different parties winning seats per urban commune, and with only one of the elections producing a majority party in a municipal council, coalition-building became an extremely important and complex activity. The immediate impulse was for most of the smaller parties to group themselves against the leader, ADEMA. Thus, although ADEMA won a plurality of the votes and hence seats in all six Bamako communes, it was able to put together a winning coalition of council members to elect a mayor in only one. By contrast, CNID, in coalition with several other parties, elected three, the US-RDA one, and PDP one mayor each in the Bamako communes.

The first, second and third vice mayors in each commune are salaried positions. In the process of coalition-building in Bamako, the party which got the job of mayor in each of the six communes allocated the remaining three salaried positions to elected councillors representing three different parties. Furthermore, the remaining members of the Commune 'Bureau' were also divided among the coalition partners. In the course of this process, a variety of trade-offs between parties, several of which were to have an impact on the National Assembly and presidential elections, were agreed.

THE NATIONAL ASSEMBLY ELECTIONS

The National Assembly elections were organised around a majority electoral system in two rounds. The 116 seats to be voted on in Mali (an additional thirteen still remain to be chosen by Malians living in other countries) are allocated among fifty-five electoral circumscriptions based on the existing administrative units, the forty-nine '*cercles*' and six Bamako communes. The distribution of seats is based on population, with one seat allocated for every 60,000 people or additional fraction of 40,000 or more, but with each '*cercle*' having a minimum of one deputy. The number of seats allocated to each electoral circumscription range from one to six. Each party must present a complete list of candidates (candidates can legally appear on one list only) equivalent to the number of deputies in the circumscription in the winner-takes-all, majority election (Ordinance No. 91-074/P/CPSP, 1991). A party receiving a majority of the votes in the first round of the election in any circumscription is declared the winner. If no party receives a majority in a given area, the two parties finishing with the most votes compete in a second-round election two weeks later. While the losing parties can endorse one of the top two parties' lists in the second round, they cannot join with them to present a new composite list.

The obvious strength of ADEMA nationally, as demonstrated in the municipal elections, frightened the opposition. Amidst fears that the transitional administration was firmly in the ADEMA camp, and charges of fraud and mismanagement in the municipal elections, the main opposition parties demanded a delay in the National Assembly elections in order to buy more time in which adequately to prepare and campaign throughout the country. In addition, time was needed to allow the government to correct problems with the ballots. The proposed delay was agreed to by the transition government and the first round of the National Assembly elections, originally scheduled for 26 January 1992 was put off until 23 February with the second round taking place two weeks later.

The level of participation in the National Assembly elections proved to be even more disappointing than that for the municipal councils (22 per cent turnout). Average turnout in the second round for the forty-four constituencies in which no party had received a majority in the first round remained at just under 22 per cent. The correlation between voter turnout in the first and second rounds of the election is quite high (r=.76), indicating little change in the relative level of participation within constituencies between the two rounds.

The only significant difference between constituencies in turnout is related to urban–rural differences. Voter turnout in the nineteen urban communes (25.8 per cent) is significantly higher (T=3.16, p<.002) than in the thirty-six rural circumscriptions (20.2 per cent). Differences in second-round voting are in the same direction but are not statistically significant. It should be noted, however, that all of the constituencies in which the election was decided during the first round are considered to be rural.

Independent observer teams, although noting some anomalies, attested to the 'adequacy' of the election procedures during both rounds of the election. Only eleven circumscriptions were decided during the first round, with five parties, ADEMA, US-RDA, CNID, PDP and UMADD, winning a total of only fifteen of the 116 seats up for grabs. Ten parties remained in contention in one or more constituencies for the second round of the elections. The level of competitiveness and relative fairness of the election is indicated by the fact that of the ten parties remaining in the race in the second round, six of them had finished first in the first-round elections in at least one circumscription. In addition, the leading party list in the first round was defeated in the second round in seven of the forty-four circumscriptions (16 per cent). In those cases ADEMA, which was involved in six of these races, lost in four (to US-RDA, PMD and CNID) and won in only two (both from US-RDA). This evidence does not suggest that any one party was given preferential treatment or that the elections were anything but fair.

The first-round National Assembly elections were contested by twenty-two officially registered parties, although to very different degrees. Only two parties, ADEMA and CNID, presented party lists of candidates in all fifty-five circumscriptions. Also competing on a national scale, the US-RDA and the RDP each presented lists of candidates in forty-nine constituencies, while the PSP contested forty-two. The UDD, RDT and PDP competed in twenty-nine, twenty-eight and twenty-seven constituencies, respectively. The remaining parties offered lists in select regions and circumscriptions only. The most localised and personalist of the parties, UMADD, presented a candidate in only one constituency (a single-member district), winning the election in the first round with nearly three-quarters of the vote (73 per cent).

The overall results of the National Assembly elections combined with a first place showing in the municipals clearly established ADEMA-PASJ as the party to beat at the national level. It is the only party that was able to win seats in all eight of Mali's regions and the Bamako district. In total it received seventy-four seats (of 116) in thirty-seven different constituencies. Its apparent victory in an additional circumscription was overturned in the courts. Rather than appealing against the court's decision, ADEMA graciously acquiesced and the two seats were awarded to the PSP. ADEMA was thus in the enviable position of being able to control the National Assembly with a strong, stable majority, without the need for coalition partners. The possibility of the emergence of a one-party-dominant government and the eventual drift to a one-party state are an obvious concern to both observers of and participants in the system.

The US-RDA, which ruled Mali from 1957 until 1968, was the only other party to demonstrate serious national strength in the legislative elections, even though it finished third in terms of the number of seats. The party, which averaged just over 19 per cent of the vote in the forty-nine constituencies in which it competed in the first round, won a total of five circumscriptions in four different regions. The US-RDA also captured a very respectable portion of the vote in every region, except the newly created Region VIII (Kidal) in the relatively inaccessible extreme northern area of the country.

The US-RDA showing is quite remarkable given the fact that the party was badly and openly split between two competing factions. It had, for all intents and purposes, divided into two separate parties (it is now officially two separate parties, the US-RDA and the PRDA, now known as the BDIA (Bloc Démocratique pour l'Integration Africaine)), over the issue of the choice of a presidential candidate. However, its lists in the National Assembly elections were designated prior to the split, so the party factions did not present competing lists in any constituencies. Throughout the years of military rule and political persecution under Moussa Traoré, the US-RDA was able clandestinely to maintain at least some of its organ-

Table 3.2 Results of Mali National Assembly elections

Party*	Circumscriptions won 1st round	Circumscriptions 1st place 1st rnd	Circumscriptions 2nd place 1st rnd	Circumscriptions won 1st + 2nd	Seats won
ADEMA	7	35	9	37**	73
CNID	1	1	4	4	9
USRDA	1	6	14	5	8
PMD	0	1	0	1	4
RDP	0	1	4	2	6
UDD	0	1	2	1	4
UFDP	0	1	0	1	3
RDT	0	0	2	1	3
PDP	1	0	3	1	2
PSP	0	0	3	1*	2
UMADD	1	0	0	1	1

*Eleven additional parties participated in the election without qualifying for the 2nd round.
**One circumscription seemingly won by ADEMA was awarded to PSP by the courts.

isation intact throughout the countryside. This, along with its name, symbol and colour (although the ballots in the National Assembly election were not in colour) recognition, past experience as the governing party, maintenance of its historic geographic base and well-known leaders, helps account for its relatively strong showing.

The CNID, very much a newcomer on the political scene, like its former ally (ADEMA) in the democratisation movement, attempted to contest the National Assembly elections in every circumscription. Buoyed by an early but highly unrepresentative poll by a local newspaper in Bamako, the party was extremely disappointed with the results. It averaged only 11 per cent of the vote, with a rather spotty showing nationally. CNID succeeded in finishing second among the parties in terms of the number of seats (nine), by winning four constituencies, one in each of three different regions and one in Bamako. The core of the party's strength in the Assembly, however, comes from the six seats it won in Ségou, the home town of the party's founder and presidential candidate, Mountaga Tall. Even there, however, CNID had to invest most of its limited resources in coming from behind with the support of the US-RDA and UDD, in order to defeat the ADEMA list in the second round. The party's strength is derived from the small but politically relevant younger, urban elements in the anti-Traoré association. Its contacts, organisation and influence in the countryside are somewhat limited, resulting in a relatively weak showing in the rural areas.

Of the remaining parties winning seats, only the RDP and the historically important PSP made efforts at running nation-wide campaigns. However, the RDP was successful in only two constituencies and the PSP in one (after a court ruling). The other parties winning seats ran campaigns in no more than half of the country, each winning in only one constituency. Basically, they are limited regional- and or ethnic-based parties, often closely tied to local notable families. In two cases, the UMADD and PDP, parties won overwhelming first-round victories in the home constituencies of their top leaders, but no seats anywhere else. The RDT and the PMD also made strong first-round showings and won second-round victories in their respective home territories.

Had the elections been run on the basis of a proportional system similar to that employed in the municipal elections, the result would have been very different (Vengroff 1994). The most important impact would be the absence of a clear majority coalition in the National Assembly. Although some have argued that a proportional system would be fairer than the current majority system, the majority system clearly has some of the advantages attributed to it by the advisers to the National Conference which adopted it for inclusion in the Constitution (Vengroff 1993; 1994). First and foremost is the greatly increased likelihood of producing a majority party or coalition in the National Assembly, as is in fact the case in Mali. In addition, any party in Mali which wishes to assert influence nationally through elections is obliged to build a relatively broad coalition of ethnic and regional groups.

THE PRESIDENTIAL ELECTIONS

The presidential elections give yet another indication of the strength of the parties and their respective bases. The election of the President, like those for the National Assembly, was conducted using a majority electoral system in two turns. If a candidate wins a majority of the vote nationally in the first round, he/she is elected. Barring a majority in the first round, only the top two candidates compete in a run-off to determine the presidency.

The presidential elections represented the fifth and sixth times respectively that the citizens of Mali were called upon to vote in a six-month period. It is therefore no surprise that voter turnout was relatively light (23.6 per cent, ranging from 17.5 to 43.4 per cent per circumscription). Turnout in the nineteen communes (28.5 per cent) was, as with the National Assembly elections, significantly higher (T=3.78, p<.001) than in the remaining thirty-six, more rural '*cercles*' (avg. = 21.3 per cent turnout). The second round of the presidential elections produced a national turnout of just 20.9 per cent, about 185,000 fewer Malians than voted in the first round. The almost certain victory of Alpha Konaré and the elimination of seven of the eight other first-round candidates undoubtedly was a contributing factor.

The distribution of the presidential vote in the first round differed from that of the National Assembly elections in one important respect. The ADEMA candidate, Alpha O. Konaré, ran significantly stronger than his party had in the parliamentary elections. Nationally, Konaré received about 45 per cent of the total vote cast, finishing in first place nationally, in first place in every region, and in first place in forty-six of the fifty-five electoral circumscriptions in the country. In eight of the remaining nine he finished in second place, and in only one, Youwarou, did he finish as low as third. In the second round of the election, Konaré and ADEMA won an overwhelming 69 per cent of the vote, finishing first in every region, first in fifty-two of the fifty-five circum-scriptions, and first among Malians living abroad.

The nine circumscriptions in which Konaré did not finish in first place in the first round are all areas which had been won by parties other than ADEMA in the National Assembly elections as well. The US-RDA (Konaté wing – now the BDIA) candidate, Tieoulé Konaté, finished second nationally and thus participated in the run-off. Konaté finished first in the first-round elections in Tenehkou and Youwarou, both RDA-held constituencies in the Mopti region, and an extremely close second in Gao and Ansongo, both in the Gao region, the historic base of the RDA. He also finished first in Koutiala, where the RDA's parliamentary ally the UDD is dominant and in Menaka, the UMADD fiefdom. In one of the two remaining US-RDA constituencies, Nara, Konaté finished a close second. If the US-RDA factions had been united, the margin between Konaté and Konaré in this constituency would have been razor thin. In the last of the RDA constituencies, Barouéli, the competing Haidara wing of the party is dominant and took most of the US-RDA vote. Once again, if the party had been united behind a single candidate, it would have finished in second place instead of third and fourth in these areas. Furthermore, the Haidara wing of the RDA endorsed the ADEMA candidate in the second round. In the second round of the election, Konaté was victorious in just three constituencies.

ADEMA demonstrated its broad-based national strength, built upon its core National Assembly constituencies, the sound reputation of its presi-dential candidate as a leader of the democratisation movement which culminated in the '*événements*' and the ousting of the Traoré regime and the solid base of supporters composed of teachers and health professionals (primarily nurses) who form the core of the party's organisation in the

Table 3.3 Mali presidential elections

Candidate	Party*	%Vote 1st Round	%Vote 2nd Round
Alpha O. Konaré	ADEMA	44.95	69.01
Tieoulé M. Konaté	US-RDA**	14.51	30.99
Mountaga Tall	CNID	11.41	
Almamy Sylla	RDP	9.44	
Baba A. Haidara	US-RDA***	7.37	
Idrissa Traoré	PDP	4.1	
Amadou Aly Niangadou	RDT	4.01	
Mamadou dit M. Diaby	PUDP	2.16	
Demba M. Diallo	UFD	2.04	
Turnout		23.9	20.9

*Officially candidates for the presidency do not run on a party designation.
**USRDA 'Congrès Extraordinaire' group, Tieoulé Konaté wing, now the BDIA.
***USRDA'Comité Directeur' group, Baba Haidara wing.

countryside. It should also be noted that the vote for the ADEMA was significantly higher in the rural than in the urban areas for both the National Assembly and presidential elections. In addition to its strong rural-based organisation, some of the ADEMA success in the presidential campaign can also be attributed to Konaré himself. During the campaign, he personally appeared in every circumscription and even in many '*arrondissements*' throughout the country. The importance of personally seeing and hearing the candidate, especially for the largely illiterate rural population, cannot be ignored. Most other candidates delegated responsibility to colleagues to speak for them in the rural circumscriptions, while confining their own campaign to the larger towns.

There is seemingly only one other party which at the moment is capable of mounting a serious national campaign, the US-RDA. The relatively high, negative correlations between the US-RDA and ADEMA votes in the first-round presidential elections indicate that these two parties are competing for the same voters, voters who in fact constitute a majority of the Malian electorate. Analysis of these data suggest that the US-RDA (the new BDIA) should be regarded as the most serious opposition party, and the party best placed potentially to challenge and succeed the ADEMA to power. For future elections it is worth noting that the Konaté wing of the party shows a good balance between support from urban and rural voters, while the smaller, Haidara wing, for a time in coalition with ADEMA, is much more urban based.

Voting data clearly indicated that the Konaté wing (BDIA) has a broader geographic base and the loyalty of the overwhelming number of US-RDA supporters and therefore the strength of the party in the future. The implications of the recent formal, legal division of the party into the RDA (Haidara) and BDIA (Konaté) for future elections remain to be seen, but the BDIA is undoubtedly the stronger of the two.

The other parties are, as currently constituted, too small or too limited in their regional bases to determine the outcome of a national election. CNID does have the ability to mobilise the youth of Bamako against the government (as it did so effectively in April 1993) and both the CNID and the RDP apparently have the core strength around which a serious opposition could coalesce. Both of these parties, which suffer from an urban bias and relatively weak organisations in the rural areas, joined the ADEMA in its second government for a brief period (L'Essor 1993). There is also an attempt by forces loyal to Moussa Traoré to bring back the UDPM under the leadership of Choguel Maiga, former administrative secretary of the UDD. They have thus far not been allowed to register the party.

THE IMPACT AND CONSEQUENCES OF DEMOCRATISATION IN MALI

Using the Charlick definition of democratic governance as a point of departure (Charlick 1992), emphasis in this paper has been placed on identifying fundamental strengths and weaknesses of the transition to democracy in Mali. The interim government tried to bring all parties into the process, signing agreements with the workers (Pacte social), with the rebelling Taureg (Pacte du nord), and the students (Memorandum de l'AEEM). By all indications, the electoral process and the emerging party system are consistent with the principles of sound democratic governance. The elections at the municipal, National Assembly, and presidential levels, in spite of some irregularities, were fair and open. All parties had the opportunity to register, to present candidates, express their views freely in open, competitive campaigns, to gain access to the media, including a number of independent newspapers and radio stations, to win seats and forge coalitions after the election results were in.

The system, which started with forty-seven organisations registered as parties is experiencing a shakeout period. Eleven parties are represented in the National Assembly, and nineteen on the municipal councils. Three national parties (ADEMA, BDIA, formerly the US-RDA, and CNID) have emerged from the fray, and several regional or local parties are likely to continue to carry some weight in the future. The danger that exists is that the parties, most of which do not have the resources necessary to sustain themselves, especially in the role of opposition, will be absorbed by the ruling party or disappear. Both of these have already begun to happen.

The strongest party, ADEMA, controls a commanding majority in the National Assembly. However, government ministers are regularly confronted by serious questions, proposals and amendments raised by both the opposition and various groups within the ruling party, its coalition, the 'Pacte républicain' and the broader society. Debate in the National Assembly is managed fairly, is open, and is often quite contentious. The nascent parliamentary groups may eventually develop the capacity to formulate serious alternatives to government policies.

At the local level, the opposition is in power (holds the mayor and the majority of the council) in a number of important communes, including five of the six in the capital, Bamako. Although relations with the central authorities have not been entirely smooth, when the appropriate texts have been modified, municipal governments should be expected to function normally. Once the rural communes are established and the whole system of the local government in place, it will be possible to get a better understanding of the degree of democratic tolerance existent in the system. The way in which the communes, urban and rural, are allowed to function should be one of the best available indicators of the degree to which the government and the ruling party are committed to democracy and increasing legitimacy. Decentralisation remains a high priority for the Malian administration, but the form of its implementation remains controversial and unclear.

A variety of arguments have been advanced to explain the relatively low turnout, including faulty voter lists, many people outside the country still appearing on the voting rolls, weak mobilisation efforts by the parties and the number and location of polling places. None of these arguments alone is compelling. However, when added to the relatively low literacy rates, confusion associated with the plethora of parties, the short time the parties had to put together new organisations and mount their campaigns, scepticism derived from years of authoritarian rule during which election results were regularly fabricated and the fact that Malians had recently gone to the polls to approve the new Constitution (with a turnout of 40 per cent), the level of participation in the free elections held in 1992 does not seem to be indicative of serious shortcomings in the development of democratic governance in Mali.

Political parties, seemingly capable of meeting the needs of a democratic polity, have begun to develop in Mali. Two key areas need to be addressed if these organisations are successfully to play a significant role in support of democratic governance:

1   the representative function – increasing capabilities to communicate regularly and effectively between the citizenry and elected representatives on the one hand and administrative authorities, at all levels, on the other;
2   policy pluralism – improving the capabilities of elected officials and representative institutions to identify, formulate and evaluate policy options and to present constructive alternatives.

In the case of the representative function, the deputies clearly view their role as involving, even being dominated by, constituency service, especially *vis à vis* the bureaucracy and the territorial administration. They clearly and uniformly stated that this form of constituency service is both the most time-consuming and one of the most important of their activities. For this purpose, in some multi-member districts, deputies on the same list divide up the circumscriptions into *arrondissements* in which they individually first campaign and, when elected, act as the representative, almost as would be the case in a single-member district. Everything from marriage licences to taxes, to land allocation are included in the list of issues addressed on behalf of constituents who must deal with the administration. Informing people of their rights and placing pressure on venal local administrators are the critical actions. Several deputies indicated that in performing this function they had been personally threatened by bureaucrats not used to having to respond to the needs and desires of the local population (Vengroff 1992; 1993). Such threats do not seem to have dampened the zeal of most deputies.

In the area of policy analysis, elected officials and parties must develop the capacity to better aggregate interests and evaluate and design legislation and/or administrative procedures presented by the government, associational groups, or individual citizens. Currently, neither the parties nor the legislature has the staff or the technical capabilities adequately to assess policy proposals brought before them. Parties have voluntary technical support committees composed of members who have a variety of backgrounds and skills. These function intermittently rather than on a regular basis, however.

Without sources of external support, the survival of the opposition may become problematic. Opposition parties may find that their only choices are to merge with the ruling party or disappear entirely. Experience in Africa and elsewhere demonstrates that without a viable opposition, democratic governance is unlikely to survive and long-term system legitimacy and stability may not be established. The proportional electoral system at the municipal level presents some important opportunities for the opposition to control at least some resources, but even these depend to a large extent on the good will of the state. At the national level, the electoral system, chosen in order to promote stability, has within it the seeds of destruction of the opposition. Since the majority electoral system disproportionately rewards the strongest party, leading to an overwhelming majority in the National Assembly, the opposition can gain access only by being coopted in a broad government coalition at the pleasure of the dominant party.

Although Mali meets most of the criteria for democratic governance, accountability, responsiveness and opportunities for policy pluralism, the legitimacy of the system is not entirely secure. Extreme economic problems faced by the country (Mali is one of the ten poorest countries in the world) may threaten the democratisation process. Because of the failure to meet the conditionalities, the IMF is now withholding funds vital to the survival of the regime. The violent street politics of the student group, the AEEM, which helped bring about the resignation of two prime ministers (Younoussi Touré and then Abdoulaye Sekou Sow and his government), is but one indicator. During those events, some raised the spectre of the return to power of the deposed dictator Moussa Traoré. In fact supporters of ousted President Moussa Traoré, led by Oumar Diallo, organised an abortive coup in December 1993.

In order to minimise further instability and because of such fears, CNID, which purportedly supported and encouraged the students, and the RDP joined the ADEMA government of Abdoulaye Sow, receiving two portfolios each. Holding the portfolio of the Ministry of Justice, CNID found itself in the untenable position of having to prosecute some of its strongest supporters, the student demonstrators who engaged in violent protests. Thus, further disturbances and dissatisfaction by the union (UNTM) and students (AEEM) have led to a second reshuffling and yet a new government, this time including an exclusively ADEMA leadership under Prime Minister Ibrahima Keita. The current Prime Minister, a close confidant of President Konaré (former ambassador to the Côte d'Ivoire), accepted the position only after receiving guarantees that he would have the authority to crack down on students if they continued to stage destructive demonstrations in which shops, homes and government property were attacked and burned.

Associational groups have developed some strength but do not find easy channels for expressing their views to the government. Structural solutions cannot, in and of themselves, ensure the survival of democracy and may not be sufficient, even in the short run. The public service unions, led by the UNTM, recently staged a one-day 'warning' strike which paralysed government. Union members, including many teachers and functionaries, continue to put pressure on the government for increased salaries. This has become an especially touchy subject since student scholarships have recently (against the demands of the IMF) been increased by 75 per cent (50 per cent in 1991 and 25 per cent in 1992), unemployment is increasing, recent graduates are not finding work in either the public or private sectors, farmers received some relief in the form of elimination of the minimum fiscal tax, and Deputies in the National Assembly received raises.

Unionists, who played a critical role in toppling Traoré, have not only not received any raises or mandated promotions, they have seen the value of their salaries significantly cut in real terms by the 50 per cent devaluation of the CFA franc. The dissatisfaction widely felt in the unions, especially among teachers and functionaries, is being exploited by the opposition as a means of gaining additional support and wooing away ADEMA supporters. The government is, consistent with the Pacte social, offering these employees land, equivalent in value to the unpaid raises, and have found the union somewhat receptive. Demands by students and unemployed youth are a continuing source of discomfort and a potentially destabilising force.

With its continuing poverty, limited prospects for economic growth and development, high illiteracy and lack of democratic traditions, democracy remains very fragile in Mali. The old UDPM of Moussa Traoré is trying to reorganise, in spite of its legally being banned, and some sympathy for the 'good old days' under the Second Republic is being voiced in some quarters. The commitment of President Konaré to democracy appears unshaken but even in his own party some are grumbling that too much leeway is being given to the opposition and their supporters. Democracy in Mali is making some progress but the nation has not yet completed the consolidation stage.

REFERENCES

Aurore (22 August 1991):2, Bamako, Mali.

Campmas, P. (1978) *L'Union Soudanaise R.D.A.*, Libreville, Gabon: UNICONTI.

Charlick, R. (1992) 'The Concept of Governance and Its Implications for A.I.D.'s Development Assistance Program', Washington, DC: Associates in Rural Development, pp. 3, 6–7.

Clark, J. (1992)'The National Conference as a Path to Democracy in Africa', African Studies Association, Seattle: unpublished paper.

Coleman, J. and Rosberg, C.G. (eds) (1966) *Political Parties and National Integration in Tropical Africa*, Berkeley and Los Angeles: University of California Press.

Decalo, S. (1992) 'The Process, Prospects and Constraints on Democratization in Africa', *African Affairs*, 91, 362, pp. 7–35.

Diamond, L. (1988) 'Introduction: Roots of Failure, Seeds of Hope', in L. Diamond, Juan J. Linz and Seymour Martin Lipset (eds) *Democracy in Developing Countries*, vol. 2, *Africa*, Boulder and London: Lynne Reinner, pp. 13–14.

Diamond, L., Linz, J., and Lipset, S. (eds) (1990) *Politics in Developing Countries: Comparing Experiences with Democracy*, Boulder and London: Lynne Reinner, pp. 10–14.

DNAT (1992) 'Direction National de L'Administration Territoriale', Bamako: Government of Mali.

Eckstein, H. (1988) 'A Culturalist Theory of Political Change', in *American Political Science Review*, 82, 3, pp. 789–804.

Hodgkin, T. (1961) *African Political Parties*, Harmondsworth: Penguin.

Imperato, P.J. (1989) *Mali: A Search for Direction*, Boulder and London: Westview.

Inglehart, R. (1988) 'The Renaissance of Political Culture', *American Political Science Review*, 82, 4, pp. 1203–1230.

L'Essor (Bamako), 19 April 1993, Bamako, Mali, p. 31.

La Palombara, J. and Weiner, M. (eds) (1966) *Political Parties and Political Development*, Princeton: Princeton University Press.

Landell-Mills, P. and Serageldin, I. (1991) 'Governance and the External Factor', World Bank's Annual Conference on Development Economics, Washington, DC: World Bank, pp. 25–26.

McKown, R. and Kauffman, R. (1973) 'Party System as a Comparative Analytic Concept in African Politics', *Comparative Politics*, 6, pp. 267–96.

Le Miroir (Bamako) 9 March 1993, pp. 1–3.

Morgenthau, R. (1964) *Political Parties in French Speaking West Africa*, Oxford: Clarendon Press.

Ngom, B. 'Mali's Judicial System', in R. Vengroff, S. Gellar, B. Ngom and B. Tessery (1992) *Democratic Governance in Mali: A Strategic Assessment*, Washington, DC: Associates in Rural Development.

Nzrankeu, J. (1993) 'The Role of the National Conference in the Transition to Democracy in Africa: The Cases of Benin and Mali', in *Issue*, 21, pp. 44–50.

Ordinance No. 91-074 P/CPSP, 18 September, 1991, Bamako, Mali.

Tessery, B. (1992) 'The National Assembly', in R. Vengroff, S. Gellar, B. Ngom and B. Tessery, *Democratic Governance in Mali: A Strategic Assessment*, Washington, DC: Associates in Rural Development.

Vengroff, R. (1977) *Botswana: Rural Development in the Shadow of Apartheid*, Cranbury, New Jersey and London: Associated University Presses.

Vengroff, R. (1979) 'Upper Volta: Africa's New Hope for Democracy', *Africa Report*, v, 23, no. 4. pp. 59–64.

Vengroff, R. (1992) 'Democratic Governance and the Party System in Mali', in R. Vengroff, S. Gellar, B. Ngom, and B. Tessery, *Democratic Governance in Mali: A Strategic Assessment*, Washington, DC: Associates in Rural Development.

Vengroff, R. (1993) 'Governance and the Transition to Democracy: Political Parties and the Party System in Mali', *Journal of Modern African Studies*, 31, 4, pp. 541–562.

Vengroff, R., Gellar, S., Ngom, B. and Tessery, B. (1992) *Democratic Governance in Mali: A Strategic Assessment*, Washington, DC: Associates in Rural Development.

Vengroff, R. (1994) 'The Impact of the Electoral System on the Transition to Democracy in Africa: The Case of Mali', in *Electoral Studies*, 13, 1, pp. 29–37.

Verité (1991), 2 Dec., pp. 2–3, Bamako, Mali.

Zolberg, A.R. (1966) *Creating Political Order: the Party-states of West Africa*, Chicago: Rand McNally and Co.

4 Nigeria: democracy and civil society

The Nigerian transition programme, 1985–1993

*Julius Ihonvbere and Olufemi Vaughan**

After three decades of authoritarian rule and a general preoccupation with issues of economic development, scholarly attention has now underscored the significance of democratic participation and governance in African states. This shift in scholarly discussions of African politics generally emphasises the interaction between major global forces and internal political and constitutional developments in the evolving struggle for democracy. In Nigeria, the interconnections between class, professional and communal factors on the one hand, and the ambiguities and un-certainties of globalisation on the other, have had serious implications for the conceptualisation of structures of society and the advancement of popular democracy. For the first time since independence, the notion of democracy transcended the elaborate constitutional manoeuvres dominated by an ethno-regional political class. Despite a carefully managed transition programme preoccupied primarily with mediating political and economic conflicts among major ethnic constituencies, a vibrant democratic move-ment has, since the late 1980s, articulated the pressing economic and political concerns of Nigeria's complex and varied structures of society.

Although essentially regional in scope and character, this popular demo-cratic movement has not only emerged as a formidable opposition to military rule, but has also sought to redefine the meaning of democratic engagement in a nation where elite behaviour is characterised by endemic corruption and a flagrant assault on human dignity. Debates and agitation for a transition to democracy are for the first time aimed at discussing the fundamental contradictions in the Nigerian social formation. The initial

*Julius Ihonvbere's field research in Nigeria was sponsored by the Aspen Institute and the National Endowment for the Humanities. Olufemi Vaughan would like to thank Dr Ihonvbere for suggesting a framework that captures an expanding political terrain. He would also like to thank the editor of this volume, Dr John Wiseman, for encouraging a perspective that focuses attention on the interconnections between civic organisations and participatory democracy.

success of this pro-democracy movement is likely to prompt new questions about a recalcitrant and unproductive ethno-regional commercial and bureaucratic structure, and consequently encourage the expansion of the public space. It is therefore critical to analyse the character and perform-ance of this burgeoning movement within the context of a military-imposed transition programme to democracy. An equally relevant issue is whether Nigeria's transient civic organisations have the capacity to fill the gap that a pro-democracy movement may succeed in creating. These critical ques-tions are informed by the monumental developments of the post-cold-war era – a phenomenon that Martin Kilson aptly describes as 'the new pluto-cracy of global capitalism in the West and its civil-society-constraining spinoffs in developing societies'.[1]

The present chapter will thus examine the dynamic interaction between this pro-democracy movement and a democratic transition programme instituted by a patrimonial military regime. It will analyse three interrelated issues. First, with a view to providing an historical background to the turbulent tradition of democratic and constitutional change in Nigeria, we will present a general assessment of political, social and economic factors in the evolution of authoritarianism and the struggle for popular democracy in Nigeria. Such a discussion is particularly pertinent because it affords us the opportunity to transcend the predominant constitutional-legalistic focus of the study of democracy and politics in Nigeria. More importantly, this background analysis will make a critical connection between the under-lying political economy, the nature of elite formation, the emergent civil society and their impact on the evolving processes of democratisation. Second, we will discuss the interaction between the structures of society and the transition programme of the Babangida regime between 1985 and 1993. We will argue that the pressure for democratic engagement by a burgeoning and ambiguously defined civil society was not only un-precedented, but further intensified the struggle for democracy and redefined the meaning of democratisation in the Babangida era. Finally, we will argue that the monumental global development of the post-cold-war period has complicated the painful and arduous process of democratisation in Nigeria. Rather than providing impetus for the country's popular demo-cratic struggle, we contend that the major political developments of the post-cold-war period only encouraged the expansion of the political space and the development of a fragile civil society.

DEMOCRACY, MILITARY RULE AND CIVIL SOCIETY: AN HISTORICAL OVERVIEW

The evolving and complex political landscape in Nigeria has provided scholars with numerous models and perspectives in the study of political organisations, social movement and style of military governance. When political independence was attained from the British in October 1960, it was assumed by liberal scholars that the country's path to democracy and development would be a smooth and steady one. The rising Western-educated elites, increasing urbanisation, vast resource endowment and a prevailing consumer culture among the dominant class were often evoked as indicators of commitment to liberal democracy and capitalist development. Nigeria was hailed as the giant of Africa and the one country in the subcontinent that could be counted upon to provide leadership in modernisation, industrialisation and economic growth.

As events in the immediate post-colonial period were to demonstrate, such expectations were ahistorical, short sighted and grossly unrealistic. The dominant liberal analysis of the era of decolonisation and the age of independence had overlooked the implications of Nigeria's historical experiences, structural distortions, underdevelopment, dependence and marginalisation in the international division of labour. In addition, these analysts had underestimated the damaging effects of factionalisation within the dominant elites and the social decay that was to provide a fertile ground for ethno-regional conflicts and political instability. The accumulative base of the dominant class was not in agriculture or in production; the regions were more viable than the central government; ethnic, regional and religious loyalties were stronger than national proclivities; corruption and social irresponsibility were rife in the ranks of the elites; the bureaucracy was inefficient and ineffective; and the British had structured the economy to be dependent on the industrial world for its survival. These conditions generated intense contradictions and instability. Within half a decade of independence law and order had broken down, the regional-based political parties and the state had lost their legitimacy, the political elites had taken refuge under the cover of primordial loyalties and, by 1966, the military had sacked the politicians from the political theatre of the nation, abrogated the Constitution, banned all political parties and imposed full military rule on the nation. By July 1967, a tragic civil war between the secessionist eastern region and the rest of the country was fully under way. This war would continue till 1970 causing untold pain, misery and dislocation.

A major consequence of the civil war was the restructuring of political relations and power balance in favour of the central government. In addition, the post-civil-war oil boom strengthened the federal government and promoted a national programme of reconstruction and rehabilitation. Yet these major political developments did not alter elite behaviour, the dominant role of the transnational corporations in the national economy nor the attempts by the state to control them. Moreover, rather than encouraging the emergence of productive economic enterprise, the indigenisation decrees of 1972 and 1977, and several national plans, created channels of corruption and mismanagement by regional oligarchies.[2] In fact, the oil boom and the rise of the rentier state which came to depend exclusively on oil rents to generate revenues, coincided with a period of social and political alienation and a regular intervention of the military in the political process. Agriculture was neglected, prestige projects were preferred to productive ones and, by strengthening lucrative but unproductive relations with foreign capital, the commercial-bureaucratic elites simply mortgaged the future and converted the country into a dumping ground for all sorts of foreign imports.

The military suffocated civil society and waged a systematic war against trade unions and other civic organisations critical to the development of an enduring process of democratisation. It failed to restructure the political terrain to contain forces of divisiveness and instability. In the midst of poverty, unemployment and grossly unequal access to basic infrastructure, primordial loyalties were strengthened and the struggle became one of confrontation between the military and a civil political class for power and opportunities. In this struggle, local people were severely marginalised as a large section of the bureaucratic elites embraced the military. Development planning simply became an avenue to open private bank accounts in foreign lands and to expand real estate holdings in Nigeria and abroad. Public institutions rapidly deteriorated and the social and moral fabric of the country experienced a severe assault. Added to these were increasing pressures from university students, social critics, the media and labour unions. Their demands were centred on pressures against the military, the quest for human rights, accountability and the democratisation of society. But there was no effective unifying national institution to reinforce and sustain these political demands.

It is in the context, therefore, of increasing challenges to military hegemony, that the military in 1979 withdrew from the political terrain and handed power to elected politicians. This withdrawal was only a temporary concession to an ethno-regional political class and not a real acknowledgement of the will of the people. At this time elements within the military were already contending that there were two political parties in Nigeria: the military and civilians! It was further argued that since the military monopolised the instrument of coercion, it emerged as the most powerful and dominant 'political party'. Nigeria's second experiment with liberal democracy of the American executive presidential model barely lasted four years, from October 1979 to December 1983. Though the Constitution had been amended to emphasise the separation of powers and had tried to strengthen the presidency, the whole arrangement collapsed like a pack of cards. Several reasons can be given for this. First, powerful elements within the military did not support the 1979 disengagement and were too eager to capitalise on the abuse of power by the civilian politicians. Second, the military in its disengagement programme had only attempted to rationalise the instruments of power at the superstructural level. Tinkering with the Constitution, debating power-sharing arrangements between regional elites, formulating policies that established uniform local government system and land reforms,[3] did not effectively address the structural contradictions within the Nigerian social structure. Practically no effort was made to mobilise and educate the public, to redefine the content and the context of politics or to encourage politicians and their supporters to reconceptualise the purpose of politics and the use of power. Third, the politicians themselves had learned nothing, and they did little to recapture the political initiative and restructure civil society. In fact, this second experiment in liberal democracy stands out as one of the country's most disorganised and corrupt political eras.[4] Within four years, the civilian government had doubled the national debt, grossly mismanaged the economy and had alienated the Nigerian public to such a level that the military intervention of Generals Idiagbon and Buhari in December 1983 was welcomed by most Nigerians with great fanfare. So much for democracy and multi-party politics; the Second Republic died an inglorious though not unexpected death and politics was once again under the control of the military. The new military government inherited a dislocated economy and demoralised society. A combination of repressive decrees, resistance to IMF conditionalities, counter-trade with several European nations, imposition of new levies and taxes and a crackdown on political expressions did not win the new regime mass support in critical sectors of the Nigerian society. A counter-coup in August 1985 witnessed the rise of General Ibrahim Babangida to power and the initiation of a new programme of transition to multi-party democracy.

THE MILITARY'S TRANSITION PROGRAMME TO DEMOCRACY

The Babangida regime was the first military government in Nigeria to institute a comprehensive programme for military disengagement from politics. Like previous military regimes, it saw itself as a temporary solution to the country's problems and was immediately committed to providing a transition programme to democratic rule. To many observers, General Babangida was initially perceived as a benevolent military dictator, a soldier/democrat and a man of great vision and unbending commitment to democracy.

The reasons why the military regime committed itself to a transition programme can be found in the complex political character of the Nigerian social formation. As in previous cases, the new administration had to declare its intentions at the beginning and made a commitment to the rapid transfer of power to civilians. The regime also tried to distance itself from the repressive attitude of its predecessors by initially embracing more liberal policies, ranging from the reorganisation of the secret service, declaration of support for human rights, abrogating repressive decrees and soliciting the support of important community-based organisations. Furthermore, this initial commitment to government by consensus and dialogue encouraged open nation-wide debates on major policies ranging from foreign policy, housing and relations with the IMF and other lending institutions. By setting up a Political Bureau in 1987 to provide recommendations for future democratic political arrangements, the regime committed itself to a timetable for military disengagement. Adept in the strategies of political diversion and manipulation, General Babangida isolated important sectors of the Nigerian society, critical to a fundamental transformation of the state and civil society. The Academic Staff Union of Universities (ASUU), the Nigerian Bar Association (NBA), the National Association of Nigerian Students (NANS), Women in Nigeria (WIN) and the Nigerian Labour Congress (NLC), to name only a few, were left out of the new 'governing coalition'. This attempt to contain civil society and restrict the country's political space brought strong opposition from these organisations and other lesser-known regional groups.

In spite of its official claims, the regime failed to make much difference on the economic front. Its structural adjustment policy was one of the worst implemented in the continent. Corruption, repression and human rights abuses gradually replaced the regime's initial policy of dialogue. Recommendations that were made by panels and boards established by the regime to deliberate over the country's many problems were abandoned for those designed by a narrow clique close to the head of state. Thus, within only two years in government, both the style and substantive policies of the Babangida administration show a regime intent on shrinking the political space and promoting a cumbersome programme of social engineering at the expense of a meaningful process of democratisation. Peter Anyang'Nyong'o notes the severe assault on egalitarian democracy in the subcontinent:

> At the centre of the failure of African states to chart viable paths for domestic accumulation is the problem of accountability and the lack of democracy. The people's role in the affairs of government has diminished, the political arena has shrunk, political demobilisation has become more the norm than the exception in regime behavior, social engineering for political mobilization . . . is the preoccupation of most governments.[5]

The attempt to contain grassroots organisations only generated deep pressures from ethnic, regional, religious, gender and socio-economic groups. The military itself was subjected to the same tensions apparent in society. Younger officers resented the rapid de-legitimisation of the military and the steady erosion of its professionalism. The April 1991 abortive coup by a group of junior officers from the south shook the confidence of the regime.[6] Finally, the end of the cold war and its political consequences in African states made authoritarian regimes increasingly anachronistic and therefore forced the Babangida regime to maintain its commitment to the transition programme.

The regime's transition programme was anchored on one fundamental assumption. Government officials argued that the previous democratic experiments ended abruptly because of the flagrant abuse of affluent politicians who had historically dominated electoral politics in all the regions of the federation.[7] For senior military officials previous attempts at representative democracy failed because regionally based political parties functioned mainly as a patronage system without any commitment to political accountability.[8] The transition programme must therefore commit itself to the establishment of a viable democratic system and a general restructuring of the country's political and economic institutions. This idea led to the creation and funding of two political parties: the Social Democratic Party (SDP) (ideologically a left-of-centre party of the West European mode) and the National Republican Convention (NRC) (a right-of-centre party).[9] The government drafted the two parties' manifestos and constitutions, appointed administrative secretaries, built their secretariats, funded their conventions and monitored all their activities. The regime also created a new electoral commission, conducted a national census, created a Centre for Democratic Studies (CDS), established political organisations such as the Directorate for Mass Mobilisation (MAMSER) to mobilise the grassroots for democracy, and the Directorate for Food, Roads and Rural Infrastructure

(DFRRI) to promote development in the rural areas.[10] Moreover, the military embarked on the containment of political dissidents, journalists, traditional rulers and other leaders with influence at the grassroots. It left no one in doubt as to its preparedness to adopt both constitutional and extra-constitutional means in its desire to monitor and control every aspect of the transition programme. In short, the Babangida regime was bent on imposing 'democracy' from the top and curtailing the country's burgeoning civil society. Indeed, the military and their advisers rejected the notion that liberal democratic traditions require at least an attempt to nurture the emergence of civic organisations. Emphasising the significance of these civic structures to any meaningful discussion on democracy in Africa, Pearl Robinson notes:

> Analyses of civil society and democratization give rise to considerations of political openings, political opportunities, structures, power asymmetries, contested meanings, and marginal as well as modal political practices. These are the channels through which a culture of politics is reconstituted.[11]

Without a doubt, the Babangida strategy failed to set Nigeria on an effective path to multi-party democracy. The two government-imposed parties quickly came under the control of the rich and powerful, a class that the regime had earlier claimed must be contained if democracy were to flourish. The favoured group of politicians (the so-called new breed) were not only inexperienced, but they also demonstrated similar political and social characteristics as their predecessors. This is not surprising given the fact that the 'new politicians' were coopted from the same political, ideological and ethno-regional arrangement that had sustained the domination of regional political classes and for well over four decades. Thus, the two parties failed to introduce anything new into the political process; once again, competitive politics was seen as a political enterprise in which contestants invest only with the intention of controlling patronage and a system of economic rewards.[12] Money was the determining factor as to who got elected to party office, who became a candidate and how the elections were generally conducted. As in the past, the politicians relied on the manipulation of ethnic, regional and religious differences in their competition for power. Indeed, despite the government's stated objectives of stemming sectoral doctrines, organisations claiming to represent vital regional and ethnic interests soon emerged as important actors in the transition programme. For example, in the earlier years of the regime, regionally based organisations such as the Committee of Northern Elders, the Egbe Ilosiwaju Yoruba (a Yoruba solidarity group led by the Ooni of

Ife), Ohe n'Eze-Igbo (a group of prominent Igbo traditional chiefs and politicians from Anambra and Imo states), all claimed to represent various groups on major federal government policies and programmes.[13] Intolerance, inexperience, a general lack of political education and the avoidance of critical issues, in particular the *national question*, characterised the cynical behaviour of the 'new breed' politicians. In fact, the military failed to conceptualise the ongoing problem of the *national question* within the appropriate context of Nigeria's tumultuous post-war history, an expanding civil society and a demand for democratisation at the grassroots level. The Babangida regime therefore ignored the lesson of major national crises such as the western region crisis of 1962–1966, the military coup of January 1966 and counter-coup of July 1967, and the civil war of 1967–1970, in its transition programme. Indeed, the regime paid little attention to the fierce contestations over religion in the emirate north and the increasing regional and ethnic conflicts in the 1980s and 1990s. These developments simply played into the hands of the General who, by the late 1980s, had assumed a more corporatist, dictatorial and patrimonial style of governance than any previous administration. In what amounted to a frantic and irrational attempt to retain power at any cost, General Babangida further corrupted regional politicians and manipulated the evolving political process.

The events leading to the presidential election of 1993 were a clear indication that the new politicians had learned little from their predecessors of the Second Republic. Referring to them with a cynical but vivid description 'casino politicians' (because they spent a lot of money and time gambling at the casinos in Abuja, the federal capital), Femi Falana, President of the National Association of Democratic Lawyers (NADL) aptly notes that

> multipartyism failed woefully because there was a total lack of encouragement and leadership coming from the political class. They were opportunistic, irresponsible, and eager to satisfy the whims and caprices of the military. They lacked the vision, courage and resolve required in the present global order to sustain a viable democratic arrangement.[14]

When a presidential election was eventually held in June 1993, with two inexperienced regional politicians (Moshood Abiola, a wealthy Yoruba philanthropist and Bashir Tofa, a rich businessman from the Emirate north) as presidential candidates of the two political parties, General Babangida annulled the results of the elections. This decision can only be explained as a desperate and irrational attempt of holding on to power at any price. The nullification of the presidential elections would prove to be the final death knoll of the eight-year Babangida saga. The repeated abuse of his excessive regime would come under the full weight of increasingly resolute Nigerian communities. In an attempt to stem a wave of persistent discontent throughout the country (especially in southern cities), Babangida installed an interim government under the leadership of a Yoruba ally, Ernest Shonekan. Lacking legitimacy throughout the country, Shonekan's government was essentially ineffective. It was in the midst of this political impasse that the military, under another General, Sanni Abacha (for many years Babangida's deputy), seized power in November 1993.[15] The Abacha coup brought an expensive and painful transition programme to an abrupt end, as the General suspended the civilian constitution, dismantled the two political parties and terminated the two-year partnership between the military and civilians by dismissing the politicians and appointing military administrators as their replacements.

Since this experiment marked a major turning point in Nigeria's history, and the country's burgeoning civil society played an unprecedented role in the termination of the Babangida regime, we will discuss the performance of this dynamic sector in the democratisation process. This is the more important because it is this reconstituted institution that provided an effective opposition to the military and is likely to feature prominently in future national democratic debates.

MILITARY RULE, CIVIL SOCIETY, AND DEMOCRATISATION

When General Babangida annulled the 12 June elections, he followed up with a set of actions aimed at restricting the political terrain, containing civil society and redefining the nature of politics. It is significant to underscore the strategies adopted by General Babangida to retain power at all cost before we proceed to discuss the spontaneous opposition mounted against the military by both old and new civic organisations. The General's strategy of maintaining power was based on the manipulation of the entrenched ethnic, regional and religious consciousness in the country. In adopting this method Babangida compromised the nationalist posture that he had projected for almost a decade. Furthermore, Babangida proceeded to stonewall on important political issues, imposed cumbersome electoral requirements and intimidated both the electorate and elected officials. In addition, the General summoned the full force of the country's media institutions in defence of his regime's policy. Throughout the crisis, the embattled dictator utilised the Federal Radio Corporation, the Kaduna-based newspaper, *New Nigerian* and its Lagos-based counterpart *Daily Times*, to discredit independent democratic organisations and their leaders.

However, he underestimated the ability of the pro-democracy organisations to mount an effective opposition against military rule. Emphasising the dangerous political manoeuvres that generally characterised military governance in the last days of the Babangida regime, a prominent former governor of Kano State, Abubakar Rimi notes:

> The cancellation of the election was a brazen act, the bravado of a man who believes he can order people about as if Nigeria was one big barrack . . . He [Babangida] has postponed the transition and banned all the candidates before. Two years ago he arrested thirteen prominent politicians in order to stop them from running for state governor. None of this provoked a response, but since June people's patience is beginning to run out.[16]

To demonstrate the opposition to the military, civic groups embarked on a massive protest across the country. For the first time since independence these organisations endeavoured to sustain mass resistance across ethnic, religious, regional and class lines. The most formidable opposition was mounted by the Campaign for Democracy (CD), an amalgamation of diverse voluntary groups cutting across political and ideological lines, formed with the specific purpose of resisting the military regime's objectives. Consisting of forty-three minor groups throughout the federation, the CD immediately embarrassed the regime by publishing the results of the presidential elections. It then embarked on a nation-wide campaign to protest the cancellation of the elections. In one instance the CD capitalised on the presence of over 80,000 football fans at the National Stadium in Lagos to distribute pamphlets calling on Nigerians to mount a one-week national protest against the military regime. Specifically, leaders of the democratic movement called on civil servants to stay away from work; for traders to lock up their stores; students and youths to engage in a non-violent demonstration and all taxi drivers to keep their vehicles away from the road. The CD made it abundantly clear that its anti-military protest was not a struggle for Abiola, the winner of the June elections, but rather a popular struggle for democratic and human rights throughout the country. Since the presidential election was between two regional candidates and in reaction to the regime's increasingly divisive strategy, pro-democracy leaders were at great pains to emphasise that their actions did not represent divisions between north and south, or between ethnic or religious groups or political parties. Excerpts from a major document of the CD clearly capture a broad range of political and economic concerns:

> There is no other time to act, to put a stop to our collective suffering other than now. If we fail to resist the Babangida dictatorship today, we

shall all be sorry for our inaction tomorrow. Posterity and future generations will not forgive and pardon us. To effectively do this we must all cooperate and work together to ensure our collective survival irrespective of ethnic/tribal origins, religious disposition and political leanings or inclinations. We must all unite to fight our common enemy: IBB. or, are we satisfied with the way the majority of us go to bed without food in our stomachs? Are we content with the rising cost of housing, medical care and transport fare? All social services like water, electricity, roads and communications etc, have been priced out of the hands of the ordinary Nigerian, these services are no longer meant for the average person in Nigeria, there is no middle class, you are either rich or poor.[17]

These political activities culminated in a five-day national protest on 5–9 July 1993. The federal government was shocked by this massive opposition. For the first time in its history, Nigeria witnessed what can be described as a relatively well-organised anti-government protest. Despite the violence reported in some Yoruba towns,[18] the CD protest had a clear vision and focus when compared to the communal riots that had become a regular feature of Nigerian politics.

Naturally, an agitation for representative democracy and economic justice of this magnitude had a serious implication for the nature and character of politics throughout Nigeria. In the north, government propaganda institutions, especially Radio Nigeria, contend that the CD was intent on splitting the country into two and installing Abiola as president of an independent southern Nigeria. To military propagandists the democratic agitations were specifically a Yoruba plot to destabilise the nation and shift the power base to the west. Moreover, government officials in the eastern states contend that the campaign was a Yoruba struggle to undermine Igbos and other southern ethnic groups. In many parts of the country, especially in the north, many of the CD supporters and their families were constantly harassed and intimidated by an increasingly notorious and restless state security agency.[19]

One immediate effect of the activities of the CD can be found in its profound impact on existing national organisations. For example, branches of the Nigerian Bar Association (NBA) in major Yoruba cities temporarily boycotted state courts until the election results were released. In Lagos, the boycott affected twenty-two courts in Ikeja and Lagos Island. In Ibadan, the capital of Oyo state, lawyers boycotted all courts, thus bringing the judicial system to a standstill. This was more than a symbolic action, as leading legal personalities were based in this section of the country. Three other major national organisations, the National Association of Nigerian Students (NANS), the Nigerian Labour Congress (NLC), and the Academic Staff Union of Universities (ASUU) declared open support for the CD by rejecting military rule and demanding the immediate implementation of the transition programme.[20] Strike actions by workers and university students in over fifteen states clearly demonstrated the widespread opposition against the Babangida regime. In fact, the prevailing political climate encouraged union members to question the leadership of their organisations[21] and to raise new questions concerning workers' conditions and the social consequences of the structural adjustment programme.

New local organisations devoted specifically to promoting democracy also sprung up during this period. The emergence of groups such as the Association for Democracy (AD); the Universal Defenders of Democracy (UDD); the Media Rights Agenda (MRA); the People's Committee for Liberty (PCL); the Movement for National Reformation (MNR), led by noted politician, Anthony Enahoro; the Movement for the Survival of Ogoni People (MSOP); the Committee for Unity and Understanding (CUU); Ethnic Minority Rights Organisation of Africa (EMROAF); and the Association for Democracy and Good Governance in Nigeria (ADGGN), led by the former Head of State, General Olusegun Obasanjo, were all an indication of the revived democratic political environment generated by the long-standing opposition to Babangida's military dictatorship. To be sure, some leaders of these organisations were opportunists with narrow political ambitions. But whatever their goals, the activities of these groups led to the reconstruction of the political terrain, encouraged a popular demand for empowerment, accountability and democracy. It is also significant to note that the pro-democracy protests cut across communal and class lines. Though this amorphous alliance of regional political groups eventually undermined the effectiveness of the protest movement, it succeeded in demonstrating that given a common objective, diverse groups are, at least in the short term, capable of establishing unifying institutions and doctrines that are essential building blocks to the construction of a viable civil society. The protests also served a critical role in public education and political organisation. Moreover, for the first time in the country's history, a national democratic movement of this kind tested its power, influence, organisational ability, the effectiveness of its branches and its ability to coordinate its activities with other minor organisations with some notable degree of success.

The democratic protest provided openings for political opportunists, aggrieved minority groups and traditional and religious leaders to form new political platforms that only complicated the crisis. Within a short period, groups such as the Eastern Forum, Ijaw People's Union, Middle Belt Elders, Consultative Committee of Western Elders, Northern Consultative Group and the Western Forum all emerged advancing sectional interests. It is, however, significant to note that two vocal minority groups, the Ijaw People's Union (IPU) and the Movement for the Survival of the Ogoni People (MOSOP) raised critical questions of political and economic self-determination. In what amounted to a litany of demands and accusations, the Action Committee of the Ijaw People's Union (IPU) condemned the three major ethnic groups, the Hausa-Fulani, the Igbos and the Yoruba, for their domination and unfair exploitation of the country's national resources. They lamented that while the Niger Delta area provided the bulk of the country's petroleum resources and has suffered severe environmental degradation, the Ijaw people have generally been marginalised in the political and economic scheme of things.[22] Similarly, representing the concerns of a relatively small ethnic group in the south-east, the Ogonis, MOSOP seized the turbulent political climate to highlight years of environmental degradation inflicted by petroleum exploitation.[23] The passionate economic and environmental demands of these minority groups not only posed new problems for the political elite, but further complicated the debate on the national question within the Nigerian body politic. In reaction to the intense rivalry of these ethnic organisations, Bolaji Akinyemi, a former Foreign Minister, reminded local leaders that,

> the crisis facing Nigeria is a national and not a sectional one, the presidential election was a national affair, contested by two national political parties which won votes across ethnic, religious, regional and military/civilian lines . . . (This) is a worrisome and retrogressive step at this stage of Nigerian politics.[24]

To Akinyemi, therefore, this development was antithetical to the construction of unifying national movements and organisations critical to an enduring process of democratisation.

The excesses of the Babangida regime, therefore, brought together both old and new organisations, that have in the past tended to operate as independent groups. These organisations, under the leadership of the CD, temporarily overlooked their divergent ideological perspectives. It is ironic, however, that the ultimate rallying force for the CD's mass mobilisation campaign would be the annulment of the presidential elections of 12 June 1993. The democratic movement emerged as the champion of an unlikely cause, an important aspect of a transition programme that it had campaigned against for many months. Ironically, Abiola, one of the country's wealthiest men and a prominent figure in the Nigerian political class for almost two decades, emerged as the symbol of the Nigerian pro-democracy movement. The issue as articulated by the leader of the CD had gone far beyond personal, ideological, regional, religious and ethnic differences which, in the past, had generally impeded the development of a unified national democratic movement. In fact, a CD document under-scored the significance of reconciling this apparent political paradox:

> The struggle to enforce the outcome of the Presidential elections of June 12, 1993 in which hundreds of Nigerians laid down their lives, limbs and liberty has been cardinal in the activities of the CD since the annulment of that election. From the onset, the CD has consistently emphasised that June 12 went beyond the *symbol* of that mandate, the Babangida parties, the entire transition programme or any ethnic group or groups . . . June 12 cannot be wished away despite the present ambivalence of its winners. It is a historic expression of the popular will transcending ethnic, religious and other primordial barriers.[25]

Yet, despite the conscious attempt to build a national political resistance against military rule, the fact still remains that the activities of the CD were most effective in the urban centres of the south (especially Lagos and major Yoruba towns). It is in reaction to this apparent weakness that the Federal Government attempted to discredit the democratic movement as the con-spiracy of a disgruntled Yoruba political class.

INTERNATIONAL REACTIONS TO THE NIGERIAN CRISIS

In keeping with major global developments of the post-cold-war period in which human rights, democratisation and economic liberalisation assumed new significance in Western foreign policy towards Third World countries, military rule in Nigeria came under the full weight of international pressure and condemnation. General Babangida had not anticipated the hostile reactions from Western powers and major multilateral institutions. He must have assumed that because of his initial popularity with key Western governments (as a result of the implementation of structural adjustment programmes) he would receive some support for his anti-democratic policies. Following the cancellation of the presidential elections, the American and British governments reacted swiftly condemning the Babangida dictatorship. They expressed their displeasure at the turn of events and gave open support to Nigeria's democratic movement. In line with the Hurd 'Doctrine of Good Governance', the British Foreign Office described the regime's action as 'regrettable' and, as an 'initial response', withdrew its military advisers from Nigeria's War College, threatened to freeze a L14.5 million aid package and denied entry visas to Nigerian government officials. In fact, the British Prime Minister, John Major, told the House of Commons that his government would seek the cooperation of other European Community members to discontinue multilateral aid to Nigeria.[26]

Similarly, the United States government described the action of the Nigerian regime as an 'outrageous decision' and threatened to lead 'an international campaign against any attempts by the Babangida administration to stay in power beyond 27 August 1993'.[27]

The premier Nigerian weekly, *Newswatch*, went as far as to report that the US ambassador to Nigeria, William Swing,[28] was instructed by Washington to 'initiate high-level contacts' with key figures opposed to the Babangida regime.[29] In reaction to some Nigerian groups based in American cities and some prominent Americans, the Congressional Black Caucus (CBC) encouraged the US government to take even tougher action against the Nigerian government.[30] In a strongly worded letter to the US Secretary of State, Warren Christopher, the CBC noted that 'The action by Nigeria's military rulers to annul the June 12, 1993 presidential election must not be allowed to stand.' It was the general view of both the Clinton administration and the CBC that the intransigence of the Nigerian military has done irrevocable damage to the legitimacy of the Babangida regime in both the country and the subcontinent. Africanists in the state department further contend that any form of support for the Nigerian regime would encourage similar actions in other African states, intensify the crisis in Nigeria itself and leave ECOWAS operations in Liberia without effective military leadership. In keeping with these pressures the US State Department announced the expulsion of the military attaché from the Nigerian Embassy in Washington, vowed to review diplomatic relations and a $22.8 million dollar aid package to Nigeria. Thus, in keeping with the Clinton administration foreign policy towards the Third World, a general disposition of the Western powers in the post-cold-war period and new CBC demands for political accountability in African states,[31] the pro-democracy movement in Nigeria had, at least for the time being, a formidable supporter in Washington.[32]

The Canadian government was not left out of the opposition to the Nigerian military regime. It imposed sanctions by suspending Nigeria's 'eligibility for military and police training and cancelled a visit to Canada by Nigerian military and civilian officials from a strategic studies institute scheduled for September'.[33] It also promised to take further bilateral measures against the Nigerian government. Important multilateral institutions such as the Commonwealth, an organisation in which Nigeria plays a prominent role, described the annulment of the elections as a 'severe setback to the course of democracy'.[34] This symbolic pronouncement by such an important international organisation further deflated the morale of the military regime and significantly reduced its prestige among member states.

The historic political development in the post-cold-war period therefore encouraged the expansion of the political space in Nigeria. Similar to other African countries where the excesses of authoritarian regimes had in the past gone unchallenged by the major powers, prevailing global conditions promoted the development of democratisation in Nigeria. The connection between global and internal factors therefore led to the expansion of the political space and consequently to the increasing fragility of the authoritarian state. The lack of support and even in some cases the hostility of major Western powers in the post-cold-war era for African dictators enabled local communities and organisations to make new politcal demands on the state. Yet, despite this important shift in the global order, it is clear that meaningful change will emerge out of the popular political struggles of Nigeria's diverse communities. The complex nature of the Nigerian crisis within the context of a rapidly changing state clearly underscores the challenge confronting Nigeria's transient and fragile democratic movement.

It is important, however, to emphasise that despite these external factors and the CD's call for sanctions from the international community,[35] Nigeria's democratic movement has consistently contested the interpretation and meaning of liberal democracy and human rights. For example, in a fascinating and critical study of human rights in contemporary African states, the eminent Nigerian political scientist Claude Ake notes that a serious analysis of this subject must underscore the political, social and cultural dimensions in local African communities.[36] Elsewhere on the debate on liberal democracy he observes:

> What is being foisted on Africa is a version of liberal democracy reduced to the crude simplicity of multi-party elections. This type of democracy is not in the least emancipatory especially in African conditions because it offers the people rights they cannot exercise, voting that never amounts to choosing, freedom which is patently spurious, and political equality which disguises highly unequal power relations.[37]

Thus, popular democratic movements in Nigeria have for the first time questioned social contradictions within the country and raised some fundamental questions about the uncertainties of globalisation, the pre-eminence of Western powers and major multilateral institutions, and Nigeria's subordinate role within this new world order.

CONCLUSION: THE FUTURE OF DEMOCRACY AND CIVIL SOCIETY IN NIGERIA

With yet another military intervention in politics, the process of developing a viable multi-party system is, at least for the moment, temporarily terminated. It would, however, be premature and incorrect to assume that with the Abacha coup of December 1993, the popular struggle for democratisation in Nigeria has come to a final halt. Through the popular struggle of the Babangida years, civil society has experienced a profound jolt. Obviously, with the return of the military, many Nigerians are disillusioned with another prolonged discussion on participatory politics. The general level of apathy is understandable when we take into account the instant cooptation of prominent SDP politicians and pro-democracy leaders by the current military regime and the fragmentation that bedevilled the CD after its initial anti-military actions. In fact, the cynicism of politicians was apparent even before the Abacha coup, as the SDP splintered into two major factions, with one supporting the decision of the Babangida regime and the other holding firmly to the results of the presidential elections. The National Assembly was also in disarray, with allegations of impropriety levied against many of its members and its President, Dr Iyorchia Ayu, impeached. By the time General Abacha intervened, therefore, the politicians were in no position to provide any credible leadership in the country. In spite of this unfortunate state of affairs, the short-lived democratic movement had shown that the military can be vulnerable to mass democratic pressures. The level of activism established through the creation of the CD has set in motion a completely new pattern of political action in Nigeria. New leaders and organisations have emerged and new questions and constituencies been established. Yet we can only be cautiously optimistic as we recognise the formidable opposition posed to democracy by a highly politicised military, a morally bankrupt civil political class and a socially fragmented society.

NOTES

1 See *Dissent*, Winter 1994.
2 For a comprehensive and critical study of multinational corporations and the Nigerian state, see Thomas J. Biersteker, *Multinationals, the State, and Control of the Nigerian Economy* (Princeton: Princeton University Press, 1987).
3 See, for example, the following documents: *Guidelines for Local Government Reform* (Lagos: Federal Government Printer, 1976); *The Report of the Panel Investigating the Issue of the Creation of more States and Boundary Adjustments in Nigeria* (Lagos: Government Printer, 1976); and *The Land Use Decree* (Lagos: Federal Government Printer, 1978).

4 See Toyin Falola and Julius O. Ihonvbere, *The Rise and Fall of Nigeria's Second Republic, 1979–1984* (London: Zed Press, 1985); and Edwin Madunagu, *Nigeria: The Economy and the People: The Political Economy of State Robbery and its Social Democratic Negation* (London: New Beacon, 1983).

5 Peter Anyang'Nyong'o, 'Introduction', Peter Anyang'Nyong'o (ed.), *Popular Struggles for Democracy in Africa* (London: Zed Press, 1987).

6 For a detailed analysis of the complex political and economic factors that led to this coup see Julius Ihonvbere, 'A Critical Evaluation of the Failed 1991 Coup in Nigeria', *Journal of Modern African Studies*, 29, 4, 1991, pp. 601–626.

7 For further discussion see William Reno, 'Old Brigades, Money Bags, New Breeds, and the Ironies of Reform in Nigeria', *Canadian Journal of African Studies*, 27, 1, 1993, pp. 66–87.

8 See Richard Joseph, *Democracy and Prebendal Politics in Nigeria* (Cambridge: Cambridge University Press, 1989).

9 For a detailed and critical analysis of the two-party system and conflict management in Nigeria see Anthony A. Akinola, 'Manufacturing the Two-Party System in Nigeria', *Journal of Commonwealth and Comparative Politics*, 28, 3, 1990, pp. 309–327.

10 For a discussion on the objectives and performance of DFRRI see Olufemi Vaughan, 'Integrated Rural Development in Nigeria: The Case of DFRRI', unpublished manuscript.

11 Pearl T. Robinson, 'Approaches to the Study of Democratisation: Scripts in Search of Reality', paper presented at the annual conference of the African Studies Association, Boston, 5 December 1993, p. 4.

12 Several studies on Nigeria's previous attempts at liberal democracy show that the country's dominant regional political elites had learnt little from their recent past. See, for example, Kenneth Post and W. Vickers, *Structure and Conflict in Nigeria 1960–1966* (London: Heinemann, 1973).

13 See *West Africa*, 29 September 1988, 20 July 1989 and the *Nigerian Economist*, 27 April 1988.

14 Interview with Femi Falana, Lagos, Nigeria, December 1993.

15 Sanni Abacha was for eight years a major actor in the Babangida regime. As Chief of Defence Staff in this military dictatorship he not only 'oversaw the persistence of power' but also emerged as 'the chief custodian of a government of false populism and deception'. Similar to Babangida's populist adminis-tration of August 1985, Abacha's Cabinet was a cooptation of prominent politicians of diverse regional and ideological persuasion. See *Nigeria Now* (London), 2 December 1993 and *Nigeria Now* (London), 3 January 1992.

16 Abubakar Rimi quoted in Paul Adams, 'Nigeria: Legacy of the General', *Africa Report*, September–October 1993, p. 68.

17 The CD document listed Beko Ransome-Kuti, Gani Fawehinmi, Olisa Agbakoba, Atahiru Jega, Glory Kilanko, Mallam Naseer Kura Jafaar, Femi Falana, Osagie Obayuwana, Chima Ubani, Chom Bagu and other leaders of human rights organisations, professionals, workers, market women and farmers' groups as those who addressed the rallies. The movement declared as its main objectives the overthrow of the Babangida regime, the recognition of the 12 June election and a call for an independent national conference.

18 It must be noted that political opposition was particularly fierce in Yoruba cities and towns. This development is not unconnected to the fact that Abiola, the winner of the presidential election, is an Egba Yoruba. There is no doubt that Yoruba passion is intimately connected to the perception that a northern military Head of State annulled the election between a victorious Yoruba candidate and a northern contender.

19 Femi Falana, 'The Struggle Has Just Started', *TELL* (Lagos), 13 September 1993.

20 See Onome Osifo-Whiskey and Ayodele Akinkuotu, 'A Dance on the Precipice', *TELL* (Lagos), 19 July 1993.

21 Union members were generally apprehensive of the relationship between some of their major national leaders and General Babangida. It is commonly known that, in keeping with his general style of leadership, Babangida had effectively manipulated and coopted major figures of the Nigerian Labour Movement such as Congress President, Pascal Bafyau. This development generated a leadership crisis among the forty-two industrial unions that make up the NLC.

22 For a detailed discussion see Ijaw People's Union, 'Our Stand on the Current Political Crisis', *Vanguard* (Lagos), 14 September 1993.

23 *Nigeria Now* (London), 3 January 1994.

24 Bolaji Akinyemi, 'Why not a Nigerian Forum'?, *Guardian* (Lagos), 25 August 1993.

25 *Campaign For Democracy: The Task Ahead of the Nigerian People* (Lagos), December 1993.

26 For a good analysis of British foreign policy in post-cold-war Africa see Stephen Riley, 'Africa's New Wind of Change', *The World Today*, July 1992.

27 Utibe Ikim, 'What Now? Will Babangida's New Game Plan Mollify US, Britain Over The Transition Programme?', *Newswatch*, 5 July 1993.

28 Ironically, the US government recalled its ambassador to Nigeria in the heat of the crisis. Ambassador Swing had been a very strong advocate of democracy in Nigeria and had given extensive support to the pro-democracy movement. There is little doubt that Mr Swing's appointment as US Ambassador to Haiti later in the year is not unconnected to his uncompromising opposition to the Babangida regime after the nullification of the July elections. See *Newswatch*, 5 July 1993.

29 Ibid.

30 Many members of the Congressional Black Caucus (CBC) were inundated with telephone calls and fax messages from concerned Americans and Nigerian organisations in the United States such as the Concerned Citizens For Nigeria (CCFN), Glendale, Arizona; the Organisation of Nigerians in America (ONA), Austin, Texas; The Movement for Democracy in Nigeria, New York; The International Alliance to Save Nigeria from IBB, Chicago, Illinois; and the International Movement for Democracy in Nigeria, Europe.

31 Recent political events in Haiti and the Republic of South Africa have gradually encouraged the CBC to raise new questions about democratisation in African and Caribbean states.

32 For a detailed discussion on the foreign policy of Western countries in the post-cold-war period see Julius Ihonvbere, 'The Third World and the New World Order in the 1990s', *Futures*, December 1992; and Olufemi Vaughan,

'The Politics of Global Marginalisation: Africa and the New World Order', *Journal of Asian and African Studies*, 29, 1994.

33 Emeka Obiagwu, 'Canada Applies Sanctions: Asks Babangida to Honour Pledge', *Guardian* (Lagos), 21 August 1993.

34 Ibid.

35 See 'Campaign for Democracy' (Lagos), 1993.

36 See Claude Ake, 'The African Context of Human Rights', *Africa Report*, November–December 1987.

37 Claude Ake, 'Is Africa Democratising?', text of the 1993 Guardian Lecture, Nigerian Institute of International Affairs. For a detailed account of this lecture see *Sunday Guardian* (Lagos), 12 December 1993.

5 Ghana: From personalist to democratic rule

Jeff Haynes

Ghanaians had little to show in concrete terms for a quarter-century of freedom from colonial rule by the time of Flt Lt Jerry Rawlings' 1981 takeover. This was ironic given Ghana's socio-economic position in 1957. Then, the country was generally recognised as sub-Saharan Africa's wealthiest state; the former Gold Coast was endowed with an impressive transportation system, a highly educated work-force, and a British-trained, professional public service bureaucracy. Much of the optimism at independence was dissipated by economic incompetence, political authoritarianism and widespread denials of basic human rights by Kwame Nkrumah's Convention People's Party (CPP) government. Its overthrow in February 1966 was greeted joyfully by most Ghanaians.

The military and police officers who overthrew Nkrumah's government formed themselves into the National Liberation Council (NLC) regime. It banned the CPP and imprisoned party leaders. Nkrumah, who was out of the country at the time of the coup in vainglorious pursuit of peace in Vietnam, died a broken man in exile in Conakry (Guinea), in 1972. The NLC's economic policy aimed to reverse the state's stranglehold, by way of privatisation of state enterprises, devaluation of the currency and galvanisation of the productive sectors (cocoa and minerals) by pricing inducements. Yet, the regime was unable to solve Ghana's problems by a reversal of Nkrumah's 'socialist' policies. As a result, the military government was happy to give way in 1969 to an elected regime of liberal pretensions.

Less than three years later, in January 1972, the ineffectual civilian government of Kofi Busia was ousted in a further military putsch. The succeeding National Redemption Council (NRC; from 1975, the Supreme Military Council [SMC]) regime announced in September that it intended to reactivate various state enterprises left uncompleted or abandoned after Nkrumah's overthrow. During the next seven years, despite some intermittent, rhetorical allusions to the desirability of socialism and the baleful effects of 'imperialism' and 'neo-colonialism', the chief attribute of the military governments was a single-minded, not to say slavish, devotion to personal wealth accumulation.[1] As popular opposition increased in the wake of economic hardships, the regime's mechanism to regularise the situation politically was by the planned creation of a 'Union Government' (UNIGOV), following a referendum: a no-party, tripartite arrangement, involving the military, police and hand-picked civilians.[2]

The referendum was held in a highly charged atmosphere in which the government blatantly advocated UNIGOV in the controlled media, whilst attempting to silence its opponents by using repressive tactics. Public meetings of the opposition People's Movement for Freedom and Justice (PMFJ) were broken up by groups of thugs.[3] The result of the referendum – a 54/46 per cent government majority – was widely understood to have been rigged, in the sense that opposition groups had been gagged as well as in the way that the official voting returns reflected more the government's aspirations than the actual numbers of votes cast. The Head of State, General Acheampong, nevertheless chose to interpret the result as conferring upon him a mandate to proceed with the introduction of UNIGOV.[4] Immediately after the referendum, the PMFJ was banned and its leaders incarcerated. Public hostility to Acheampong's actions led senior officers in the SMC to calculate that their best chance of managing the transition to a suitable civilian regime lay in removing him from power.[5] As a result, in July 1978 Acheampong was removed from office in a palace coup and replaced by his second-in-command, General Fred Akuffo. Akuffo, in a measure designed to gain public support, legalised the formation of political parties to contest the general election scheduled for June 1979. In addition, his regime released those imprisoned for anti-UNIGOV activities and appointed a Constituent Assembly to formulate a new constitution. Acheampong was not brought to trial, but merely banished to his home village and stripped of his military ranks and titles. As the date of the elections approached, rumours spread that Akuffo had made a deal with aspirant politicians to give himself and other SMC members immunity from prosecution after the handover of power.[6]

It was chiefly a burning sense of outrage and injustice occasioned by such rumours, as well as a serious, prolonged decline in living standards, which led Flt Lt Jerry Rawlings to lead a small-scale, armed forces mutiny on 15 May 1979. Although Rawlings was arrested, two weeks later a successful military uprising erupted which resulted in his release and appointment as Head of State, followed by the executions of *inter alia* Generals Acheampong and Akuffo. Following elections in September, a civilian government – led by Hilla Limann, whose party, the People's

National Party, was moulded on Nkrumah's CPP – came to power. The incompetence and corruption of this regime contributed to its short life. In addition, its assiduous hounding of Rawlings helped to precipitate a further military *coup d'état* on 31 December 1981. This time Rawlings said he wanted a 'revolution', something that would lead to an appreciably more just, equitable order in Ghana, in which ordinary people would have a say in the formulation and execution of government policies. Initially it appeared that his regime might institute a one-party system. Later, however, its political focus changed: an early socialist orientation gave way to a concern to build local-level democracy with a 'developmentalist' focus. The Rawlings regime later set in train a transition to multi-party national politics; this resulted in presidential and legislative elections in late 1992. The progress of the transition from personalist rule with socialist pretensions to an increasingly stable pluralist democracy forms the focus of much of the rest of the chapter.

Ghana's political history between 1957 and 1981 is a common enough saga in Africa of democratic aspirations and visions increasingly sacrificed on the day-to-day exigencies of governmental rule. Nkrumah's populist nationalist regime disappointed mightily various status constituencies; in response sections of the police and military seized power officially to rectify things. The senior military figures found that running a state was rather more complex than they had bargained for. They handed over to civilians who proved inadequate to the task of turning round an economy already showing signs of serious mismanagement. Re-enter the military, this time with very few real pretensions to rule wisely or well; access to state resources became little more than a gravy train for those with the know- how to benefit. Developments in Ghana may well have turned out like the economic and political débâcle of Zaire, or even the ghastly civil war which afflicted Liberia from the late 1980s. In Ghana, however, authoritarian rule by Jerry Rawlings led to significant, and prolonged, economic gains.

The country became the International Monetary Fund's 'star pupil' in the mid-1980s, although many ordinary Ghanaians found that much-vaunted macro-economic success was not reflected in comparative increases in living standards. By 1993, the minimum day's wage of C460 was the equivalent of US$0.33. With petrol at C1,600 a gallon, a minimum-waged worker earning C12,420 a month could buy 7.76 gallons of petrol with his monthly salary, *and nothing else.*[7] Worker opposition to government policy was forthright and condemnatory; in the Fourth Republic (from 1993) economic issues rather than democracy were the focus of popular discontent.

FROM PROVISIONAL REGIME TO DEMOCRATIC GOVERNMENT

The gradual emergence of the constitutional regime of the Fourth Republic began with the tenth anniversary of Rawlings' Provisional National Defence Council (PNDC) regime's inception at the end of 1991. It was followed in 1992 by two important political developments: first, a referendum on future political arrangements was successfully conducted in April 1992; second, presidential and parliamentary elections were held in November and December. Rawlings was elected President of Ghana, and his party, the National Democratic Congress (NDC), achieved controversial success, winning virtually all the seats in the legislature.[8] The ban on party politics between 1982 and 1992 served to give him a headstart over competitors in the presidential race, as he was the generally respected incumbent. At the same time, what was striking after a decade of PNDC rule was the inability of the regime to maintain a broad, secure support base, despite the macro-economic successes. Between 1984 and 1991 Ghana's economy grew by an average of 5 per cent annually, when population grew each year by 2.6 per cent.[9] Real growth of nearly 2.5 per cent a year was one of the best records in sub-Saharan Africa. The acceptance by much of the political opposition of the thrust of the PNDC's economic policies was clear; the election campaigns did not focus on their desirability, but rather on the legitimacy, accountability and human rights record of Rawlings' regime.[10]

Rawlings' regime remained a provisional one from 1981 until 1992. It was the dramatic end of communist rule in Eastern Europe which helped to focus attention in Ghana, as elsewhere in the region, on the issue of appropriate democratic political reforms. Many autocratic and dictatorial governments including Ghana's were challenged by calls for multi-party democracy and increased government accountability. Such demands were initially refused by Rawlings, but finally heeded in mid-1991 when pressures for reform became virtually overwhelming. In addition to the changed international climate following the fall of communist regimes and the cessation of the cold war, three factors led to the decision. First, international financial agencies, such as the International Monetary Fund (IMF) and the World Bank, and foreign governments, including those of Britain and America, made it plain that aid flows could be reduced or held up if fairly speedy democratic reforms did not take place.[11] Second, what appeared at the time to be successful political reforms Nigeria helped to persuade the PNDC leaders that it was b a pace and, hopefully, in a style they could control, rath speed and direction of events carried by unforeseeable

Third, and perhaps most importantly, the government came under prolonged pressure from leaders of domestic opposition groups, particularly
the umbrella Movement for Freedom and Justice (MFJ) and the smaller,
less influential, socialist-inspired Kwame Nkrumah Revolutionary Guards
(KNRG), impatient for multi-party democracy and the opportunity to take
their place in the sun. From its founding in mid-1990 until early 1992, most
anti-PNDC elements were coordinated by the MFJ. Yet, once Rawlings
announced that multi-party politics would be allowed from mid-1992, the
coalition of interests represented by the MFJ fractured. The Movement
criticised Rawlings' regime on four counts: failure to spread the gains of
economic growth relatively equitably, the declining standard of cash-
starved higher education and social services, the claimed diminution of the
rule of law, and finally, the absence of civilian, elected government respect-
ful of human rights.

The MFJ was launched on 1 August 1990, at a time when the regime was
calling for a widespread debate on the future framework for politics in
Ghana. It was regarded by many as a fairly serious threat to the PNDC's
continued domination since it was supported by politicians from both of
Ghana's two main political traditions: the Convention People's Party of
Kwame Nkrumah and the United Party of the late Kofi Busia. Leaders were
a remarkable mixture of socialists and liberals long committed to the
restoration of party political rule. The Chair of the Movement was the
historian, Professor Adu Boahen, who incurred the wrath of the PNDC in
1988 by a series of public lectures in Accra which vociferously attacked the
regime and its form of government. Other MFJ leaders included Johnny
Hansen and John Ndebugre (PNDC Secretaries [Ministers] during the
'radical' phase of 1982–1983), both socialists, the liberal Kumasi lawyer,
Obeng Manu, and Akoto Ampaw and Kwesi Pratt, former members of the
Marxist–Leninist National Democratic Movement, incarcerated briefly in
1987 because of their political activities. The Kwame Nkrumah Revolutionary Guards (KNRG), claiming to be the 'true' heirs to Nkrumah's
social democratic principles, also called for the reintroduction of party
political rule in Ghana.

Despite the dismissiveness which the government affected to regard the
MFJ, an attempt to launch it in Kumasi in September 1990 was prevented
by riot police. By this time the trade union movement and students were
independently calling for a national referendum on the issue of multi-party
politics in Ghana. Gradually, the weight of informed public opinion was
coalescing behind opposition groups' position of a phased reintroduction of
democracy. The problem for the PNDC was that in the context of local
debate on the political future and international pressure for qualitative

democratisation, it could not be seen to be cracking down too hard on such groups as the MFJ or ignoring their demands wholesale. While the PNDC could take credit for initiating the political debate about Ghana's constitutional future in 1990, the controlled nature of the national discussions on economic and political reform added credence to the MFJ's argument that the PNDC government had no real intention of introducing a pluralist political system and thus run the risk of losing power. By the end of 1990, the PNDC had done little concrete about setting up a permanent political framework for the country and nothing at all about a timetable for a return to constitutional government. Yet, it would not be correct to perceive the PNDC's moves towards multi-party democracy as entirely a defensive and begrudging reaction to foreign and domestic demands, given that the first democratisation programme was announced (although not implemented) in 1983, but it is not by any means certain that reforms would have come as quickly or in the form they did without the combination of domestic and international pressures.[13]

The PNDC – and Rawlings particularly – was very sceptical about the desirability of the reintroduction of a pluralist political system. The solution to the problem of the country's political future was initially to refer to an idealised version of Ghana's pre-colonial political past as a model for the future. Some government representatives appeared to want to develop an indigenous system of democracy structured on institutions, without 'inappropriate' competing political parties.[14] Kofi Awoonor, initially Ghana's ambassador to Brazil and then to Cuba, waxed lyrical in print about how in the past, following debate, community decisions were arrived at through the mediation and coordination of the local chief.[15] Colonialism, he argued, destroyed the local democratic systems, replacing them with a political agenda and processes based on the experiences and development of Britain which were quite inappropriate to the needs of Ghana. The imposition of this alien system, he claimed, was the root cause of the country's remarkable political instability since independence.

The PNDC attempted to stage-manage regional seminars held in 1990 and 1991 to discuss the country's political future. Most of the speakers were in agreement with the PNDC's plan for the future form of politics; no dissenting groups were allowed to address the audiences.[16] In the event, however, the PNDC plan was too much like the vilified UNIGOV proposal of the late 1970s to elicit much popular support. Rawlings' support of the 'no-party' option was to many Ghanaians unfortunately reminiscent of the attempt in 1978 to legitimise the breathtakingly corrupt military regime of General Acheampong. On that occasion it was envisaged that Acheampong's regime would metamorphose into a so-called 'Union Government', a corporate entity with significant involvement by senior security forces personnel. The still vivid memory of this flagrant attempt to legitimise such an unpopular and unrespected regime was enough to make Rawlings' plan anathema to many Ghanaians. In addition, the international trend of opinion and of events was firmly towards wholesale democratisation of authoritarian rule: Latin America, the former Soviet Union and Eastern Europe, East Asia and parts of North Africa were all undergoing demo-cratisation 'experiments' at the beginning of the 1990s. In this climate, plans for corporate government, while having the virtue of respect for prevailing patterns of power distribution, had the overwhelming dis-advantage of attempting to buck the democratising trend. Opponents of the PNDC shrewdly realised that to equate the PNDC plan with that of Acheampong's would be to link in the minds of Ghanaians, albeit un-warrantedly, the otherwise quite different Rawlings and Acheampong regimes. As a result of perceptive opposition attacks upon the 'no-party' government plan, the then Secretary (i.e. Minister) for Local Government, Kwamena Ahwoi, intimated in August 1990 that democratic political reforms would be implemented over a three-to-five-year timescale, later revised to between two and three years.[17] The interim results of the national debate on the political future were presented in mid-1991; the impetus by then was firmly towards a system characterised by competing political parties. The results were to form the basis for discussions on the content and form of a new Ghanaian constitution. It was to be drafted by the end of that year by a government-appointed 258-member Consultative Assembly, made up largely of representatives of corporate groups.[18]

The Consultative Assembly finished its deliberations in March 1992 after an unexpectedly rigorous series of debates. Initially, many considered that it would endorse without full deliberation what the government wanted. Yet, it did show an expected degree of independence in rejecting three of the PNDC's key draft proposals: a powerful President with a subordinate Prime Minister (along the lines of the French system); significant military representation in the President's advisory bodies; PNDC-created Committees for the Defence of the Revolution to survive the end of the regime's rule.[19] Its recommendations – including unfettered multi-party democracy and a four-year presidential term – were backed in a national referendum by a ratio of more than four to one (87 per cent to 13 per cent on a turnout of 3,500,000 voters). This was slightly lower than the almost 60 per cent of registered voters achieved in district-level elections in 1988 and 1989. The issue of the numbers of registered voters in the country was later to become a *cause célèbre* as opposition parties attacked the government for allegedly inflating the numbers of those eligible to vote

– by up to one and a half million names – for purposes of electoral fraud. The fact of the matter, however, was in part more prosaic: the voters' list had been compiled for district assembly elections in 1987 when the political climate had been quite different. Many potential opposition voters may not have registered as a complaint against the form of elections, i.e. *district* elections rather than *national*-level ballots. Opposition parties boycotted the second round of elections for the National Assembly in December 1992 in protest against alleged electoral fraud in the first round.

GHANA'S ELECTIONS IN 1992

During elections in the forty years between the Gold Coast's legislative elections in the early 1950s and the polls of 1992 and 1993, politicians campaigning for power sought ideological focus by allusion either to the socialist ideals of Kwame Nkrumah or by reference to the more pro-Western, economically liberal ideas associated with Kofi Busia and J.B. Danquah. When in government, however, leaders of whatever claimed ideological complexion often found economic success to be elusive, the pursuit of personal wealth and aggrandisement, uniformly seductive. For this reason the emergence of a third strand – a Rawlings or PNDC approach – was welcomed by many Ghanaians. Its centrepiece and *raison d'être* was Rawlings' decade of purposive, effective, dynamic and relatively uncorrupt personalist rule. Rawlings' ideological approach melded nationalism and anti-imperialism with an economic philosophy which stressed the qualities and attributes of private individuals and their capital. Clearly, the emergence of the PNDC approach made the former two-party tradition redundant, yet certain factors must be made clear in relation to the formation of the NDC party in 1992 which help explain both its electoral successes and Rawlings' apparent volte face on the issue of the introduction of multi-party politics.

The first factor is related to a continuing economic vulnerability which Ghana faced despite receiving foreign loans of more than US$9 billion dollars between 1983 and 1992. The structural adjustment programme supported by the International Monetary Fund (IMF) and World Bank could almost certainly not have been maintained during a period of democratic politics. It was clear, however, that continued economic success would hinge to a large extent on factors beyond the control of any government. A combination of international recession and over-supply reduced real world prices for Ghana's major exports, cocoa and gold, in 1992. There was not much foreign investment in the country, and only limited success in diversifying Ghana's exports. It would be difficult to set the stage for a transition to democracy, in which members of the PNDC wished to feature, when economic resources were reduced by circumstances beyond the government's control. Much foreign and domestic effort had been put into the rejuvenation of the Ghanaian economy. For Western donors the continuation of rule by the strongman, Rawlings, was the best of a not particularly inspiring set of options. Given the slow pace and disappointing levels of foreign investment even *during* the stability of the PNDC period, Western donors considered that his removal might be only too conducive to economic, and perhaps political and social, upheaval. An editorial in *West Africa* magazine on 16 November 1992, quoting a recent edition of the London *Financial Times*, put it thus: 'Western donors feel that *at the very least* a defeat of Flt-Lt Rawlings would cause a period of economic policy instability' (emphasis added). Opposition politicians made it clear that if any gained power their first priority would be settling scores with Rawlings. While carefully avoiding direct threats, opposition figures, such as J.H. Mensah (former Finance Minister in the Busia-led Progress Party government of 1969–1972), J.W.S de Graft Johnson (former Vice President of the Hilla Limann-led Third Republic, 1979–1981) and Kweku Danso (of the Ghana Democratic Republican Party), stressed that the main problem was Rawlings himself. He was considered to be a man who would stop at nothing to achieve his ends. Human rights abuses had been common during Rawlings' tenure; these had to be investigated after Rawlings' political demise and, if found guilty, Rawlings would be made personally to pay the price. The desirability and continuation of economic reform was agreed by all political groupings. The outraged opposition was overwhelmingly drawn from Ghana's middle classes; leaders represented those who had often personally suffered under PNDC rule. By targeting Rawlings personally they were extending their own experiences to Ghanaians *en masse*; they expected everybody else to see Rawlings in the same light as they did. This not only demonstrated the social gulf between most opposition politicians and their putative supporters, in contrast to Rawlings' 'man of the people' style, but also led them to attack the *style* of rule rather than its substance. Rawlings' leadership had led to a degree of political stability and economic growth which many Ghanaians appreciated. The opposition tactics proved to be a costly error when none of their leaders, other than Adu Boahen with around 30 per cent of the vote, scored credibly in the presidential elections.[20]

The second issue was straightforwardly political. The situation for Rawlings was complicated by the PNDC's nationalistic response to calls for political reforms. The Rawlings-inspired coup in December 1981 had overthrown the democratically elected Limann government; it could be regarded as both inconsistent and defeatist to bow to pressures to reintroduce the same kind of system. Rawlings was strongly opposed to a pluralist political system because he considered that it was merely a front for the corrupt and self-serving behaviour of politicians. Yet, after a decade of a provisional regime, and frequent but unfulfilled promises to 'pass power to the people', he was in an untenable position without movement towards political reform. The initial response – the introduction of district assemblies – was an attempt to develop a form of democracy based on a party-less system at local level from which national politics would gradually develop. The popular rejection of this idea was a serious rebuff which encouraged the formulation of an alternative. The dangers of social instability and strife if the PNDC did not continue in some form helped to persuade Rawlings that the introduction of pluralist politics was a step which, however unwillingly, he must take. The only way to 'keep those punks out' of power (i.e. opposition politicians) was to ensure the perpetuation of his regime in one form or another; for this Rawlings needed not only to exploit his still considerable personal popularity, but also to 'sell' the PNDC's record to a healthily sceptical electorate during the election campaign.[21]

The PNDC's opinion research in late 1990 – i.e. 18 months before the end of the ban on the formation of political parties was announced – indicated that a PNDC party could expect to win more than 50 per cent of the votes in four of Ghana's ten poorest regions: the Upper East, Upper West, Northern and Volta (sixty-two of 200 constituencies). It would probably divide the vote with a party in the Nkrumaist tradition in the Eastern and Central regions (forty-three seats), but would lose to such a party in the remainder of the regions: Ashanti, Brong-Ahafo, Greater Accra and Western (ninety-five seats).[22] Fighting on its own a PNDC party would hope to win nearly half the available seats; partnering a Nkrumahist group it might do very much better. It is significant that any party proclaiming the tradition of Busia and Danquah appeared to have its work cut out to gain a substantive position in a legislature or to achieve the presidency. Clearly the paramount 'social democratic' welfarist objectives, within the context of a mixed economy with a strong state role, of both the Rawlings and Nkrumah traditions were highly popular amongst many Ghanaians, even before a sustained period of campaigning by Rawlings in the country's rural areas which later bore electoral fruit.

Initially, Rawlings appeared to be prevaricating between three options: to retire from politics, to throw in his lot with the Nkrumaists, or to front his own party. Opinion within the PNDC itself was initially divided between those who urged Rawlings to front a Nkrumaist party and those who considered that a PNDC group, by manipulating the advantages of incumbency (controlling the media, targeting financial sources to certain areas, cultivating influential figures, extolling the successes of the PNDC's economic reform programme and stressing the dangers of political instability), could expect electoral victory in its own right. Significantly, Rawlings managed to keep nearly all senior and middle-ranking government figures either within the confines of a PNDC party or within the ranks of one of its allies. This allowed him and his party to stress that the current 'team' would continue its effective work in the future Fourth Republic, a position epitomised by the PNDC's (and later the NDC's) slogan: 'Unity, Stability and Development'.

The announcement of a return to constitutional rule was quickly followed by the reformation of the traditional political parties albeit under new names. The Busia/Danquah strand was strongly pro-business, liberal and supportive of democratic freedoms, while the Nkrumaist stance was nebulous enough to defy easy categorisation, beyond the espousal of socialist aims and objectives (full employment, strong state role in both political and economic contexts, equitable distribution of wealth). In effect, the distinction was largely reducible to the role of the state in the economy and the position of individual (as opposed to collective) freedoms. There was no clear-cut ethnic division between the two parties, although Akan-speakers tended to gravitate towards the Busia/ Danquah position, while ethnic minorities, especially 'northerners', often found themselves within the Nkrumaist camp.

The Busia/Danquah tradition's chosen vehicle was the New Patriotic Party (NPP), led by Adu Boahen, a former university history professor. He had come to public prominence following a highly critical series of public lectures in mid-1988, which served to highlight the PNDC's authoritarianism. The NPP's electoral programme did not focus upon the continuation or cessation of the economic reforms instituted by the PNDC – which it supported – but rather upon the authoritarian nature of PNDC rule and the particular position of Rawlings, who it saw as an unelected dictator of eleven years' standing. Several of its leading figures such as Kwame Safu-Adu and Boahen himself, had either been imprisoned or severely harassed by the PNDC's security forces. As Safu-Adu put it in July 1992: 'We're going to campaign first of all on human rights – detention without trial, lack of accountability. It's been very expensive to criticise the PNDC, the rule of law has disappeared.'[23] The NPP's liberal leanings were tempered by a burning desire for revenge against Rawlings, a characteristic which endeared it to the elitist strata of Ghana's so-called 'professionals' – lawyers, medical doctors, intellectuals – but which failed as it turned out to convince many 'ordinary' Ghanaians outside of Ashanti, the home region of many of its leaders, of its fitness to rule.

Followers of Nkrumah, perhaps scenting victory as a result of favourable national opinion polls, his posthumous political renaissance in Ghana and his reputation as a pan-Africanist hero, were nevertheless seriously split. Factions were not distinguishable by ideological differences so much as reflective of the aspirations of various individuals who imagined that they were the 'real' standard bearer of Nkrumaism, which was, in fact, an amorphous set of ideas. The picture was confused by the personal links between certain PNDC figures (such as Kojo Tsikata) who were close to former followers of Nkrumah, including the PNDC's former High Commissioner to Zimbabwe, John Tettigah, and Kojo Botsio, once Nkrumah's Foreign Minister.

The leading Nkrumaist party was initially 'Our Heritage', later the People's Heritage Party (PHP). Leaders included former PNDC Secretaries Johnny Hansen and John Ndebugre, as well as Tommy Thompson, publisher of the defunct Independent *Free Press* newspaper which had been a thorn in the PNDC's side in the mid-1980s. The PHP's presidential candidate was former Lt Gen. Emmanuel Erskine. Erskine's main appeal was thought to be that, as a former military man with a highly commendable record as Force Commander of the United Nations Interim Force in Lebanon, he had called upon the military to disengage from politics and for popular resistance to any further coup attempts.[24] Despite this, the PHP's lack of a distinctive platform, shortage of funds and inability to organise nationally counted against it.

A second Nkrumaist group, the National Independence Party (NIP), suffered from a similar disability to project itself as a credible electoral force. Its presidential candidate, Kwabena Darko, a wealthy businessman, gained his position by assiduous use of his fortune, but never managed to develop his party into a viable national grouping. Not offering Ghanaians any special reason to vote for him, Darko fared inauspiciously in the presidential poll. Despite the poor showing of the NIP and the PHP, both did better than the most radical group claiming Nkrumah as inspiration, the Popular Party for Democracy and Development (PPDD). One of the PPDD's leading figures was Kwesi Pratt, a long-standing opponent of Rawlings from the left. His party was so short of funds that it failed even to register for the electoral competitions.

The People's National Convention led by former President Hilla Limann (deposed by Rawlings in 1981) did best of the Nkrumaist parties in the presidential poll. Limann from the Upper West region emphasised his success in the north as a 'local boy made good' to attract voters in his home region and from the neighbouring Upper East and, to an extent, the Northern region. In the Upper (East and West) regions he gained a third of the vote, but lost to Rawlings even there. Despite his regional appeal, he was generally seen as a 'loser' who had been unable to make his mark when leader of the government.

The National Convention Party (NCP) also claimed the mantle of Nkrumah. The NCP was notable for two things. First, several of its leaders were PNDC-appointed diplomats, including John Tettegah, Kofi Awoonor (Ghana's representative to the United Nations) and Chris Hesse (Moscow High Commissioner). They were not convinced that the PNDC could build a party with electoral attraction, and thus refused to join Rawlings' party. Tettegah claimed that the PNDC 'never (had) got popular power off the ground'.[25] Nevertheless, in the event the NCP forged an electoral alliance with the PNDC which resulted in it gaining eight seats in the legislative elections. Thus, no less than five parties claimed Nkrumah as their ideological referent. The splintering of the broad church of Nkrumaism (spanning left-wing socialism to right-wing social democracy) reflected the positions of senior Nkrumaists who were unwilling to forget their personal aspirations for the greater good of a putative movement. They were also out-manoeuvred by the decisions of followers of Nkrumah in the PNDC regime to throw their lot behind the NDC once Rawlings had made the decision to stand for the presidency.

Rawlings' NDC was an assemblage of interest groups and popular movements united by their wish to see a further period of (P)NDC rule. Senior PNDC figures, including Obed Asamoah (Secretary for Foreign Affairs), Ebo Tawiah (PNDC member), Kofi Totobi Quakyi (Secretary for Information) and Huudu Yahaya (Secretary for Committees for the Defence of the Revolution [CDRs]), were senior figures in the NDC. Yahaya's three deputies, Sam Garba, Kofi Portuphy and Cecilia Johnson, each had extensive links with PNDC activists throughout the country. Garba was linked to the community and workplace CDRs which, following a period in the mid-1980s when it seems that they would be abolished, rose to become a quasi-PNDC movement, although the CDR network never developed into a *de facto* PNDC political party. This role was filled by the populist June Four Movement, which had branches throughout the country.[26] Portuphy was the director of the National Mobilisation Programme which had helped to resettle economic refugees expelled from Nigeria in the 1980s and set them to work in farming cooperatives. Johnson was the full-time secretary of the December 31st Women's Movement (DWM), which enjoyed the patronage of Rawlings' wife, Nana Konadu Rawlings, and was popular amongst women generally. The DWM was instrumental in constructing much-needed day-care centres, markets for local produce, and for leading public education campaigns. Johnson's appointment as Yahaya's deputy was an attempt to bring the CDRs and DWM closer together.

Support for the NDC was expressed by successful cocoa farmers through the Cocoa, Coffee and Sheanut Farmers' Association, and represented in the NDC by the National Vice Chief Farmer, R.A. Achaab. The NDC also encompassed a number of Rawlings' loyalist groups, including the numerous grassroots 'Rawlings Fan Clubs', the New Nation Club, the Development Union and the Eagle Club. The latter initially appeared as a challenger to the NDC, by seeking to invoke Rawlings' name as its guiding philosophy. It unwisely attempted to adopt Rawlings as its presidential candidate without his agreement. For his part, Rawlings regarded leading figures in the Eagle Club, such as his cousin, Michael Soussoudis and the founder, Captain Felix Okai, as 'opportunists' using his name 'to pursue their own private political agendas', and rejected their advances.[27] The Eagle Club changed its name to the Egle (sic) Party, which was an acronym for 'Every Ghanaian Living Everywhere'. It became part of the NDC's so-called 'progressive coalition' in 1992, along with the Nkrumahist National Convention Party. It gained one seat in its own right in the legislative polls.

The success of attending to grassroots issues helps to explain Rawlings' sweeping success in the presidential elections, the extent of which can be gauged from the results presented below in Table 5.1. It is clear from the table that three of the presidential candidates did very poorly indeed. The PHP's presidential candidate, former Lt Gen. Emmanuel Erskine gained a derisory 1.7 per cent of the votes in the presidential poll, while Kwabena Darko of the NIP fared little better, achieving just 2.8 per cent of the votes. Former President Limann gained 6.7 per cent of the votes cast. Their collective failure to do better was in part reflective of Rawlings' clear dominance, while the bulk of anti-Rawlings votes were cast for his main rival, Adu Boahen of the NPP. The key to an appreciation of Rawlings' electoral success is not to be found only in his undoubted personal popularity. There is also the role of the PNDC-created community organisations which formed a country-wide network and included the community Committees for the Defence of the Revolution (CDRs), the December 31st Women's Movement and the June Four Movement. Such organisations were instrumental, in tandem with traditional chiefs, in delivering the vote both for Rawlings and the NDC more generally. Indeed, the PNDC, by Law 107 of 1983, made a chief's legal status dependent on recognition by the government. As a result, the PNDC was able to use its power for political purposes. In Brong-Ahafo over fifteen chiefs were elevated to paramount status in 1988; this meant that their own personal powers were increased by

Table 5.1 Presidential election results by region, November 1992

Region	turnout (%)	Valid votes	1 (%)	2 (%)	3 (%)	4 (%)	5 (%)	Cons
Western	45.9	394,286	22.8	0.6	5.6	60.7	2.4	19
Central	45.6	334,031	26.0	1.9	3.5	66.5	2.2	17
Accra	46.2	507,445	37.0	4.3	4.1	53.4	1.2	22
Volta	60.8	478,417	3.6	1.6	0.7	93.3	0.8	19
Eastern	50.9	516,874	38.5	1.9	2.3	56.7	0.7	26
Ashanti	49.1	712,584	60.5	2.5	3.6	32.9	0.6	33
Brong-Ahafo	43.2	392,864	29.5	5.3	2.3	61.9	1.0	21
Northern	47.3	320,973	16.4	11.0	1.5	63.2	7.9	23
Upper West	47.7	129,600	8.9	37.1	1.8	51.0	1.2	8
Upper East	47.5	201,946	10.5	32.5	1.4	54.0	1.7	12
Country total	48.3	3,989,020	30.4	6.7	2.8	58.3	1.7	200

1 = A. Boahen (New Patriotic Party); 2 = H. Limann (People's National Convention); 3 = K. Darko (National Independence Party); 4 = J. Rawlings (National Democratic Congress); 5 = E. Erskine (People's Heritage Party). Cons = Constituencies.

Source: *West Africa*, 16 November 1992, p. 1963

their heading their own Area Traditional Councils. They also benefited personally from the receipt of royalties garnered from mineral exploitation and other activities.[28] Perhaps not coincidentally, Brong-Ahafo recorded the highest percentage of adults over eighteen years to register on the electoral roll. Not too much should be made of this, however: electoral results in the presidential poll indicate that voters in Brong-Ahafo had the lowest turnout (43 per cent) in the country. In another example of attending to local concerns, the PNDC allowed a number of commercially important towns originally extracted from the control of Krachi to be reincorporated into that district upon appeal. Krachi district recorded the highest level of voter registration in the Volta region.

It was noted above that the PNDC's private opinion research in late 1990 indicated that a PNDC party would be likely to win outright only the most impoverished regions: Upper East, Upper West, Volta and Northern. Similar levels of electoral success looked unlikely in Ashanti, Brong-Ahafo, Greater Accra and Western regions, while the result appeared to be in the balance in the Eastern and Central regions. One reason for Rawlings' presidential success was provided by the opposition parties' claims that the vote was rigged. According to the opposition politicians, a combination of ballot box stuffing, electoral register inflation and intimidation of political opponents provided the reason for the outcome. Despite such charges, international electoral observers found the conduct of the poll exemplary, with voter intimidation at a minimum.[29] More serious was the charge of electoral register inflation; a number of sources claimed that it was inflated by between one and two million names. After observation of the registration of voters process in April 1992, the International Foundation for Electoral Systems, a US-based organisation, concluded that the list was 'grossly inflated: the total number of registered voters (8.41 million) is improbable given an estimated population of 16 million of whom half are under 15 years of age. An estimate of a million erroneous entries is not inappropriate'.[30] Such a verdict was backed by other foreign organisations including the Organisation of African Unity and a team from the Commonwealth Secretariat. Despite the fact that an apparently inaccurate register could facilitate vote-rigging the opposition parties still agreed to fight the presidential election. Once they had been comprehensively beaten by Rawlings, they turned round to claim 'foul'. It is impossible to know the extent to which the register was inaccurate; if the figure was inflated by one million votes, and all these votes went to Rawlings in the presidential poll, then they would have been instrumental in his victory. At the same time, it should be stressed that it is hard to envisage any of Rawlings' frankly uninspiring challengers, other than perhaps the NPP's leader Adu Boahen, beating him in a two-way contest. There was a probably fatal drawback with Boahen as a national challenger to Rawlings; he would have been associated with Ashanti aspirations and would not, as a result, have enjoyed much support from non-Ashantis. In any case, no international observers recorded incidents *to their knowledge* of ballot box stuffing. It would seem appropriate to see Rawlings' victory as largely due to legitimate reasons, although it is by no means certain that there was not a degree of chicanery resulting from the probably inflated electoral register.

The most persuasive explanation for Rawlings' victory is one alluded to above: effective work by the CDRs and other community organisations, with support from a significant proportion of chiefs, resulted in the backing of many Ghanaians living in the rural areas. Rawlings achieved much less success in the ethnically mixed urban centres.[31] Although by no means as significant as, for example, in the recent Kenyan and Angolan elections, there was undoubtedly an ethnic dimension to Ghana's presidential elections. Rawlings, half-Scottish and half-Ewe, secured over 90 per cent of the votes in Volta region, the Ewe's homeland. Adu Boahen of the NPP, on the other hand, secured over 70 per cent of the votes in Ashanti, his home region. Yet, despite this, the relatively low political salience of ethnicity coupled with the illegality of political parties based on region, 'tribe' or religion, ensured that such allegiances remained relatively unimportant issues in the elections. The issues of economic progress and human rights were of much greater importance. Boahen's NPP failed to attract a majority of votes by campaigning on the human rights issue, whereas Rawlings and the NDC appeared to most Ghanaians to be the best chance for economic progress. Solid support for Rawlings in the four poorest regions was, at least in part, because people there had benefited for the first time from being the targets of development efforts including rural electrification, water supply, road-building, and health and education improvements.

The account above indicates that the presidential elections were substantially 'free and fair'. Because of this the decision by the main opposition parties to boycott the legislative poll needs a comment. Two clear, yet contrasting, explanations may be suggested for their course of action. First, such was the pique and discomfort felt by the opposition parties at the sweeping victory for Rawlings that they decided not to fight the legislative polls because they expected a further electoral débâcle. Second, the official reason for the opposition boycotting the legislative poll was twofold: first, that the electoral register was so inaccurate that there was no chance of a fair competition; second, that the PNDC government had *additionally* resorted to unfair measures (such as ballot box stuffing) to win the presidential poll; it would certainly do the same in the legislative elections. There was also a tactical manoeuvre at work: if all the main opposition parties could reach consensus about boycotting the second election, then the charges about electoral fraud would appear much stronger. In the event, however, the opposition parties were unable to present convincing evidence of clear-cut electoral malpractice. The international community had already stated that it was happy that the presidential poll had been fair; the opposition was unable to prove otherwise. Thus, the conclusion must be that the opposition, in order to obscure its inability to win electoral success by normal inter-party competition, attempted to belittle without ultimate success the efficacy of the elections themselves. In the event, all the anti-Rawlings parties succeeded in doing was to condemn themselves to political marginality.

Once all the opposition parties made it clear that they would boycott the legislative elections on 29 December 1992, the significance of the polls was greatly diminished. Unsurprisingly, the turnout was much lower than in the earlier round of voting, although there were regional variations. The highest was recorded in Volta region, and the lowest in Greater Accra. Table 5.2 illustrates this by region. Despite attempts by Rawlings to establish a dialogue with the opposition by postponing the legislative elections for two weeks, the Fourth Republic commenced in January 1993 under a

Table 5.2 Legislative election results by region, December 1992

Region turnout (%)		NDC	Seats gained			
			Egle	NCP	Independent	Cons
Western	29.8	16	–	3	–	19
Central	28.2	16	–	1	–	17
Greater Accra	18.0	22	–	–	–	22
Volta	51.2	18	–	1	–	19
Eastern	25.9	22	1	3	–	26
Ashanti	19.9	33	–	–	–	33
Brong-Ahafo	32.4	20	–	–	1	21
Northern	33.1	23	–	–	–	23
Upper West	34.5	8	–	–	–	8
Upper East	40.5	11	–	–	1	12
Country total	29.0*	189	1	8	2	200

*This was the average turnout in the 177 constituencies where the seat was contested. In 23, individuals were returned unopposed.
NDC = National Democratic Congress; Egle = Every Ghanaian Living Everywhere; NCP = National Convention Party.

Source: Compiled from information in *West Africa*, 11 January 1993, pp. 11–12

serious handicap. The NDC and its electoral allies controlled 198 of the 200 seats. The National Convention Party and the Egle Party were *de facto* aspects of Rawlings' NDC, although they continued to claim independence after the elections. The two independents, both women (Abena Nsoah, Kintampo constituency, Brong-Ahafo region; and Hawa Yakubu, Bawku Central constituency, Upper East region), were clearly unable on their own to form a meaningful opposition. In effect, the long process of normalisation of the political arrangements had resulted in the institution of a *de facto* one-party state by the ballot box; the very situation which the opposition had campaigned against. The opposition parties, coordinated as the Inter-Party Coordinating Committee, agreed to fulfil a constitutional role as the governmental opposition. They refused to take part in the electoral process, however, until three conditions were met: a new voters' register compiled, citizen identity cards distributed and a new Electoral Commissioner installed to replace the incumbent, Justice J. Ofori-Boateng who, they argued, was too closely linked to the government.

With the opposition parties playing a tentatively supportive political role in the Fourth Republic, i.e. they agreed upon the efficacy of the political system if not the NDC's and Rawlings' dominant role within it, attention quickly refocused on the economic position of the country which, overshadowed by the dramatic political events of 1992, loomed in 1993 as the most intractable issue. The PNDC's last budget was announced on 5 January 1993, just two days before the 'handing over of power' to the NDC government. A 60 per cent increase in fuel prices was announced, with petrol up from C990 to C1,600 a gallon; the move was unsurprisingly unpopular and served to highlight how desperate the regime was for increased tax revenues. The overriding objective of the government's fiscal policy, encouraged by the World Bank, was to seek to correct its fiscal imbalances.[32] It seemed likely, however, that the hike in fuel prices would throttle economic recovery rather than engender it: businesses would be badly affected, inflation would rise, the *cedi* would continue its precipitous devaluation (it had already dropped from C2.75=US$1 in early 1983 to more than C600=US$1 ten years later, a cumulative 218-fold reduction in its value *vis-à-vis* the US dollar), while the trade union movement would be unlikely to take the unwelcome impact upon wage and salary levels with equanimity.

The first year of the Fourth Republic was dominated by labour unrest and strikes owing to the inflationary effects of the January 1993 oil price rises, and by the inadequate wage levels of ordinary workers in Ghana. The rebuilding of the links between the union movement and the government from the mid-1980s had not resulted in concrete improvements in salary levels for most workers or even the maintenance of real wage levels. Since the mid-1980s both individual union and Trades Union Congress leaders, on the one hand, and the Rawlings-led PNDC government, on the other, appeared to understand that it was self-defeating for both sides to engage in constant conflict with each other. The PNDC government proffered the olive branch by inviting union leaders into a tripartite consultative forum in tandem with employers' representatives. Over time, however, this began to be perceived by many workers as little more than a 'talking shop' whose deliberations did not result in palpable benefits for working people. In 1987, government statistics indicated a rate of inflation of 39.8 per cent as against the projected rate of 15 per cent. To maintain the real wage of C90 at the beginning of 1986, workers on the minimum wage should have been paid C145 (US$1) in 1987. In 1988 the inflation rate was 31.4 per cent against the projected figure of 20 per cent. Thus, to maintain the 1986 purchasing power such workers should have received C190 rather than the C146.25 they actually received. The inflation rate in 1989 was 25 per cent, so a minimum wage of C237 was necessary to maintain the 1986 wage

Table 5.3 Changes in the real and nominal minimum wage 1974–1993

Year	Minimum wage (cedi): day	Index (nominal)	Index (real, 1963=100)
1974	2.00	67	292
1975	2.00	67	225
1976	2.00	67	144
1977	3.00	100	100
1978	4.00	133	77
1979	4.00	133	50
1980	5.33	178	44
1981	12.00	400	46
1982	12.00	400	38
1983	25.00	833	32
1984	35.00	1,167	39
1985	70.00	2,333	72
1986	90.00	3,000	70
1987	112.50	3,750	70
1988	146.25	4,875	70
1989	170.00	5,666	59
1990	218.00	7,266	58
1991	218.00	7,266	41
1992	300.00	8,122	34
1993	460.00	15,332	51

Source: Figures received from the Trades Union Congress, Accra, May 1993

level, rather than C170. The inflation rate between 1990 and 1992 averaged 30 per cent a year. Between 1986 and 1990 the minimum wage lost about 20 per cent of its value; with a further 13 per cent drop between 1991 and 1993. Changes in the real and nominal value of the minimum wage since 1974 are shown in Table 5.3.

Many, if not most, of Ghana's politically crucial half a million unionised workers considered that the government was unwilling rather than unable to institute significant increases in the real value of the minimum wage. Yet, the fact of the matter was that the government was under intense pressure from the World Bank to reduce wage levels in order to make the economy attractive for foreign investment as well as to reduce the state's own wage bill. There was more than just economic rationality involved: World Bank analysts indicated that they considered that Ghana could become Africa's first 'economic miracle' if it followed the accelerated growth strategy as pursued by newly industrialising countries in south-east Asia.[33] What this would entail would be a much more radical privatisation strategy and continuing – even increased – pressures on wage levels which are already acknowledged to be among the world's lowest. World Bank concern was stimulated by the end of IMF balance of payments support in 1992. The issue of the desirability of authoritarian government in stimulating economic growth was viewed ambiguously by the Bank; for example, it appeared to view favourably China's continued authoritarian rule as it had apparently led to a much higher rate of growth than democratic India's. The World Bank considered that democratic governments 'have proved less able than authoritarian ones to manage economic reform in polarised societies'.[34]

The NDC government faced a particularly intransigent issue: to what extent, and with what effects, would economic restructuring unravel now that there was a democratically elected government in power, whose elected representatives would need to be responsive to their constituents? It was by no means certain that the election of an NDC-dominated government under the close personal supervision of Rawlings would ensure the continued downward pressure on real wage levels essential for the type of economic success envisaged by the World Bank. The NDC government's 'Accelerated Growth Strategy' (AGS), announced in mid-1992 and implemented from the following January, aimed at growth rates of *10 per cent a year over the medium-term*. Although probably unprecedented in sub-Saharan Africa, such growth rates were accomplished by the East Asian 'miracles' – Hong Kong, Singapore, South Korea and Taiwan – over a thirty-year period from the early 1960s. Ghana's plans in this respect were crucially dependent upon foreign donors' pledges of $2,100 million in concessionary funding and on the acquiescence of a low-pay work-force. The World Bank was highly sceptical of the NDC government's political will to privatise the economy further, and threatened bluntly to cut its funding unless certain objective criteria were met. These included selling off of more state-owned enterprises and cutting government employee levels.[35]

During early 1993 the opposition Inter-party Co-ordinating Committee (ICC) of the four opposition parties sent mixed signals; it produced a measured realistic response to the NDC government's first budget, setting out alternative budgetary proposals which were particularly concerned with taxation and the stimulation of both domestic and foreign investment. On the other hand, it was reported that Adu Boahen, leader of the NPP, urged Ghanaians to take to the streets in protest against the 'bogus and fraudulent' budget.[36] In the event, Bahen's lack of popular support for this course of action was exemplified by Ghanaians ignoring his seditious advice.

The ICC's opposition to the budget was in part a calculated political move to gain the support of disaffected trade unionists. Widespread strikes and labour unrest were a feature of the 1990–1993 period. In late 1990 and early 1991 doctors, teachers, laboratory technicians and nurses took industrial action in pursuit of wage claims and better working conditions. In mid-1992 the previously quiescent civil servants took to the streets in a coordinated campaign to force the government to increase salary levels commensurate with comparative workers in the private sector. In an attempt to cut government spending civil servants' salaries had been whittled away during the 1980s. In the run-up to the elections, the PNDC found it expedient to capitulate to the civil servants' demands. Wage increases of between 50 and 70 per cent were announced for them just before the 1992 elections, which stimulated university lecturers to strike and bank employees to think about striking in mid-1993.

After the elections the government wanted to show the World Bank that its capitulation to the civil servants was merely a tactic to help it gain electoral success. It tried to sack nearly ten and a half thousand Cocoa Board (Cocobod) employees, which precipitated an all-out clash with the Trades Union Congress (TUC). Leaders of the TUC were under pressure to show that they would use the freer political climate to attack government over wage issues, while the NDC government was being watched by foreign donors to see whether political liberalisation had weakened its resolve in labour disputes. An uneasy truce was declared in October 1993 when the TUC, mindful that the NPP and other opposition parties were attempting to use the Cocobud dispute as a means of whipping up political – as opposed to economic – opposition to the NDC government, advised the Cocobod workers to return to work, having gained better severance conditions for the redundant employees.[37] Four things emerged from the Cocobod incident: first, that the NDC government and the TUC leaders could agree that labour unrest was damaging to the country's political stability; second, that the World Bank would see that the government had once again capitulated to labour unrest; third, that potential foreign investors might think again about investing in Ghana if the government failed to control unionised workers; fourth, that the opposition parties had failed to manipulate an important industrial dispute for their own advantage.

Prospects for the three years of NDC government before the 1996 elections depend crucially upon it reaching a *modus operandi* with unionised workers. The World Bank would be unlikely to deprive the government of funding provided that it appeared to be serious about reforms. The sale of half the government's stake in the Ashanti goldfields for an estimated US$250 million in 1993 was a clear signal to the Bank that it was serious about reform, as well as a welcome injection of funds. Democracy in Ghana, as elsewhere in Africa, seems inextricably linked with acceptable levels of economic growth. Rawlings and the NDC's electoral successes in 1992 were a sign that Ghanaians were willing to give them the benefit of the doubt, at least in the short term, that they were the team to lead Ghana into self-perpetuating economic growth. If economic conditions are not significantly ameliorated by the time of the next elections in late 1996, it seems unlikely that either the NDC or Rawlings would have a further chance. Although this presupposes that an opposition marked by distrust, discord and distinctive ideological positions can produce a viable alternative to Rawlings.

NOTES

1   Richard Jeffries, 'Ghana: The Political Economy of Personal Rule', in Donal B. Cruise O'Brien, John Dunn and Richard Rathbone (eds), *Contemporary West African States* (Cambridge: Cambridge University Press, 1989), pp. 75–83.
2   Naomi Chazan and Victor Le Vine,'Politics in a "Non-Political System": the March 30, 1978 Referendum in Ghana', *African Studies Review*, Vol. 22, No. 1 (1979), pp. 177–207.
3   Jeffries, 'Ghana', p. 82.
4   Naomi Chazan, *An Anatomy of Ghanaian Politics: Managing Political Recession, 1969–82* (Boulder, CO: Westview Press, 1983), pp. 260–267.
5   Emmanuel Hansen, 'The Case of Ghana, 1966–83', in C. Alger and J. Balazs (eds), *Conflict Crisis for International Order: New Tasks for Peace Research* (Budapest: Hungarian Academy of Sciences, 1985), p. 96.
6   Jeffries, 'Ghana', p. 83.
7   Ghana TUC Secretary General's May Day Address, 1 May 1993, mimeo, p. 2.
8   See *West Africa*, 28 December 1992, pp. 2233–2234, for an account of why the opposition parties boycotted the parliamentary elections.
9   Ibid., 23 December 1991, p. 2143.
10 V. Brittain, 'Ghana's Leader Tries to Buck Africa's Election Trend', *Guardian* (London), 4 July 1992.
11 *Guardian* (London), 19 September 1990.
12 'Ghana: The Return of the Old Parties', *Africa Confidential*, Vol. 32, No. 18, 13 September 1991, p. 6.
13 Republic of Ghana, *Two Years of Transformation: 1982–83* (Accra: 1983).
14 K. Ingram, *Politics in Modern Africa. The Uneven Tribal Dimension* (London: Routledge, 1990), pp. 41–42.
15 K. Awoonor, *Ghana. A Political History* (Accra: Sedco, 1990).
16 These sentiments were expressed at seminars on Ghana's political future at Koforidua and Cape Coast in August 1990 when the author was present.

17 Author's interview with Kwamena Ahwoi, PNDC Secretary for Local Government, Accra, 1 August 1990.
18 *West Africa*, 18 November 1991, p. 1924.
19 'Ghana: Dusting off the Political Suits', *Africa Confidential*, Vol. 33, No. 3, 7 February 1992, p. 2.
20 For a general account of opposition parties and their attitude to Rawlings and the question of electoral fraud, see Ajoa Yeboah-Afari, 'The Postponement and the Boycott', *West Africa*, 30 November 1992, pp. 2054–2055. For individual opposition figures' comments about Rawlings and the nature of his regime, see J.H. Mensah, 'Contradictory Intentions', ibid., 16 March 1992, p. 453; J.W.S. de Graft Johnson, 'Questions of Honesty', ibid., 30 March 1992; and 'Waking a New Generation', interview with Ghana Democratic Republican Party leaders, ibid., 20 April 1992, p. 673.
21 K. Blay-Amihere, 'Keeping the punks out', *New African*, July 1992, p. 18.
22 *Africa Confidential*, Vol. 32, No. 20, 11 October 1991.
23 V. Brittain 'Ghana's Leader Tries to Buck Africa's Election Trend', *Guardian* (London), 4 July 1992.
24 *Africa Confidential*, Vol. 33, No. 3, 7 February 1992.
25 Ibid., Vol. 32, No. 18, 13 September 1991.
26 The June Four Movement was named after the day in 1979 that Rawlings first assumed power, albeit briefly. Until September of that year, he headed a populist military regime whose goal was to 'clean up' society and purge those from positions of influence who were found to be corrupt. Initially, the June Four Movement was of a socialist orientation; later it developed into a populist movement involved in community development initiatives. There was a low-key yet evident rivalry with the CDRs, although activists were often members of both organisations.
27 *Africa Confidential*, Vol. 33, No. 16, 14 August 1992.
28 Ibid., Vol. 33, No. 23, 6 November 1992.
29 *West Africa*, 9 November 1992, pp. 1908–1909.
30 *Africa Confidential*, Vol. 33, No. 23, 20 November 1992.
31 Ibid.
32 *West Africa*, 11 January 1993, p. 12.
33 *Africa Confidential*, Vol. 33, No. 16, 25 September 1992.
34 Ibid.
35 Ibid., Vol. 34, No. 19, 24 September 1993.
36 *West Africa*, 18 January 1993, p. 53.
37 Ibid., 4 October 1993, p. 1176.

6 Ethiopia and Eritrea: the politics of post-insurgency

Christopher Clapham

INTRODUCTION: THE PROBLEM OF ETHIOPIAN EXCEPTIONALISM

The inclusion of Ethiopia in any comparative study of sub-Saharan Africa invariably raises issues that derive from the country's peculiar historical record. Ethiopia's transition to democracy, in so far as there can be said to have been one, is no different. Even though an ostensible process of democratisation has been under way since the overthrow of the Marxist–Leninist regime of Mengistu Haile-Mariam in May 1991, both the route which Ethiopia followed up to that point and the discernible outcomes in what are now the two separate states of Ethiopia and Eritrea, are appreciably different from much of the rest of Africa.

At the same time, Ethiopia has shared in intensified form many of the features of the recent African experience which have shaped the transition to multi-party democracy in other parts of the continent. Domestically, there are few if any African states in which the failure of a centralising autocracy has been more convincingly demonstrated, and in which the need for some structure of accountability and consent is more evidently needed. Externally, no other African state has been so strongly affected by the cold war and its sudden ending, which in the Ethiopian case has been accompanied by a rapid transition from dependence on the Soviet Union to a renewed association with the United States. But, at the same time, these influences have been mediated by specific national circumstances in a way that illuminates both the universality of the demand for some new form of 'democracy' in Africa and the variable circumstances which affect its outcome. Rather than invalidating comparison, therefore, the Ethiopian case – in addition to being of considerable interest in its own right – should enable us to gain an enhanced understanding of the processes involved in the movement towards multi-party democracy in Africa as a whole.

THE EXPERIENCE OF STATE FORMATION

Every study of democratisation pays at least lip service to the need for democratic institutions to be adapted to the particular circumstances and mores of the society concerned. In Ethiopia, which has never during its long record of statehood experienced any regime that could plausibly be described as democratic, the problem of reconciling an accountable political structure with the social order in which it would have to be placed is especially acute. This is not simply a matter of ethnic, religious and regional differences, though these are as great in Ethiopia as in any other African state; such differences have not, after all, prevented countries such as Nigeria from managing at least brief periods of multi-party electoral competition. The problem in Ethiopia lies in the way in which such differences have been built into the very structure of the state; and as a state formed ultimately by internal rather than colonial conquest, it has in particular been marked by major sources of inequality which are in some measure inherent in the state itself, and which any movement towards democracy must necessarily call into question.

The first and most important is that whereas elsewhere in Africa an externally imposed colonial state was more or less autonomous from its individual local communities, in Ethiopia the state was 'owned' by one distinctive group within the domestic population. Regardless of its capacity to recruit individuals from other peoples, all the way up to the highest positions, the Ethiopian state is essentially that formed by the Amhara and Tigrayan peoples of the northern Ethiopian plateau. The Amharic language is the language of government, and even though orthodox Christianity has ceased to be the recognised state religion, people of Christian origin are disproportionately represented at every level of government. The critical issue in Ethiopian politics has thus been not so much which group controls the central government, as the relationship between a Christian-dominated and Amharic-speaking centre, and the various peripheral peoples and regions – or, to put it slightly differently, between Ethiopian 'nationalism' and regional autonomy. Although a strong sense of regional identity and rivalry has marked relations even between those parts of the country that have historically formed the Ethiopian state, the introduction of a participant political structure must almost inevitably bring this issue to the centre of political debate, and raise vital questions about what it means to be 'Ethiopian'. For Ethiopia as for the former Soviet Union, the first issue raised by democratisation is the survival of the state itself.

In a state marked by a dominant ethnic and cultural core, the potential relationship between democratisation and political culture also takes on a different colouring from that in states which are more autonomous from their own populations. Both African politicians and academic observers writing on African democracy have sought to relate it to the pre-colonial political arrangements of the societies concerned, and the values which these embodied.[1] These efforts have generally been futile: it has proved extremely difficult to activate indigenous values of accountability, no matter how authentic, in such a way as to impose effective constraints on the management of independent African states. In Ethiopia, where the values and structures at least of the northern highlands have been closely associated with the state, these have been markedly hierarchical and inegalitarian. Every aspect of Amhara society, it has been observed, is founded in authority relations.[2] These relations culminate in a political hierarchy which has enabled highland Ethiopia to maintain a recognisable state over a vastly longer period than anywhere else in sub-Saharan Africa; but they create attitudes to authority which are difficult to reconcile with the exercise of open criticism and legitimate opposition that characterise multi-party democracy. In particular, it has been difficult to criticise any individual in a position of authority without appearing to challenge that authority. There has been a place for open revolt, and also for tacit opposition through delay, intrigue and the manipulation of a language which is noted for its range of double meanings. The open accountability of the ruler to the ruled has not, however, been a feature of Ethiopian political culture.

It has been plausibly argued that such cultural constraints apply only to some of Ethiopia's numerous peoples, and that there are other groups in which decision-making is characteristically consensual rather than autocratic, and in which free discussion and open criticism are acceptable. This case has been made especially for the Oromo, who are sometimes regarded – especially by the proponents of a separate Oromo political identity – as embodying the antithesis of the cultural values ascribed to the Amhara.[3] There is some countervailing evidence from nineteenth-century Oromo monarchies which were as autocratically ruled as any Amhara political system.[4] But in any event, exactly the same problems arise in extrapolating from these local structures to the level of the state as in other parts of independent Africa.

The combination of a hierarchical political structure within the historic Ethiopian state, and its imposition from the nineteenth century on the peripheral peoples of an enlarged Ethiopian empire, also led to a level of social and economic inequality which was, by African standards, exceptional. The most important form this took was the large-scale alienation of land in what is now southern and western Ethiopia in the course of Ethiopian conquest and state consolidation in the late nineteenth and early twentieth centuries, and its allocation – together with the services of the peasants who worked on it – to nominees of the imperial regime. Much of this land was allotted in massive holdings to courtiers and military leaders; some of it was given in small amounts to retired soldiers, called *neftenya*, who thus became the local representatives of imperial rule. Effective as a means of consolidating central control, this system aroused indigenous resentments which were expressed through a demand for land reform, and intensified the ultimate dangers to the state of any process of democratisation.

THE EXPERIENCE OF POLITICAL MOBILISATION

Ethiopia likewise differs from other African states in the form taken by the ultimately inevitable process of popular mobilisation into political life. Notably, since it was already independent, it did not experience the period of nationalist mobilisation against colonial rule, which at the same time often intensified internal rivalries, that continues to define the context for multi-party democratisation in much of the rest of Africa. Though Emperor Haile Selassie had established a parliament under the first Ethiopian Constitution of 1931, and elections to its lower chamber were conducted by universal adult suffrage under the revised constitution promulgated in 1955, this did not become an effective forum for the creation of political constituencies or the pressing of popular demands. It was no more than an adjunct to an existing system of imperial government and, notably, lacked any party system.[5]

With the sole but extremely important exception of Eritrea, popular political mobilisation in Ethiopia was effectively repressed under the imperial regime and only erupted into national political life with the revolution of 1974. Originating as a series of urban protests against imperial rule, the revolution was extended to the countryside through the land reform of 1975, which nationalised all rural land, and led to the establishment of a network of peasants' associations and other organisations which for the first time created institutional linkages between the state and the rural population. This went a long way towards resolving the legacy of land alienation, even though it could not dissolve much of the resentment which that had caused, while eventually new structures of central control over agricultural production and marketing were to nullify the initial effects of the reform. At the same time, however, the seizure of national political power by a radical military regime led by Mengistu Haile-Mariam pre-empted the construction of any liberal political order on the base laid by social and economic reform.

Some observers have pointed to the bloodlessness of the early period of the 1974 revolution, and argued that a process of peaceful democratisation was under way, only to be aborted by the seizure of power by the ruthless military faction led by Mengistu Haile-Mariam. This is, in my view, doubtful. Quite apart from the structural problems already noted, virtually all of the major contestants in the bitter and bloody struggles for power which followed the revolution were wedded to some form of Marxism, and virtually all of them likewise were essentially concerned with the seizure of power at the centre. In the event, the victorious Mengistu regime, which was based in the military but could draw on a legacy of Ethiopian nationalism which appealed to a much wider constituency, promoted a Jacobin project of national consolidation, in which the destruction of privilege was intended to provide the social and economic basis for the construction of a powerful and centralised state. This project was justified in terms of revolutionary Marxism–Leninism, and backed by a close alliance with the Soviet Union.

This process was accompanied by the creation of the formal structures of Soviet-style communism, including a vanguard single party, the Workers Party of Ethiopia (WPE) formed in 1984 and the promulgation of the People's Democratic Republic of Ethiopia (PDRE) in 1987. It scarcely needs to be said that any 'democratic' element in the new structures, such as popular consultations over the PDRE constitution and its subsequent approval by referendum, or the election of a supreme soviet (known as the National Shengo), was entirely a matter of window dressing. In one respect, however, the Mengistu regime helped to lay the groundwork for its successor, since in taking over the Stalinist concept of 'nationality', it provided at least a nominal basis for the articulation of ethnic identities and for the programme of ethnic federalism introduced after 1991.

One part of Ethiopia, as it then was, experienced a very different form of political awakening. The Italian colony of Eritrea, conquered by the wartime allies in 1941, came under British military administration pending eventual disposal by the United Nations. This set in train a process of political party formation which much more closely resembled the familiar African experience, even though the parties were formed to present alternative scenarios for the territory's future, rather than to press for independence against a colonial government. These revealed considerable divisions, notably though not entirely between the Christian highland areas which had historically formed part of the Ethiopian state and Muslim lowland zones which had been associated with it only tangentially, if at all; there were also divisions between Muslim groups – especially between the western lowlands and the coastal peoples – and considerable misgivings among some sections of the highland community about association with Ethiopia. The Ethiopian government was able to take advantage of these differences, and – with the aid of its diplomatic standing and of a Unionist Party formed within Eritrea – to secure the association of Eritrea under a federal arrangement with Ethiopia.[6] The federation was subsequently abrogated in 1962, leading to Eritrea's full incorporation into Ethiopia.

The rapid undermining of the democratic elements in the Eritrean Constitution provided by the United Nations in many ways resembled the post-independence suppression of democracy in other parts of Africa. But whereas in other African territories, the imposition of single-party rule was at least carried out by the party with the greatest amount of electoral support, and within the nominally democratic framework of an independent republic, the Eritrean Constitution and political parties were subverted and suppressed by a monarchical state from outside the territory, and served to promote a sense of Eritrean identity which had previously been slight. Since no democratic means of resolving Eritrean grievances was available, it also led to the formation of a guerrilla insurgent movement, the Eritrean Liberation Front (ELF), which even before 1974 posed a considerable challenge to the Ethiopian government's control of the territory. It was to set the pattern for opposition to central rule in other parts of Ethiopia.

THE DEVELOPMENT OF OPPOSITION

The passage to democracy throughout Africa has been critically affected by the political forces that developed in opposition to autocratic regimes and the mechanisms through which these were able to articulate their demands for change. Much attention has rightly been focused on the emergent institutions of 'civil society', such as churches, trade unions and professional associations, which in Africa as in Eastern Europe have often come to the fore as the cracks in the structure of autocracy have become increasingly evident. Ethiopia, however, has lacked not only an established (even if suppressed) political party structure, but even the ostensibly non-political organisations which have generally formed the basis for emergent democratic institutions and demands elsewhere. The orthodox Church has never acquired, within the Ethiopian political tradition, the autonomous role which both the Roman Catholic Church (with its international structure) and the Protestant churches (with their appeal to biblical authority and independent conscience) have gained both in Europe and among the missionary churches of Africa; nor did mission churches in Ethiopia fill the gap, since their role was restricted and their foreignness excluded them from an accepted place in national society. Other associations, such as the trade unions, grew up beneath the shadow of autocracy. Most of all, however, there fell across Ethiopia the shadow of the revolutionary terror of 1976/1978, during which thousands of Ethiopians were ruthlessly destroyed, especially amongst the urban intelligentsia, while others fled abroad or disappeared into long imprisonment. The level of repression under the Mengistu regime has been amply documented and had a traumatic effect on many of those who experienced it.[7] In some places, notably Addis Ababa University, a culture of independence and hence of opposition survived. But whatever their feelings and beliefs, for those Ethiopians who remained in government-controlled areas of the country, there was no alternative to public acquiescence; for those bent on opposition, there was no alternative to exile or insurgent warfare.

The exile community, much of it in the United States, has been notably ineffectual. Its leading members are drawn heavily from Addis Ababa-based academics and intellectuals, and from former high officials from the Haile Sellassie regime and those who, after a period in office after the revolution, ultimately broke with Mengistu and fled. They formed a number of political organisations, several of them grouped together into the Coalition of Ethiopian Democratic Forces (COEDF). They have suffered, however, from a failure to establish themselves inside the country, and have often been out of touch with realities – such as recognition of the fact that the independence of Eritrea was beyond the capacity of any government in Addis Ababa to prevent – which any viable political movement would have to take into account.[8] Many of its members hold established positions, especially in academic life, which they could not expect to equal in Ethiopia, and are caught between being Ethiopians on the one hand, hyphenated Americans on the other. Like other African exiles, they help to show that effective political action has to come from within the country and cannot be orchestrated from abroad.

Insurgency, on the other hand, proved to be very effective indeed. Ethiopia has a tradition of insurgency, dating back to rebels who took to the hills to fight against incumbent emperors, and reinforced by the resistance to Italian rule in 1936–1941; some rural revolts took place under Haile Sellassie.[9] After the revolution, initial rebellions by displaced landlords and noblemen were relatively easily snuffed out, but these were eventually replaced by some of the most effective insurgent movements not only in Africa but in the world. Given both the historical tension between core and periphery in the Ethiopian state and the practical need for insurgent movements to build up support in their base areas, these insurgents almost invariably sought to distinguish themselves in ethnic or regional terms. The uncompromising centralism of the Mengistu regime, despite formal concessions to national self-determination and regional autonomy which could readily be dismissed as window dressing, provided them with ample opportunities to do so. Their strategies none the less differed. In Eritrea, and also in some degree in the Somali-inhabited areas of the south-east, the insurgents could make some claim to total independence from Ethiopia, whether as a separate state or (in the Somali case) by joining another existing one. Groups in the rest of Ethiopia, which were not in a position to make such a claim, were obliged to fall back on demands for regional autonomy accompanied by changes in the structure of central government. With the capture of power in May 1991 by the Ethiopian People's Revolutionary Democratic Front (EPRDF) in Addis Ababa and the Eritrean People's Liberation Front (EPLF) in Asmara, these movements were in a position to put their programmes into effect. The distinctiveness of the new political order in Ethiopia and Eritrea, matched only by Uganda elsewhere in Africa, thus springs immediately from the fact that it has been instituted by successful insurgent movements, not by an effective challenge to established regimes at central level.

DEMOCRATISATION AND INSURGENCY

Insurgency rarely provides a conducive basis for the development of multi-party democratic forms of government. Seldom if ever, in Africa or in other parts of the world, has the overthrow of an established autocracy by insurgent warfare led to multi-party democracy, and many of the problems of democratisation both in Ethiopia and in Eritrea derive from the origins of the new regimes.

For a start, insurgency necessarily militarises the society in which it occurs. Populations on either side are mobilised into the struggle, whether through the insurgents' organisation of the peoples in their base areas or through the conscription of soldiers on the government side. Fighting becomes the normal means through which political action is expressed, and when the insurgents are ultimately able to defeat the government and take over control of the state, the recourse to arms is reinforced by success. Throughout the Horn of Africa, the ready accessibility of armaments – most of them supplied by the Soviet Union, first in support of the Somali government and subsequently in much larger quantities in support of the Mengistu regime in Ethiopia – likewise reinforced the temptation to seek power through the barrel of a gun.

Successful insurgency also creates a characteristic set of attitudes in the minds of those who have undertaken it. The members of the victorious guerrilla army have, after all, risked their lives in the pursuit of goals which are readily expressed in terms of democracy and liberation. Often, they have seen many of their comrades killed along the way. They view themselves, not as a professional army, but as the representatives of the people whom they have helped to organise and among whom they have fought. They often retain a particular contempt for those people who have remained in the cities while they have been fighting in the mountains and the countryside and who have at the very least compromised with the previous regime, and very possibly supported it. These people, often holding positions in the bureaucracy, academic life and other comfortable bourgeois professions, are also those who most readily articulate the liberal values of multi-party democracy and – in the eyes of the insurgents – seek to wrest from them by political manipulation the victories which they have won on the battlefield. Such divisions between the 'fighters' and the urban professionals help to account for the hostility between the EPRDF regime and the university in post-1991 Addis Ababa. Corresponding to this negative attitude towards those who did not take part in the 'struggle' is the tightness of the internal leadership group, composed of individuals who fought together, who are likely to retain their secretive attitude towards decision-making. Even in a country as vast as China, the veterans of the Long March continued to occupy the inner sanctum of the regime for decades afterwards. These attitudes are unlikely to prompt the openness to criticism and to coalition-building that multi-party democracy requires.

In many cases, the self-image of the guerrilla is reinforced by explicit doctrines of 'people's war' derived from Mao Tse-Tung. These not only provide a powerful set of organisational principles, but also present the liberation army as the authentic representatives of the masses and the countryside against the corrupt forces of urban government. The abandonment of power to party politicians, readily identifiable as members of the very class against which they have been fighting, is thus a betrayal of the cause for which they have fought. The capture of power, indeed, is no more than the prelude to the task of creating a new form of political organisation, in which the former guerrilla army becomes the vanguard of a new people's government. Both the EPRDF in Ethiopia and the EPLF in Eritrea, whose leaders were members of the Marxist intelligentsia which had fought in vain against the Mengistu regime in the cities and then retreated in classic Maoist fashion to the countryside, were strongly infused with the principles of people's war. Both movements were Marxist in organisation, and although their appeal to the international communist bloc was impeded by the Soviet Union's strong support for the central Ethiopian government, the EPRDF maintained an explicitly Marxist ideology and vanguard party until shortly before its takeover of power in Addis Ababa. Neither in Ethiopia nor in Eritrea did successful insurgency lead to the installation of governments with any commitment to multi-party democracy as this was understood by Western liberals.

ERITREA: THE TRIUMPH OF PERIPHERAL NATIONALISM

The situation in Eritrea was the more straightforward of the two. The Eritrean People's Liberation Front was an extraordinarily effective and well-organised insurgent movement, which had fought for the creation of an independent Eritrea, and in the process had sought to create a sense of Eritrean nationhood, of the kind that had been so evidently lacking during the period of permitted political organisation that had eventually culminated in – and been aborted by – federation in 1952. The success with which it had first maintained itself in being, and then extended its control over most of Eritrean territory, in the face of a massive Ethiopian army which enjoyed the full support of the Soviet Union, could only reinforce its sense of itself as the authentic embodiment of the Eritrean people. Its crushing victory over the Ethiopian army at Afabet in northern Eritrea in March 1988 marked the breakout from the essentially defensive position which it had maintained since 1978, and its takeover of all of northern and western Eritrea. With the capture of the key port of Massawa in January 1990, the central government forces were penned into an enclave around the capital, Asmara, and had to be supplied by air. By the time Mengistu Haile-Mariam fled the country in May 1991, only Asmara remained to be captured. As soon as this took place, almost at the same time as the EPRDF capture of Addis Ababa, the EPLF created a Transitional Government of Eritrea, and acted as an effectively independent government, pending the formal declaration of independence in 1993.[10]

The victory of the EPLF thus represents the triumph of insurgent nationalism, complete with all its characteristic problems for the creation of multi-party democracy. While in some respects the EPLF may be regarded as analogous to the nationalist single-party regimes that took over at independence in other parts of Africa, its reluctance to admit the legitimacy of opposition was intensified by the long and bitter struggle for independence. This struggle, moreover, was one that had taken place on two fronts. It was most evidently directed against the central Ethiopian government, and against those Eritreans who favoured continued union with Ethiopia. These were by no means as negligible as EPLF propaganda suggested. During the 1940s and early 1950s, it had been possible to create a viable Unionist Party, which certainly enjoyed strong Ethiopian government support, but which could also mobilise a substantial vote, especially in the rural areas of the Christian highlands; educated Eritreans were able to gain employment in the central government, where their representation under Haile Sellassie was second only to those from the central province of Shoa. Even though the Ethiopian government alienated much of this support through its heavy-handed suppression of regional autonomy, pockets of unionism remained – especially in the Seray district close to the Tigray border – and the central administration in Eritrea continued to rely to an appreciable extent on locally appointed officials. In some areas, notably the Kunama territory around Barentu in the west, the central government was able to profit from local ethnic rivalries. Immediately following the EPLF's capture of Asmara, it expelled from Eritrea large numbers of people – including longtime residents and famine orphans – whom it did not regard as authentically Eritrean. Several hundred Eritrean officials in the former government were detained. The promulgation of a nationality law, to distinguish between Eritreans and other Ethiopians and thus determine who would have the right to vote in the referendum on independence, further enabled the EPLF to define the boundaries of the nation. Given that several of the most important communities in Eritrea, notably the Tigrinya-speakers of the highlands and the Afar of the Red Sea coast, also lived across the artificial frontier in the rest of Ethiopia, this gave some latitude for discretion as to who was, and was not, Eritrean.

Second, however, the right of the EPLF to represent a united Eritrean nation was also contested. The first insurgent movement to launch any effective challenge to Ethiopian control of Eritrea was, as already noted, not the EPLF but the Eritrean Liberation Front (ELF), which started operations in western Eritrea in the early 1960s.[11] Given that the Unionist Party was largely Christian in composition, and that the western Muslims had the slightest links with Ethiopia of any of the Eritrean peoples, this was not surprising. Given equally the explicitly Christian identity of the imperial government in Addis Ababa, and the potential availability of external support from radical Arab states, it was not surprising either that the ELF should identify itself as Muslim and even Arab. As Christians were progressively alienated from the Ethiopian regime, many of them – including the eventual EPLF leader Isaias Afewerki – joined the ELF, but were alienated from it in turn by its Muslim leadership and identity, as well as by its organisational ineffectiveness. Since Eritrea is almost equally divided between Christians and Muslims, it was evident to them that any effective nationalist movement would have to be non-confessional. This they sought to create in the EPLF, in which Marxist and Maoist organisational principles replaced the ELF's adherence to Islam and Arabism. The validity of this strategy was proved by the EPLF's success in ousting the ELF even from Muslim areas, which – since the more heavily populated highlands remained under central government control – became the EPLF's base zones. The ELF splintered into a series of factions, with different local affiliations and sources of external support, and ceased to present any serious military challenge to the EPLF by the early 1980s. A multi-party political system, particularly at a time when the appeal of political Islam was rapidly growing in several neighbouring states, would however raise obvious dangers of the reintroduction of religion as a source of internal division, splitting apart the facade of national unity which the EPLF had fought so hard to create. When four opposition movements, three of them factions from the ELF, formed an alliance in September 1992 in Saudi Arabia, the EPLF accused the Saudis of interference in Eritrea's domestic affairs. The continued presence of a large Eritrean Muslim population in Sudan intensified the danger, and early in 1994 the Eritrean government accused the National Islamic Front in Sudan of fomenting Islamic fundamentalism among these refugees and using them to infiltrate Eritrea.[12]

In the aftermath of victory, the EPLF therefore declared a two-year transitional period, leading up to the referendum on national independence, during which it would itself act as the transitional government, and the army which it had formed would continue in being as an agency of national reconstruction. There was indeed a vast amount of reconstruction to be undertaken, in a territory which had been shattered by war over nearly three decades, and the EPLF armed forces provided the obvious instrument for the purpose. They were also expected to work on an unpaid basis, as they had done during the war, and thus helped to relieve the budget of the embryonic state – at the price of some discontent which surfaced immediately before independence in May 1993. At the same time, Isayas announced that the EPLF would be disbanded once independence had been achieved, and that multiple political parties would then be allowed to form, though not on any ethnic or religious basis.[13] Given the newly dominant position of the United States, following the collapse of the Soviet Union and the end of the cold war, this formal commitment to liberal democracy may readily be regarded as following from Eritrea's urgent need for international acceptance, and especially for aid. Had the EPLF come to power at some more propitious time, it could have been expected to follow the normal trajectory of revolutionary insurgent movements, and opt for a single-party socialist state with a centrally planned economy.

During the period leading up to the independence referendum in April 1993, there was no opposition political activity within Eritrea, and although Isaias Afewerki had conceded under strong external pressure that 'anti-people elements' would be permitted to campaign for a 'No' vote in the referendum, no one was foolhardy enough to do so. The eventual vote, in which 99.8 per cent of the voters opted for independence on a turnout of 98.2 per cent, and only 1,882 'No' votes were cast, could therefore be regarded as a foregone conclusion, though it need not be regarded with the cynicism which voting figures of this kind are apt to excite.[14] The referendum was amply monitored by large numbers of external observers, and even though those with misgivings about independence may well have kept their heads down, there could be no doubt about the enthusiasm with which the occasion was greeted throughout Eritrea. So massive a majority could likewise, of course, be regarded as conferring popular legitimacy on the movement which had fought for it. It did not, however, lead to the introduction of any system of multi-party democracy. At independence, a further transitional government was instituted for a period of up to four years, and the introduction of multi-party elections was postponed until a constitution had been drafted. In the interim, Isaias Afewerki became president, and the EPLF Central Committee was converted into the National Assembly, with the addition of sixty coopted members. The EPLF held a Congress in February 1994, at which it changed its name to the People's Front for Democracy and Justice (PFDJ), and the institutions of the government were formally separated from those of the Front. In the following month, the National Assembly was enlarged to seventy-five PFDJ central council members, with an equal number of popularly elected ones, but there was no indication that these elections would allow for multi-party competition.[15]

Following independence, Eritrea may be expected to follow the trajectory of territories that preceded it thirty years or more earlier. It is a single-party state with a powerful military, faced by the triple challenges of potential internal divisions, a threatening international environment and a virtually derelict economy. The normal response to all of these challenges has been to seek to strengthen the leadership of the state and to resist calls for pluralism. Despite changes in the international order, there is no reason to expect Eritrea to be any different. Sooner or later, the inherent defects of the single-party system, allied to the real and serious problems that an independent Eritrea has to face, are likely to prompt a reappraisal; but the 'democracy' represented by the PFDJ continues to be that of nationalism, unity and independence, rather than of multi-party competition.

THE EPRDF REGIME IN ETHIOPIA

The EPRDF had much in common with the EPLF and generally enjoyed close and friendly relations with it. The two movements fought against the same centralising autocracy and sought independence or autonomy for those on whose behalf they saw themselves as struggling. They none the less faced very different situations, and this led to contrasting approaches to the issues of pluralism and multi-partyism. The EPLF viewed itself as a national movement, seeking national independence and promoting national unity; though it recognised different 'nationalities' within Eritrea, these were subordinate to the Eritrean nation as a whole. Within Eritrea, it stuck as rigidly as the Mengistu government had done in Ethiopia to the sanctity of the national boundaries, and the need to control 'narrow nationalism' or 'chauvinism' in the interests of the wider nation.

The EPRDF, on the other hand, was formed by the Tigray People's Liberation Front (TPLF) in the Tigray region immediately south of Eritrea, and the option of independence was not open to it; whereas Eritrea had experienced a separate existence as an Italian colony, and been subject to the explicit jurisdiction of the United Nations, Tigray had at no time in two thousand years been separated from the Ethiopian state. Conversely, whereas Eritrea was ethnically diverse, Tigray was – save for small Afar and Oromo populations on its eastern side – ethnically homogeneous. Virtually all of its people spoke Tigrinya, and despite considerable internal factionalism this gave them a pronounced sense of regional self-identity as against the Amharas to the south. The rallying point for the TPLF was therefore Tigray ethnicity, and this provided the basis – again by way of the Stalinist doctrine of nationality – for a programme which sought a radical decentralisation of power in Ethiopia to autonomous nationalities. This programme likewise provided a basis for alliance formation with other groups in Ethiopia, and such an alliance was constituted as the EPRDF. The first of its other units, formed with the Amhara in Gonder and northern Wollo, was significantly called the Ethiopian (not Amhara) People's Democratic Movement (EPDM), but the subsequent partners – starting with the Oromo People's Democratic Organisation (OPDO) – all took the names of their respective ethnicities.

On the face of it, this offered a challenging and innovative approach to the issues of democracy, ethnicity and statehood. The centralised state, more evidently in Mengistu's Ethiopia even than elsewhere in Africa, had failed to meet the needs of its people and could only be maintained by force. But though Eritrea's independence had to be conceded, the fragmentation of Ethiopia into a collection of ethnic microstates had little to offer. Whereas most African states have sought to suppress ethnicity in the interests of a wider national unity, the TPLF programme recognised the futility of this approach and proposed a system in which self-governing regions would gain the identity and legitimacy conferred by their common ethnic basis while retaining the ability to cooperate over matters of common concern. The governments of all these regions would likewise be democratically accountable to the people within them.[16]

This programme led to a dramatic proliferation of ethnically based movements, many of which were affiliated to the EPRDF. By January 1992 it was possible to identify fifty-seven of them, twenty-nine of which were represented in the Council of Representatives which had been established by the EPRDF in July 1991; this excluded Eritrea, which was already being governed as a separate administration. In numerous cases, rival groups contested the right to speak for the same nationality, though only in the case of the Oromo was more than one of these represented in the assembly. Their origins were varied. A few of them, notably the Oromo Liberation Front (OLF) and the Western Somali Liberation Front (WSLF), had an auto-nomous existence prior to the EPRDF takeover and had fought (if ineffec-tually) against the Mengistu regime. Several of the groups claiming to represent southern peoples, by far the most significant of which was the OPDO, had been formed by the EPRDF during the later stages of the war against the Mengistu government, largely from conscripts in the central government army who had surrendered to the EPRDF. These were gener-ally the first people from their respective groups with whom the EPRDF had made contact, and since they were thoroughly alienated from the regime which had conscripted them, it made sense to use them as the agents of their captors; on the other hand, they had no particular status within their home communities and their premature recognition by the EPRDF regime as representatives of their nationalities was to create serious problems. Other groupings sprang up from nowhere, often led by opportunists in the capital who could carve out a niche for themselves in the new political structure by claiming to represent their people in the provinces. None of these groups, the TPLF included, had any kind of democratic mandate, and what or whom they represented was largely a matter of self-assertion. In establishing the interim assembly, the EPRDF clearly favoured those movements which were affiliated to its own organisation, and could not ignore such groups as the OLF, but were otherwise largely concerned to ensure that every major ethnic grouping in the country had someone in there who claimed to represent them.

But while the parts were represented (however uncertainly), the whole was not. The Council of Representatives included, among its eighty-two members, one seat apiece for four different movements which described themselves as 'Ethiopian'; but the idea of any overarching Ethiopian identity scarcely figured. The contrast with African states where the emphasis – even within multi-party systems – has constantly been on the nation as a whole could scarcely be more strikingly expressed, and it is all the more remarkable in that Ethiopia has a history as a multi-ethnic political unit which long predates any other state in sub-Saharan Africa. There is moreover a substantial political community, centred on Addis Ababa and the Shoan region but by no means exclusively Amhara, which views itself simply as Ethiopian and disclaims affiliation with any particular ethnicity. From the viewpoint of the EPRDF, this community was so discredited by association with the policies of the Mengistu regime that it scarcely needed to be taken into account. From the very first days of its takeover of power, the new regime was thus opposed by an articulate section of the national elite which was entrenched in central institutions such as the bureaucracy and the university. These institutions were subjected to a series of purges which culminated in the dismissal of over forty leading members of staff of Addis Ababa University in May 1993, while the bureaucracy was likewise dismembered. The other major national institution, the Army, had been disbanded after the EPRDF takeover.

The EPRDF regime's programme of ethnic federalism also ran into trouble. Its problems lay not only in the doubtful representativeness of many of the constituent members of the EPRDF coalition, but more basically in the ethnic structure of the country itself. Ethnic politics inevitably raises the issue of numbers, and the Tigrinya-speakers who provided the bedrock of EPRDF support form no more than a small minority of the total population. Though Oromo claims to constitute half of the Ethiopian population are grossly inflated, 29 per cent of respondents in the 1984 census identified themselves as Oromo, closely followed by 28 per cent who identified themselves as Amhara; when allowance is made for Eritrean independence, these numbers rise to about 31 per cent and 30 per cent respectively. Tigrinya-speakers constitute well under 10 per cent of the total.[17] This crude arithmetic is reinforced by the fact that Tigray, one of the poorest regions in the country, produces virtually no exportable surplus of any kind, and is heavily dependent on other regions and external aid even to feed its own population. Any elected central government would thus – unlike the EPRDF regime – be unlikely to accord any great weight to the Tigrinya-speaking population, while a devolved regional government would result in each ethnic administration controlling a high proportion of its own economy and leave Tigray dependent on the charity of other regions. When it came to the point, therefore, the TPLF-dominated EPRDF regime could not afford to implement the programme which it had espoused.

This became evident in the first elections to be contested in Ethiopia after the EPRDF takeover, which were held for the new regional councils in June 1992. These were preceded by intense wrangling between the EPRDF and other movements, notably the OLF, and culminated in an OLF boycott. The elections were not held at all in the Afar and Somali areas and the city of Harar, where the security situation was precarious. In areas where they were held, the election process was controlled by the EPRDF, and results which showed non-EPRDF victories were suppressed. Though some 250 election observers from a wide variety of countries and international bodies monitored the proceedings, they could not agree on a final report, as a result of differences between those who wished to word it in a form which was more or less critical of the regime. Even the observers from the United States, which was anxious to present the impression of an orderly transition to democracy, were obliged to conclude (in unofficial but reported comments) that the elections were not free or fair. Though some of the problems can be ascribed to the difficulties of organising contested elections in a country which had never previously had them, it was also evident that the regime was not prepared to see its opponents win.[18] The OLF withdrew its members from the Council of Representatives immediately after the elections, and a demand for the annulment of the results made by ten opposition parties was refused. The government's announcement of the establishment of a board to 'correct election errors' appears to have been a sop to external opinion.

Although the government had previously announced that a general election would be held in 1993, this was postponed while a new constitution was drafted, and elections to a Constituent Assembly were eventually held on 5 June 1994. Virtually all of the opposition movements boycotted the elections, on grounds of harassment and a suspicion that the results would be fixed in the government's favour anyway; while disputes of this kind characteristically take the form of name-calling on each side, the regime's pursuit of Professor Asrat Woldeyes, an Amhara surgeon who had taken the EPRDF at its word and started his own ethnically based opposition movement, the All Amhara People's Organisation (AAPO), allowed very little room to doubt its unwillingness to permit any organised opposition. Many would-be voters also boycotted the registration process, especially in Addis Ababa where only just over half of the estimated voting-age population registered.[19] Some independent monitoring groups, notably an Ethiopian Human Rights Council, were permitted to operate, and in addition to foreign observers, an indigenous group called the Ethiopian Congress for Democracy also monitored the poll.

The election was held on a single-member constituency basis, with constituencies organised on ethnic and regional lines; although there were a notional 100,000 voters per constituency, a number of much smaller ethnic groups had special constituencies of their own. Former members of the Workers' Party of Ethiopia and of the pre-1991 Ethiopian Army were not allowed to vote unless they had gone through a process of rehabilitation approved by the regime, a provision which may potentially have excluded several hundred thousand people from voting.[20]

Given that almost all the opposition parties boycotted the poll, the forty-two competing parties very largely consisted of ethnically based parties affiliated to the EPRDF, each of which stood only within its own ethnic area.[21] Only in Addis Ababa did the EPRDF candidates stand as such, rather than under a local ethnic label. Most of these ethnic parties, such as the splendidly named Silti Azernet Berbere Meskan Weleni Gedebano People's Democratic Movement (SABMWGPDM) stood in a very small number of constituencies. In very few constituencies, notably in the Afar, Gurage and Harer areas, did rival candidates from different parties stand against one another, and only in two of these did opposition candidates – in each case from the Afar Liberation Front (ALF) – actually win. In sixty-eight of the 525 constituencies (excluding the Somali region where the elections were postponed) EPRDF candidates were returned unopposed, but the normal pattern was for the EPRDF candidate to be formally opposed by independent candidates. Given that these candidates were in most cases virtually unknown, whereas the EPRDF candidates were normally people already well established in local administration, there must be a strong presumption that they were normally straw candidates, put up in order to convey the impression of a contest, especially to external observers. Foreign observers in some constituencies were unable to track down candidates who were nominally standing, and the number of votes they obtained were often derisory. In four constituencies outside Addis Ababa, one each in Welega, Gambela, Hadiya and Harer, independents defeated EPRDF candidates. In Addis Ababa by contrast, though EPRDF candidates were returned unopposed in five of the twenty-three constituencies, independents won ten of the remainder.[22]

The reactions of external monitors were guarded. In the words of the European Union statement:

> The European Union believes that the elections of a constituent assembly in Ethiopia were satisfactory from the technical point of view. These elections were thus an improvement on the 1992 regional elections and represent progress in the democratic development of the country. The conduct of the elections indicated that there are grounds for believing that the opinions of the Ethiopian people could be properly reflected at the planned election for a parliamentary government.
> The European Union considers that there is still some way to go, particularly regarding the climate in which opposition parties are able to campaign.[23]

The independent Ethiopian monitoring organisation, A-Bu-Gi-Da, reached very similar conclusions, noting that it was 'doubtful whether the elected members of the assembly would satisfactorily represent the range of Ethiopian opinions on the constitution', and that 'allegations about parties being unable to freely operate and other forms of harassment must be taken seriously'.[24]

CONCLUSION

In Ethiopia and Eritrea, as in much of Africa, the immediate impetus for a movement towards multi-party democracy has been provided by the evident collapse of an autocratic and overcentralised form of government, in an international context dominated by the failure of the Soviet Union and the model of state-building which it represented. The peculiarity of the Ethiopian experience lies partly in the displacement of the former regime by insurgent warfare rather than urban protest, but also in the structure of the Ethiopian state itself and the difficulty of reconciling democratic accountability with state survival. In Eritrea, the successful insurgent movement has been able to lead a movement for independence, and form an effective new state in which, however, multi-party democracy on the Western model has been progressively postponed. In the residual national territory, what might well be regarded as an imaginative scheme for ethnic devolution and local-level democracy has in practice been derailed, not merely by the determination of the new regime to maintain a control over government which free elections would be unlikely to confirm, but equally by the extraordinary difficulty of creating an ethnic confederation which would combine the requirements of accountability, order and the equitable distribution of resources. However evident the need for any viable system of government to rest on popular support or at least acquiescence, it cannot be said that a stable and democratic multi-party political structure has yet emerged in either Ethiopia or Eritrea, and there is little sign of it doing so in the immediate future.

NOTES

1 The appeal to indigenous political structures and cultures can be used to make an argument for different forms of political arrangement: Julius Nyerere, in 'Democracy and the Party System', *Freedom and Unity* (Oxford University Press, 1967) pp. 195–203, used it to support a single-party system; Dennis Austin, in 'Opposition in Ghana: 1947–67', *Government and Opposition*, Vol. 2, No. 4, 1967, made a case for an indigenous basis for multi-party politics.

2 See D.N. Levine, 'Ethiopia: Identity, Authority, and Realism', in L.W. Pye and S. Verba, *Political Culture and Political Development* (Princeton University Press, 1965), notably pp. 250–256.

3 This point was made by the anthropologist of the Oromo, Professor Herbert Lewis, at the Symposium on the Making of the New Ethiopian Constitution, Addis Ababa, May 1993.

4 See Mohammed Hassen, *The Oromo of Ethiopia: A History 1570–1860* (Cambridge University Press, 1990), notably pp. 173–174, 190–191.

5 See Clapham, *Haile-Selassie's Government* (Longman, 1969), ch. 10; and R.L. Hess and G. Loewenberg, 'Ethiopian No-Party State', *American Political Science Review*, Vol. 58, 1964, pp. 947–950.

6 The period immediately preceding and following federation in Eritrea has been extensively examined, though often from a partisan viewpoint; for a selection, see H. Ehrlich, *The Struggle over Eritrea, 1962–1978* (Hoover Press, 1983); Jordon Gebre-Medhin, *Peasants and Nationalism in Eritrea* (Trenton: Red Sea Press, 1989); K. Trevaskis, *Eritrea: A Colony in Transition, 1941–1952* (Oxford, 1960).

7 See, for example, Amnesty International Reports, Afr 25/07/77, 25/10/78, 25/05/91; and Africa Watch, *Evil Days: Thirty Years of War and Famine in Ethiopia* (New York, 1991); though the last of these is open to charges of political bias, the overall picture is incontestable. For fictional vignettes of the period by an Ethiopian novelist, see Hama Tuma, *The Case of the Socialist Witchdoctor and Other Stories* (Heinemann, 1993).

8 The monthly journal *Ethiopian Review*, published in Los Angeles, provides an excellent forum for the exile community, but in so doing often reflects its political impotence.

9 See Gebru Tareke, *Ethiopia: Power and Protest* (Cambridge University Press, 1991).

10 See D. Pool, 'Eritrean Independence', *African Affairs*, Vol. 92, No. 368, 1993.

11 See J. Markakis, *National and Class Conflict in the Horn of Africa* (Cambridge, 1987), ch. 5.

12 *Eritrea Update* (published by the Government of Eritrea Mission to the UK), January 1994.

13 BBC *Summary of World Broadcasts*, ME/0859 B/6–7, 3 Sep 1990.

14 *Keesings*, 1993, p. 39403.

15 *Keesings*, 1994, pp. 39850, 39899.

16 For an appraisal of the EPRDF's programme, and the progress made towards achieving it, see John M. Cohen, 'Transition toward Democracy and Governance in Post Mengistu Ethiopia', Harvard Institute for International Development: Development Discussion Paper No. 493, June 1994.

17 Population and Housing Census Commission, *Ethiopia 1984 Population & Housing Census Preliminary Report* (Addis Ababa, September 1984); and *1984 Population & Housing Census of Ethiopia Analytical Report at National Level* (Addis Ababa, May 1991). These census figures are inevitably disputed. The 1984 census was undertaken at a time when ethnicity was not high on the political agenda, and there was no strong pressure on individuals to identify themselves in other ways than they wished, though the Amhara numbers may well have been inflated by the higher social status accorded to Amharas. The number of Tigrinya-speakers, which was recorded as 9.8 per cent, was almost

certainly underestimated as a result of the wars in the major Tingrinya-speaking areas, Tigray and Eritrea. On the other hand, Eritrean independence removed from Ethiopia a large proportion of the Tigrinya-speakers recorded in the 1984 census, while not affecting the numbers of Oromos and Amharas.

18   See *Keesings*, June 1992, p. 38952.
19   *The Ethiopian Herald*, 5 June 1994.
20   Electoral Law of Ethiopia, *Negarit Gazeta*, 52nd Year No. 56, 23 August 1993.
21   *The Ethiopian Herald*, 5 June 1994, names thirty-nine parties, and three others not noted on that list appear in the electoral returns.
22   The formal announcement of results was not available at the time of writing in July 1994; these results are provisional ones supplied by the National Election Board to observers in Addis Ababa after the election.
23   European Union, 'Communique of the Presidency', Brussels, 24 June 1994.
24   June 5, 1994 Constitutional Assembly Election Monitoring Mission, *Summary Report by A-Bu-Gi-Da Ethiopian Congress for Democracy* (Addis Ababa, 22 June 1994).

7 Uganda: the advent of no-party democracy

Holger Bernt Hansen and Michael Twaddle

Uganda is notable nowadays both for its comparative tranquillity and for the radical nature of its economic reforms. This is in a part of the world better known in recent years for communal strife and negative economic growth. Zaire, Sudan, Somalia, Rwanda, even Kenya hit the headlines more frequently nowadays for political disorder and economic decay than for development or democracy. Uganda, by contrast, now seems in another league. Twenty or even ten years ago, it appeared a hopeless economic and political case during the presidencies of Idi Amin (1971–1979) and, for a second time, of Milton Obote (1980–1985). Now, however, it is treated widely as a regional trendsetter. Economically, it is hailed by international financial experts for the energy with which its current president, Yoweri Museveni, supports 'structural adjustment' policies validated by the World Bank and the International Monetary Fund. Politically, Museveni astonishes students of Third World politics still further by the vigour and eloquence with which he attacks multi-party democracy as inappropriate for Africa and, in Uganda in particular, a cause of the country's continuing problems rather than one of their potential solutions.[1]

Is this largely cynicism on Museveni's part, designed in essence to ensure his own continuance in power? In the absence of an opportunity to interview President Museveni personally on an analyst's couch, it is unwise to be dogmatic in suggesting any definitive answer to this question. However, this much may be said with some confidence: Uganda's economic reforms in the 1980s and 1990s were imposed upon it mostly from outside by international financial institutions. To be sure, upon winning power in January 1986, after a guerrilla war with, first, the second Obote government of the early 1980s and then the Okellos' regime which replaced Milton Obote in power in 1985, Yoweri Museveni's National Resistance Movement did attempt to fix the Ugandan shilling at an artificially high level against the US dollar and the British pound.[2] But this strategy did not prove a success. With the collapse of the Soviet Union and of other centrally controlled economies in Eastern Europe shortly afterwards, Museveni's Uganda had little alternative but to submit to World Bank and IMF 'medicine' for economic reform floating the Ugandan shilling, cutting back on state expenditure and liberalising both internal marketing and foreign trade arrangements.[3] What Museveni was able to do subsequently, was to apply policies of economic liberalisation and development to Uganda with intelligence and panache.

What he was not able to do was to obtain his Cabinet Ministers' undivided support for these new policies. This was because, once the NRM had established its presence militarily in a substantial part of Uganda, it attempted to strengthen its hold further by coopting into top decision-making bodies representatives of other organised political forces in the country. This was in order to create a government of national unity. Militarily, the policy was a resounding success, pacifying the greater part of Uganda and leaving only a small strip of land bordering the southern Sudan prone to popular millenarian protest and external disruption. Politic-ally, however, there were costs. Under earlier governments in post-colonial Uganda, political leaders had been able to control Cabinets by hiring and firing subordinates on classic patronage terms: if a subordinate became disloyal, or politically objectionable on other grounds, he or she could be, and usually was, fired. That was no longer possible in quite the same way after January 1986. In Museveni's Uganda, concern to create a government of national unity drawn from as many effectively autonomous or semi-autonomous political forces as possible, basically in order to bring the country's internal wars to a close, meant that Ministers were no longer subject to quite the same patron–client restraints on their political behaviour as before.

Balancing, and to some extent constraining the resultant broad-based but weak centre of government in Uganda after January 1986, were stronger representations of the multifarious political grassroots of the country in the form of resistance councils. These councils had been established initially in the early 1980s, as small-scale, face-to-face support groups during the NRM's guerrilla struggle against Milton Obote's second presidency and the shortlived dictatorship of the Okellos. After its successful seizure of supreme power in January 1986, resistance councils were spread through-out Uganda by conscious NRM policy.

These particular institutions have been defended subsequently by NRM leaders as being essentially more democratic institutions than earlier political parties operating at the territorial level. This is because the Demo-cratic Party, the Uganda Peoples' Congress, and the *Kabaka Yekka* ('the

king alone') movement in Buganda made Uganda's transition to independence from Britain in 1962 an intensely fraught and divisive affair.
Admittedly, Britain too is condemned by NRM leaders for deepening the
country's divisions during its period of protectorate rule. But DP, UPC and
KY deepened these divisions further after independence from Britain, by
continuing to encourage ethnic, regional and what Museveni's government
calls 'sectarian' differences (by which it means the politico-religious
cleavages still dividing Ugandans today).

To start with, these divisions operated in the first years of independence
within a framework of multi-party politics. But, as the 1960s progressed,
the KY–UPC alliance and competition with DP gave way increasingly to
rule by the UPC alone. In the period 1966–1967 the central government of
Uganda came to blows with the Buganda government, Kabaka Mutesa fled
abroad and a unitary constitution was imposed upon Buganda and other
parts of the country by President Milton Obote. In January 1971, Obote was
ousted from office by his Army Commander, Idi Amin. Amin's tyranny
lasted for eight years. After Amin's overthrow in 1979 as a consequence of
an invasion by Tanzanian security forces in alliance with Ugandan
opponents of Amin's regime organised under the banner of the Uganda
National Liberation Front, there was a brief return to non-military government in Uganda. But, after a succession of short-lived civilian regimes, in
mid-1980 another military coup took place. Under the auspices of the
resultant military commission, a controversial general election was held at
the end of 1980 and the UPC was returned to power for a second time.
Milton Obote was still its leader and 'Obote 2', as his second presidency
became known popularly in Uganda, lasted until mid-1985. Then yet
another military coup took place under the Generals Bazilio and Tito
Okello. It was their regime which the National Resistance Movement
displaced in January 1986.

After its seizure of power, the NRM installed an intricate structure of
resistance councils from village to district level wherever its writ ran in
Uganda. Elections to the various councils were held in February 1989 at the
lowest village or R1 level, followed by indirect elections to higher councils
in a steadily tapering pyramid of politicians.[4] In February 1992 there were
further elections at the lowest village or R1 level by queuing, again
followed by a succession of indirect elections for higher councils. Overall,
popular participation in these two sets of elections was considered at the
time to have been widespread, successful and to have provided positive
evidence of the NRM's commitment to its own kind of democracy. However, a notable omission in the February 1992 elections was any arrangement for even indirect elections to the most important council of all, the

National Resistance Council or parliament. The omission was justified on the grounds of congruence with the decision, taken shortly beforehand, to prolong the tenure of the NRM government and, with it, of Yoweri Museveni's presidency until 1995. By this time, constitutional reforms and a proposed Constituent Assembly were assumed to have been likely to have been in place and even possibly to have led to direct elections at the highest as well as at lower levels in the country.

This brings us to the NRM's principal contribution to constitution-making in Uganda after its installation of resistance councils: the Constitutional Commission. The Commission started its work in February 1989 and was supposed to complete a final report and to submit a new draft constitution for the country by 1991. Subsequently, it was granted an additional year in which to complete its work. Then it was allowed yet another year, making effectively four years of work for the Uganda Constitutional Commission altogether. Was this too much? During its first years of deliberation, some donors expressed serious concern about the seemingly slow and meagre results of the UCC's activities, only two interim reports by 1992, and this at a time when demands for greater respect for democracy and human rights in Third World countries were moving to the top of the list of conditions for overseas aid imposed by the richer capitalist countries following the ending of the cold war between the First and Second Worlds. Indeed, by the early 1990s the World Bank was declaring openly in its publications that sustainable economic development in African countries presupposed the existence of democratic governments with sufficient accountability to combat corruption and misuse of public funds.[5]

A considerable embarrassment at this time was the suggestion that the power base of Museveni's government lay more in the National Resistance Army than in the National Resistance Council and the various councils between district and village level throughout the country. After all, the Army still consumed a considerable percentage of the national budget, more than education and social services combined. There had also been continued violations of human rights by the NRA; not as numerous nor as serious as those which occurred under the Amin and Obote 2 regimes but embarrassing and regrettable incidents none the less. One such incident took place at Mukura in northern Uganda, where presumed opponents of the NRM government were imprisoned and later perished in a railway container. Such incidents suggested at the very least a lack of control by the civilian government.

None the less, it would be a mistake to accept uncritically the claim by certain exiles opposed to Yoweri Museveni's continuance in power, that donors have withheld substantial funds because of unease about his dependence upon army rather than civilian support in Uganda. Donors who have made cuts, such as Sweden or Germany in 1992, appear to have done so mainly for reasons relating to their own countries. To be sure, Museveni's government pre-empted other reductions in external assistance by announcing substantial cuts in military expenditure shortly before the meeting of the Paris Club of Western donor countries considered Uganda's public needs in April 1992. Later President Museveni also announced that army officers would suffer progressive stages of retrenchment along with other public servants. And he has proved as good as his word. This is evidenced by, among other things, the current programme, financed by the World Bank as lead agency, to demobilise and resettle 30,000 soldiers in 1992–1993 and 20,000 annually until Uganda is left with an army numbering roughly 30,000 by the end of 1995.[6]

Other critics attribute delays in the constitution-making process in Uganda since 1986 to undue influence by an army concerned, despite its steadily decreasing size, not to lose power to old political parties whose support remains considerable throughout the country. Here it must be admitted that the extension by Museveni's government of its period in power without further elections of even an internal kind has inevitably increased criticism of it. This is particularly the case among exile groups already suspicious of many of its actions since 1986. Nevertheless, it would be wrong to attribute this extension of the NRC and the President's tenure of office to 1995, together with the earlier delays which occurred in the Constitutional Commission's activities between 1989 and 1993, principally to undue influence upon Museveni's government by the National Resistance Army. Indeed, in several respects, that charge is almost the exact opposite of the truth.

Initially the NRA had been stirred into action as a guerrilla force by the return to power of the Uganda Peoples' Congress through a seemingly shamelessly rigged general election. As a perceptive Ugandan journalist has pointed out:

> Civilians who had never fought before rallied to the NRA and took up arms. Though many senior NRA [personnel] were police officers or had been active in the UNLA [that is, the armed wing of the Uganda National Liberation Front which overthrew Idi Amin] or the Museveni-led exile force, Front for National Salvation [FRONASA] before, the majority were not professional soldiers. And Museveni himself had been a militant intellectual rather than an intellectual soldier. . . . A naked military dictatorship was out of the question. The NRA did not begin to democratise as a gift. First, because ordinary people had paid the price

for the overthrow of Obote 2 and had been the largest element in the NRA force. Secondly, precisely because the NRA leadership was more enlightened than its predecessors (give the devil his due), it recognised that democratisation, however limited, was the best strategy of consolidation – not more gun rule.[7]

During their formative years in the Ugandan bush, NRA guerrillas thrashed out a 'ten-point programme' proposing not only the extension of resistance councils to other areas of Uganda, but also stressing 'the need for national unity and "the elimination of all forms of sectarianism"'.[8] Indeed, it is in part because these latter proposals have been treated as seriously as those for resistance councils by NRA personnel that the deliberations of the Constitutional Commission in Museveni's Uganda have proved so protracted.

Uganda's lively and free press has also criticised delays in the constitution-making process in recent years. Sometimes it is asserted that the NRM government did not take the process seriously enough to allocate sufficient resources to enable it to be completed speedily. On other occasions it is said that a new constitution has already been written in secret, so why all the delay? On yet others, that just a few constitutional experts could compose a draft constitution in a matter of months, so why is it taking several years?

Similar criticisms were made of the Uganda Constitutional Commission by the Ugandan cabinet ministers. Politicians supportive of Yoweri Museveni's policies, as well as those opposed to them, asked repeatedly whether a new constitution was necessary at all. Why not return to the Independence Constitution of 1962 and delete all subsequent amendments made to it by Idi Amin's regime and by both the Obote 1 and 2 governments? Akena Adoko, a relative of Milton Obote, even suggested the establishment of a caretaker government composed essentially of the heads of the three main religious denominations in Uganda – Anglican, Roman Catholic and Muslim – to run the country for six months until multi-party elections might be organised under the 1962 Constitution.[9]

When the National Resistance Movement took over the government of Uganda in January 1986, it banned campaigning by the old political parties. This was done in order to make possible an interim period of reconciliation and reconstruction in the country. However, political parties as such were not banned. The parties continued to issue newspapers and to collect revenues from properties registered in their names as well as to receive gifts from party supporters. None the less, the ban on party campaigning and electioneering irked party leaders, all the more so as Western countries and international financial institutions increased pressures upon African countries to return to multi-party democracy. Paulo Semogerere, the leading representative of the Democratic Party in the NRM government, has stressed his support in public on several occasions for a return to multi-party competition.[10] Cecilia Ogwal has made even stronger statements on behalf of the UPC: she denounces any informal or formal agreement with the NRM government and demands the right to return to 'normal politics' at the earliest opportunity.[11] President Museveni has responded repeatedly to such statements by reminding their authors that the suspension of political party activity still stands but, as soon as the constitution-making process makes it possible, the people of Uganda themselves will decide whether or not to return to multi-party politics.

Paradoxically, these demands by leaders of old parties for a speedy return to multi-party politics proved counter-productive in the short term by making it even more difficult for the Uganda Constitutional Commission to reach a speedy consensual decision on the issue.

Already, in its first Interim Report of December 1990, the UCC admitted that the issue of political organisations in Uganda was 'a highly controversial point'.[12] After reviewing the various options and dismissing from consideration the one-party system, there remained essentially two alternatives: the multi-party system of political competition followed between the 1950s and 1966–1967 and between 1980 and 1985, and the 'no-party' or 'movement' system (by which was meant a system embracing representatives from all political parties under a single organisational umbrella such as the NRM itself had been attempting to administer since 1986). As the UCC had not made up its mind which of these two systems to recommend, pressure at the start of its deliberations by DP and UPC leaders in support of the multi-party option probably had two effects. One was that, in order to maintain its appearance of impartiality, the Commission delayed its final decision on this matter as long as possible. A second effect was that the Constitutional Commission eventually attempted to avoid making a decision altogether by recommending a referendum on the issue in its final report.

Throughout its four years of deliberations, it was important for the UCC to remain independent of conflicting interests in order to retain the basic confidence of the majority of Ugandans in its essential impartiality of judgement. Its twenty-one members themselves represented the cultural and linguistic diversity of Uganda and had been appointed because of their individual professional skills and expertise. Its chairman was a Ugandan judge. He proved an excellent chairman. None the less, it was an embarrassment to both him and his colleagues that delays in their deliberations should have led to the charge of collusion with the government of the day's presumed reluctance to face Uganda's old political parties in a multi-party general electoral showdown. The very terms of this charge assumed an identity of interest between the Uganda Constitutional Commission and the NRM government which called into question the Commission's credibility.

To assess it adequately in retrospect, we need to place the UCC in its context. After the overthrow of Amin's tyranny and the passing of several short-lived successor regimes – Obote 2, and the Okellos' dictatorship – Ugandans asked themselves insistently: 'What went wrong?' As insistently as they declared to themselves and to the wider world: 'Never again!' This much was clear at the very start of the present NRM government's term of office in January 1986 to one of the present writers.[13] During its armed struggle against Obote 2 immediately beforehand, it had been clear that a new constitution would be an important instrument to correct past political mistakes and introduce fundamental political changes desired by Ugandans in order to prevent their country tearing itself apart again so disastrously. Clearly, earlier constitutions could not simply now be reintroduced without changes. The Lancaster House Constitution at independence in 1962 had imposed an unworkable federal structure upon the country. Milton Obote's 'pigeonhole' constitution of 1966–1967 had been approved by Uganda's parliament immediately after MPs had discovered its proposed contents in their respective pigeonholes at the parliament building.

These experiences have set the context for the country's latest experiment in constitution-making. The Uganda Constitutional Commission of 1989–1993 had no mandate to present a draft constitution based on the advice of just a handful of constitutional experts either from abroad or from within Uganda itself. On the contrary, a new constitution needed to be built up from below upon the basis of widespread popular participation and opinion.[14] Ugandans at large, and not just the Constitutional Commissioners, needed to identify the principal issues to be considered. Hence the Commissioners' desire to collect Ugandans' views in the field, as it were, before attempting to compile a draft constitution based upon these views. It was to be a very bold experiment. Necessarily, it would also be an experiment which would take time. First, meetings had to be conducted throughout the country to explain what a new constitution would be about. Then information needed to be disseminated and seminars held in many parts of it in order to encourage Ugandans to submit memoranda. From the outset the Uganda Constitutional Commission promised to take all submissions received into account. This was a brave promise. As John Waliggo makes clear, it was to prove an enormous undertaking even with external assistance in the form of computers and an Australian constitutional expert, Anthony Regan.[15]

None the less, despite the enormity of the task and difficulties in raising the necessary funds, summaries of all memoranda submitted to the Commission had been made by the beginning of 1992. By this time, too, a second interim report had been issued. This recommended the election of a separate Constituent Assembly to approve the contents of a new constitution rather than that the existing National Resistance Council should itself perform this function. The CA should also be elected by secret ballot rather than through a continuance of the queuing system. At the beginning of 1992, it was assumed that the CA elections would take place in the first half of 1993. In fact, the CA elections were not to be held until March 1994.

However, by the beginning of 1992 it was clear that some things would almost certainly be in the draft constitution to be debated by the Constituent Assembly, other items might not be in it and yet others might or might not be included. Falling within the first category were likely to be a Bill of Rights providing provisions for the election of representatives for women, children and other disadvantaged groups along with a developed democratic system of substance. A single-chamber legislature based on free and fair elections would ensure regular and peaceful changes of government. The precise electoral system remained to be decided. But, assuming the proposals for electing the CA were repeated in subsequent general elections, it was highly likely that significant but limited percentages of parliamentary seats would be reserved for special groups like the Army, religious leaders, trades unionists, youth and women.

According to the second interim report, the President of Uganda would in future be elected directly. He would have to be well educated, but it was not essential that he should have a university degree. There was also agreement that the Army should be placed under civilian control as well as being specially represented in parliament for a transitional period along with other special interests.[16]

Besides the matter of multi-party politics, to which attention has already been drawn, three other vital issues remained to be resolved. One was whether Uganda would have a unitary or federal form of government. Another was whether traditional rulers would be restored: here the basic question was what would happen to the Kabakaship of the Buganda kingdom – would it be revived as a social and cultural institution without any substantive political role to play? Also still to be resolved at the start of 1992 was the identity of the national language – which one? A recent government paper on education had indicated that this issue was likely to revive old debates over the respective merits of Luganda and Swahili and whether other languages should be privileged at the possible expense of more minor languages in the country.[17]

In 1993 a final report was issued by the Uganda Constitutional [Odoki] Commission, together with statistical analyses of memoranda submitted to it and a draft constitution to be considered by the forthcoming Constituent Assembly.[18] On language, the claims of both Swahili and Luganda were shelved in favour of English, though:

> Nothing in this Constitution prohibits the use of any other language as a medium of instruction in schools or other educational institutions or the use of any other language for legislative, administrative or judicial purposes as may be prescribed by law.[19]

On Uganda's kings, the Odoki Commission agreed that

> for the peace, prosperity and unity of Uganda, traditional institutions should not be shaped in a way that gives particular regions, ethnic groups or districts a constitutionally privileged position over other regions, ethnic groups or districts. Such constitutionally privileged positions could lead to tensions and harm the well-being of the nation.[20]

Titles and local customs, however, were another matter.

> The titles to be given to the traditional leaders of any ethnic group or region should be left to the people concerned. The four monarchs and Kyabazinga [of Busoga] who were recognised traditional rulers in the 1962 Constitution can, if their respective people desire to restore them, enjoy the same titles as those of 1962.[21]

'If their respective people desire to restore them' – the overwhelming message of memoranda received by the Commission from the area of the former kingdom of Buganda was in favour of the restoration of their king to his former glory. Shortly after taking over control of Uganda in January 1986, the NRM government had recognised Mutebi II as 'head of the clans' or *Ssaabataka* in Buganda, partly as a reward for his support for its five-year bush war against the second Obote government.[22] Now, nearly a year before elections were held for a Constituent Assembly to finalise all aspects of the new constitution, Mutebi II was recognised as King of Buganda. His coronation was held in July 1993, to widespread rejoicing throughout Buganda.

But what did this mean? What were the coronation's implications for the future constitution of the whole of Uganda and its pattern of party competition? Battle was intensified by Conservative Party leaders seemingly espousing many of the earlier objectives of the *Kabaka Yekka* movement of the 1960s, along with DP and UPC notables demanding an early return to multi-party politics so popular with Western donor nations in the 1990s. The political temperature was raised further by a disputed coronation in late

1993 in Ankole, where the Omugabe was much less popular as king than Mutebi, because kings' wives there were drawn from far more restricted social circles than their counterparts in Buganda. The anointing of a new Omukama for Bunyoro was delayed until mid-1994 because of a legal case brought by a disappointed prince of the Nyoro royal house. In Toro the king was crowned already but was absent as he was also Uganda's ambassador to Cuba and opposed by Ugandans emanating from those parts of his kingdom incorporated into it during the period of British protectorate rule. As for the Kyabazinga, the situation in Busoga was still such as to make the complexities of nineteenth-century Schleswig–Holstein which so bemused nineteenth-century European politicians appear simple by comparison.

Dynastic complexities apart, there were the difficulties of slotting the revived kingships into both the new constitution to be decided by the Constituent Assembly and the new era of democratisation and 'good governance' desired by Western donor nations who had funded much of the Odoki Commission's work. How *will* the revived kingships fit into the new order?

The principal problem is Buganda. In *Uganda Now: Between Decay and Development* published in 1988, Christopher Wrigley stressed how, geopolitically, the country had been unhinged by Buganda.[23] The Uganda Protectorate was built around the kingdom of Buganda. British protectorate officials made their principal base there in the 1890s and employed Ganda chiefs to pacify many surrounding areas.[24] Ganda catechists and evangelists introduced Anglican and Roman Catholic Christianity into many of these areas also from the 1890s onwards.[25] Sometimes a neighbouring kingdom was sliced in half, sometimes surrounding kingdoms were enlarged in size. Sometimes there were no kingdoms in sight, only politically decentralised peoples upon whom appointive chiefs were imposed by British protectorate officials. It has been in many of these areas that resistance councils have proved most popular since the NRM government came to power in January 1986. But, centralised or decentralised, Ugandans nowadays live in a landlocked state in the heart of Africa, surrounded by potentially (and, sometimes, actually) hostile neighbours and defended by an army steadily being reduced in size because of the 'structural adjustment' policies encouraged by Western donor countries. In these circumstances, geopolitical coherence is crucial, and the Odoki Commission's recommendation of a basically unitary state seems hardly surprising: Buganda should be allowed cultural independence, if its peoples so desire, but not federalism of the sort that brought the state of Uganda to its knees in 1966–1967.

Since Odoki, the Kabakaship of Buganda has been revived in accordance with popular demand in the old kingdom area and further buttressed financially by the return of the Kabaka's lands and market dues along with 'historic sites' of symbolic significance. How much further demands for a 'cultural king' may go in Buganda and the smaller western kingdoms in Uganda is clearly critical.

At issue, crucially, here, are several implications of Yoweri Museveni's government's policies on decentralisation with respect to these kingdoms. There are at least two important sets of questions. First, will the districts falling geographically within these kingdoms, to which powers are increasingly to be devolved in coming years, be allowed to group themselves together in practice as kingdoms? If so, would a weaker pattern of federalism be acceptable?

Second, what are the powers to be devolved to district level by central government in coming years? Are real powers to be devolved, or only functions?

Clearly, both sets of questions cannot be answered definitively until the Constituent Assembly has completed its work in 1995, if then.

Two further matters should also be mentioned. One concerns the merits of proportional voting in culturally and linguistically divided states like Uganda. The arguments in its favour are by no means new but they were passed over by the Odoki Commission in favour of the traditional British first-past-the-post single-member-constituency system. However, should the Constituent Assembly or some future government in Uganda take them seriously, a subsequent transition to multi-party democracy in Uganda might prove both much smoother and more just. As Goran Hyden points out:

> By providing an opportunity for more than one winner in each constituency, PR mitigates the centrifugal tendencies present in plural societies. When this system was first introduced in Europe, it was specifically designed to provide minority representation and thereby to counteract potential threats to national unity and political stability. Uganda and much of the rest of Africa face similar challenges today.[26]

Then there is the most difficult question: the role of the military in transitions to democratic politics in Third World societies. That this question does not presently appear to be the most difficult one confronting students of Ugandan politics is a tribute not only to President Yoweri Museveni and his government, but also to the National Resistance Army in general and to its principal commander in particular. Earlier we noted the predominantly civilian values pervading the NRA in its bush war against the grosser features of the Obote 2 and Okello regimes, and the powerful forces influencing Ugandans since January 1986 towards the domestication and progressive reductions in size of the country's armed forces. Equally important before the Constituent Assembly elections of March 1994 was the attitude of Major General Mugisha Muntu. As James Katorobo reports, he 'chastised the politicians for fearing to face the electorate' in such elections and for suggesting instead that the existing National Resistance Council should transform itself into the Constituent Assembly. As Katorobo remarks:

> His nationalist statesmanship will remain memorable as a rare demo-cratic sentiment from a military source in Africa. In the end the NRC enacted the Constituent Assembly statute and the business of establish-ing a Constituent Assembly went like clockwork.[27]

In another expert observer's opinion, 'The CA elections [of March 1994] could lay claim to being the most free and fair of Uganda's nation-wide elections since independence.' This is because

> in the 1980 elections, the first after independence, the DP probably won enough seats to control parliament, but – with the help of widespread intimidation and manipulation – the UPC declared themselves the winners. The 1989 national elections were undoubtedly more free and fair in terms of respecting the choices made by voters, but under rules that suffered from the democratic defects of allowing an open ballot and tiny indirect electoral colleges in each constituency and [moreover] prohibiting party activity.[28]

In March 1994, by contrast, balloting was secret and the franchise universal, but overt party competition was still banned. However, though candidates competed for CA seats as individuals rather than party members, their party preferences were widely known. As soon as the successful CADs' names were declared, it also became clear that 'no-party democracy' supporters outnumbered proponents of an early resumption of 'multi-party politics' in Uganda by roughly two to one.[29]

Granted this outcome, why did 'multi-party' CADs take part in the Constituent Assembly's debates and sub-committees with such seriousness in the second half of 1994? Basically, we suggest, because there is still much to play for. Towards the end of 1994, moreover, President Museveni replaced his elderly male Vice President from Buganda (Samson Kisekka) with a woman from Busoga (Spesiosa Kazibwe) and also sacked from the national government two leading supporters within it of stronger powers for Buganda in the new constitution (Abu Mayanja and Samuel Njuba). Around the same time, Cecilia Ogwal and other CADs supporting both the UPC and an early return to multi-party politics at national level in Uganda, changed their minds on the federal option for Buganda; in future, they now declared publicly, they would vote for, rather than against, this option. If

UPC supporters keep this particular promise, Ugandan politics in the later 1990s may repeat the pattern of the earlier 1960s, when, in the country's second general election, *federo* activists from Buganda joined with UPC supporters from areas of Uganda outside Buganda to defeat the Democratic Party at the polls. Only time will tell whether history will repeat itself in this way. However, already the National Resistance Movement seems set upon turning itself into a political party and, despite President Museveni's continuing protestations regarding the unsuitability of multi-party politics for sub-Saharan African states,[30] the principal debate in the Constituent Assembly would appear to have become largely a matter of when, not whether, no-party democracy will give way to the multi-party kind again in Uganda.

NOTES

1 This chapter is an expansion and revised version of our contribution to *From Chaos to Order: The Politics of Constitution-making in Uganda*, edited by ourselves and published in 1994 by Fountain Publishers, P.O. Box 488, Kampala, Uganda.

2 See Michael Twaddle, 'Museveni's Uganda: Notes Towards an Analysis', pp 332-3 in our earlier edited *Uganda Now: Between Decay and Development* (London: James Currey, 1988).

3 See Joshua Mugyenyi, 'IMF Conditionality and Structural Adjustment under the National Resistance Movement', in Holger Bernt Hansen and Michael Twaddle (eds), *Changing Uganda: The Dilemmas of Structural Adjustment and Revolutionary Change* (London: Currey/Athens, Ohio: Ohio University Press, 1991) for a fuller discussion.

4 See Nelson Kasfir, 'The Ugandan Elections of 1989: Power, Populism and Democratization' in *Changing Uganda*, pp. 247–288.

5 Chapter 7 in *World Development Report 1991: The Challenge of Development* provides fuller details.

6 Information from the Danish development agency DANIDA, November 1992. DANIDA was a member of the Western donors' group.

7 Charles Onyango-Obbo in *The Monitor*, 23 August 1994.

8 Quoted by Michael Twaddle in *Uganda Now*, p. 320.

9 *The Citizen* newspaper for week ending 5 August 1992. See also A.G.G. Gingyera-Pinycwa, 'Towards Constitutional Renovation: Some Political Considerations' in *Changing Uganda*, pp. 224–229.

10 *The New Vision*, 11 July 1992.

11 Ibid., 3 August 1992

12 See pp. 20 *ff.*

13 See Michael Twaddle, 'Museveni's Uganda: Notes Towards an Analysis' in *Uganda Now*.

14 See Sam Njuba, 'Legal Adjustment to Revolutionary Change' in *Changing Uganda*, pp. 210–216.

15 See John Mary Waliggo, 'Constitution-making and the Politics of Demo-cratisation in Uganda' in Holger Bernt Hansen and Michael Twaddle (eds), *From Chaos to Order: The Politics of Constitution-making in Uganda* (Kampala: Fountain Publishers, 1994), pp. 18–40. See also Anthony Regan's own account, 'Transforming Uganda? Constitutional and Political Change 1986–1994' in *Newsletter of the African Studies Association of Australia and the Pacific*, xvi (June 1994), pp. 8–13.

16 See further Dan Mudoola, 'Institution-building: The Case of the NRM and the Military 1986–9' in *Changing Uganda*, pp. 230–246.

17 Government White Paper on *Implementation of the Recommendations of the Educational Review Committee* [Uganda], April 1992, pp. 15*ff*. See also Ruth Mukama, 'Recent Developments in the Language Situation and Prospects for the Future' in *Changing Uganda*, pp. 334–350.

18 *The Draft Constitution of the Republic of Uganda* and *Report of the Uganda Constitutional Commission* [Odoki Commission]: *Analysis and Recommen-dations*, 28 May 1993.

19 *Draft Constitution*, 5 (2).

20 *Report* [Odoki Commission], 19. 109, pp. 547–548.

21 Ibid., 19. 116 (p. 549).

22 See Michael Twaddle, 'Museveni's Uganda' in *Uganda Now*, pp. 326–327.

23 'Four Steps towards Disaster' in ibid., pp. 27–35.

24 See Michael Twaddle, *Kakungulu and the Creation of Uganda 1868–1928* (London: Currey/Kampala: Fountain/Athens, Ohio: Ohio University Press, 1993) for one case study.

25 Holger Bernt Hansen, *Mission, Church and State in a Colonial Setting: Uganda 1890–1925* (London: Heinemann, 1984) and Louise Pirouet, *Black Evangelists* (London: Rex Collings, 1978) are the standard studies.

26 Goran Hyden, 'Political Representation and the Future of Uganda' in *From Chaos to Order*, p. 185.

27 James Katorobo, 'Electoral Choices in the Constitutent Assembly Elections' in ibid., p. 119.

28 Nelson Kasfir, 'Ugandan Politics and the Constituent Assembly Elections' in ibid., p. 151.

29 See also Judith Geist for an account of the 'Political Significance of the Constituent Assembly Elections' of March 1994 in *From Chaos to Order*, pp. 90–113.

30 For example, 'Museveni says No to Political Parties again' was one of the headlines in the Kampala *Monitor* on 14 December 1994.

8 Malawi: the transition to multi-party politics

Denis Venter

The identity of pre-colonial Malawi centred on the Maravi Empire, a very loosely organised society covering a large expanse of territory which extended well beyond present-day Malawi[1] and initially encompassed the Chewa and later the Tumbuka peoples. During the nineteenth century, the empire was subjected to multiple successful invasions by the Yao from the north, who became heavily involved in commercial slave trading as agents of the coastal Arabs on the East African seaboard, and by the warlike Ngoni from the south. Although the Chewa, Tumbuka, Yao and Ngoni form the basis of Malawi's ethnic groups, the contemporary boundaries of Malawi owe as much to British, and especially Scottish, missionary activity along the Shire River and the shores of Lake Malawi as to the influence of ancient ethnic loyalties. Following David Livingstone's arrival in the late 1850s, missionaries were highly active in the latter half of the nineteenth century. The pattern of endemic tribal conflict and disruption caused by the slave trade, however, to a great extent promoted social instability and even detribalisation in pre-colonial Nyasaland.

INTRODUCTION

A strong sense of national identity followed the formation of the British Protectorate of Nyasaland in 1891. The early administration succeeded within a relatively short timespan in establishing physical power and legal authority. By the introduction of a system of district administration it also achieved a high degree of administrative and legal penetration of the traditional, mainly rural, African population. The general process of Westernisation during the colonial era – through Christianisation, education, modern commercial practices, urbanisation and so forth – also facilitated the replacement of parochial affinities, at first gradually and then more readily, by a commitment and loyalty to a more inclusive societal entity. The creation of a feeling of nationhood – a common identification with Nyasaland as a territory – was therefore less problematic than in other colonised African territories.

However, from the early 1920s onwards a new political awareness became apparent. The so-called 'Native Associations' – essentially interest groups geared towards articulating African public opinion – continually focused on issues such as the inadequacy of educational facilities and the assault on African land rights. In addition, by the 1930s it had become clear that the colonial policy of undermining the traditional authority of chiefs and headmen and of attempting to implement a form of direct rule in traditional administration, had met with failure. This problem was temporarily resolved by the introduction of a system of indirect rule. Meanwhile, the African associations also started to petition for direct representation in decision-making institutions such as the Legislative Council. After the Second World War, the volume and intensity of these demands increased and they were reinforced by the insistence on universal adult suffrage.

At the same time, the contact of migrant workers with conditions in neighbouring territories, as well as the experiences abroad of African soldiers during the Second World War, generated a growing sense of dissatisfaction among Nyasaland Africans with their general state of under-development and lack of material benefits. In the 1950s the consequences of incorporation into the Federation of the Rhodesias and Nyasaland accentuated this awareness, and the practical manifestation of their economic deprivation and inadequate social services consolidated African opposition to federation. A general disgruntlement with the system of traditional authorities within the context of local government, and the enforcement of unpopular agricultural measures, resulted in a growing radicalisation of the rural masses and the consequent collapse of district administration.

In fact, the imposition of federation on the African peoples of Nyasaland served as a catalyst for political discontent. Whereas the African associations and the Nyasaland African Congress (NAC) had previously always been prepared to operate within the parameters of the colonial framework and utilise constitutional mechanisms in bargaining about grievances, the nationalist movement now not only questioned the legitimacy of the existing colonial system but also actively challenged it. The goal was the overthrow of the *status quo*, as manifested in the colonial system, and the establishment of a new social and political order. A campaign of civil disobedience – aimed especially at agricultural measures and land rights – was launched and strikes, disturbances and violence became everyday events.

Thus, the reactivation of the NAC and its subsequent conversion by the late 1950s into a mass political movement – the Malawi Congress Party, MCP – through the mobilisation of the rural African population, exerted almost intolerable pressure on the colonial government. Anti-federation nationalist campaigning was vigorous, and in 1958 Dr Hastings Kamuzu Banda returned to Malawi from Ghana to add his seniority to a movement led by young activists. The nationalist movement, in particular, was to play a key role in fostering a sense of national consciousness throughout Nyasaland. The rapidly growing radicalisation of the African population, and the general condition of unrest and violence precipitated the crisis of 1959, when a state of emergency had to be declared. Scores of nationalists, including Banda, were imprisoned and accused of plotting armed rebellion, but an enquiry led by Lord Devlin largely exonerated them.

Following in the slipstream of the march towards decolonisation elsewhere in Africa, two constitutional conferences were held in London in the early 1960s. First, the British government conceded representative government to Nyasaland; and in quick succession, the principle of African majority rule was confirmed with the introduction of responsible government, internal self-government and the granting of independence on 6 July 1964. Banda was now Prime Minister; two years later Malawi was a republic within the Commonwealth – and a *de jure* one-party state to boot – with Banda as Executive President. Within three months of independence, however, Banda was constitutionally challenged by a coalition of younger politicians who, besides differences on issues of policy, objected to the centralisation of power in his hands. The security forces intervened decisively in his favour and, from this point until the early 1990s, the regime became progressively more authoritarian and dictatorial, with most important decision-making powers concentrated solely in the hands of Banda.[2]

ONE-MAN, ONE-PARTY RULE

While countries all around it fell into wars and were bankrupted by ill-conceived economic planning and weakened by conflict, Malawi maintained a remarkably even keel after independence. Unlike its neighbours, Malawi could at least have been said to work – although the peace, stability and relative economic success which the country enjoyed until the early 1990s was bought at an exceptionally high price. While Malawi was the darling of international refugee agencies for its generous treatment of more than a million Mozambican refugees congesting the southern districts of the country, it was also found guilty by the international media and donor governments of committing outrageous acts against its own citizens. For all intents and purposes Malawi was not even a one-party state: it was a one-man state, a political despotism in which the state apparatus was answerable to only one man. The result was a climate of fear almost unparalleled anywhere in Africa, even in countries wracked by violence.[3]

Although Banda was seen as the 'father' of Malawian nationalism and independence, his return home – after practising for years as a medical doctor in Britain and Ghana – had been organised by a number of dynamic young nationalists who asked him, as an older figure, to lead their campaign for independence under the banner of the Nyasaland African Congress (NAC) – later to become the Malawi Congress Party (MCP). In fact, Banda eventually came to power on one issue: the leading role he played in the 'break-up' of the Federation of the Rhodesias and Nyasaland. It was his greatest achievement. No sooner had Malawi become independent, however, than Banda's repressive instincts emerged and he turned on those who had helped organise his return. The new country was rapidly drained of some of the best and the brightest in the African continent as leading party members were jailed, killed or fled into exile. Banda soon entrenched his paternalistic ruling style by setting rigid and arbitrary standards for political, social and cultural behaviour, and heavy penalties for dissent.[4] Essentially, Banda was his own source of legitimacy and was widely respected, if also feared. However, he had been able to maintain his rule only with the help of 'the Family' – his closest advisers, John Tembo, and Tembo's niece, Cecilia Kadzamira.

At one time suspicions were voiced that the powerful Tembo–Kadzamira duo – a strange entourage, intent on perpetuating the system after Banda had gone – were the *de facto* rulers of the country. Tembo was believed to be the real brain and motivator behind 'the Family'. He was Treasurer General of the MCP, Malawian co-chairman of the Joint Security Commission with Mozambique, and was also appointed to the position of Minister of State in the Office of the President. This, in effect, made him 'prime minister' and, for all intents and purposes, the real ruler of Malawi as he handled – at least initially – all the important ministries the President had allocated himself.[5] But the critical link to Banda lay with Cecilia Kadzamira – commonly known as Mama – a large woman with a flashing smile who, as official hostess, was at the diminutive President's side during official engagements. Being closest to Banda, she was believed to have had the President's ear and therefore had the greatest influence on him. However, neither Tembo nor Kadzamira enjoyed broadly based, independent political support and both had by the early 1990s incurred the unpopularity of being too close to the then widely discredited President.

To be sure, the Malawian state was a strong and authoritarian, one-party state, dominated by a small, autocratic and dictatorial political clique and characterised by a 'top-down' flow of policy directives and government decrees – an archetype of the 'Leviathan' state. In this respect, the ministerial and parliamentary structures were purely nominal and had the facile function of rubber-stamping and rationalising handed down policies. The 'predatory' behaviour of the Malawian state, on the other hand, entailed a mutually reinforcing political and economic system in which the dominant minority of the political elite and their economic agencies preyed on the populace for their own benefit and at the expense of the absolute welfare of a majority of the population and long-term development goals.[6]

PRESSURES FOR A MULTI-PARTY SYSTEM

Since the beginning of 1992, Malawi had begun to show all the usual symptoms of a country approaching the end of a long-standing autocratic regime. In what must rank as the biggest blow to Banda's declining prestige, eight Roman Catholic bishops – for the first time daring to criticise Dr Banda in public in an unusual challenge to Malawi's authoritarian government – issued a pastoral letter[7] on Sunday, 8 March 1992 condemning *inter alia* Malawi's human rights record (the continued detention without trial of scores of political prisoners and extremely harsh treatment of prison inmates), calling for democratic reform and greater political freedom (especially an end to curbs on freedom of expression and other civil liberties). This attempt to unleash public debate on a whole range of issues met with harsh criticism from the MCP and the government, who accused the bishops of sowing 'disunity' and of disturbing 'peace, security and progress'. Banda summoned and berated the clerics; and two days later they were detained and interrogated for several hours by the police and then put under house arrest.

The pastoral letter and the treatment meted out to the Catholic bishops sparked off protests that arguably became the country's first overt act of disenchantment with, and the most direct form of criticism against, Dr Banda's government for nearly three decades. Finally, the democratic tide that had swept throughout the rest of Africa began to seep into Malawi. Despite the cruel fate that had overtaken so many of Banda's critics in the past, political protest now became much more open.

The politics of dissent

There had been a current of political opposition to Banda's regime since the early 1960s, but it had largely been based abroad around exiled politicians and intellectual dissidents. Sadly, Malawian opposition movements had been plagued by mutual suspicion, ethnic rivalry and inaction, owing to long years of exile, failed armed rebellion, harassment by Malawian security agents and lack of international support. However, following the emergence of the Movement for Multi-Party Democracy (MMD) in Zambia, changes in the international political climate in the post-cold-war era, and the growing recognition among Malawian exiles of the need for unity, representatives of the Malawi Freedom Movement (Mafremo), the League for a Socialist Malawi (Lesoma), the Congress for the Second Republic (CSR), the Malawi Democratic Union (MDU), and the Malawi People's Party (MPP) formed the United Front for Multi-Party Democracy (UFMD) with a view to bringing together all the forces of democracy within and outside Malawi.

The challenge to Banda's iron-fisted rule was joined by a conference of over eighty Malawian pro-democracy exiles from around the world – most of them members of the UFMD – held in Lusaka from 20 to 23 March 1992. Ironically, it was Chakufwa Chihana, the only home-based opposition figure present in Lusaka, who was instrumental in shifting the focus of the democratic movement back home. He saw his mission as spearheading a campaign for multi-party democracy inside Malawi. And he did so in the teeth of dogged resistance from veteran exiles who feared their years of largely ineffective campaigning would be left behind by the new phase in the struggle. A clear schism developed, and there was bitter discussion on the question of transferring the struggle inside Malawi and particularly on mandating Chihana to lead the way.

Key members of the UFMD walked out in disgust, subsequently resigned from the Front and, with Chihana, set up the Interim Committee for a Democratic Alliance (ICDA): a decision based on proposals contained in Chihana's keynote address[8] to the conference, when he urged that a more representative organisation should be formed to press ahead with demands for multi-party democracy. Thus, a major new lobbying organisation for democratic reform was emerging inside Malawi for the first time. The ICDA would consult and work with representatives of the churches, students and academics, professional bodies, the business community, the labour movement and non-governmental organisations inside Malawi. It was essentially a pressure group, whose objectives were to campaign peacefully for the restoration of basic human rights and democracy in Malawi.

Charged with the weighty responsibility of uniting opposition forces in favour of democracy inside Malawi, Chihana returned to the country on 6 April 1992 bravely to defy the Banda regime from within. Predictably, he was immediately detained; but his incarceration helped to focus the minds

of both regional and international governments and effectively placed the
onus on the Western world to spur on the country's democratic movement.
It caused instant outrage in neighbouring countries and considerable concern among the country's Western aid donors.

A turning point: the May 1992 disturbances

The sporadic and rather spontaneous events of March and April 1992
reached a climax in Blantyre – the industrial and commercial centre of
Malawi. Demonstrations began in that city early on Wednesday, 6 May,
when a few hundred workers at Lonrho's David Whitehead textile factory
started strike action, calling on others to join the work stoppage and protest
against poor working conditions, low wages and the high cost of living.
Violence broke out when police tried to disperse demonstrators. In panic,
paramilitary riot squads later opened fire as they fought running battles
with rioting crowds. There was widespread looting, much of it targeting the
supermarkets of the People's Trading Centre (PTC) – a subsidiary of Press
Corporation Limited, wholly owned by Banda, which controls large sectors
of the Malawian economy – signifying the anti-establishment nature of the
riots. Clearly, the MCP had lost its aura and grip on the people: MCP
district and regional offices in Limbe and Ndirande townships were destroyed, and women wearing cloth emblazoned with Banda's portrait were
attacked. Thus, although the 6 May riots had been sparked by an industrial
dispute, political discontent emerged as an important undercurrent.

In Lilongwe, however, the situation was clearly different: the High Court of
Malawi had ordered the state to bring Chihana to court and press charges
against him or furnish reasons for his continued detention. When, on 7 May,
the state once again failed to produce him, this sparked off an angry demonstration by over 6,000 people who marched into town, calling for the immediate and unconditional release of Chihana, and demanding a multi-party
system and freedom from one-party rule. The police used tear gas and a baton
charge to break up the essentially peaceful demonstration, and this led to
rioting when the crowd rampaged through the market area and clashed with riot
police. Unrest continued throughout that Thursday night in the high-density
suburbs of Lilongwe. The district MCP offices were burnt down, and again the
first targets for looting were PTC supermarkets. The demonstrations and
resultant disturbances following Chihana's failure to appear in court were,
therefore, clearly politically motivated.

For Malawi, this was the worst violence ever. Indeed, the 6 and 7 May
rioting was the first large-scale expression and spontaneous outburst of
discontent with the Banda regime. Though in some places the police

refused to intervene, in others they used live ammunition. Protesters fought back; some people were killed, others injured. Significantly, while the regular and paramilitary police forces were on the streets trying to quell the violence, the Army kept its distance and did nothing to stop the looting.

Malawi's small, 7,000-strong Army is said to be neutral. The Army, one of Malawi's few institutions with a reputation for honesty and an interest in upholding the Constitution,[9] had a particular dislike for Tembo and the police force he used to silence opponents. At that stage, the most crucial question was the role that the Army would play. For a while, a coup by the military seemed to be a possibility that could not be discounted. Although some of the top officers still appeared to be loyal, there were reports that at the end of April 1992 twenty-seven senior and middle-ranking officers had met the President and informed him they would be unwilling to undertake policing duties against citizens calling for a multi-party constitution. It thus seemed that a schism was developing between the police and the Army.

The initial strike action and demonstrations on 6 and 7 May had a ripple effect throughout the country and in the following days there were strikes in most major companies: after civil servants in the lower categories and city council workers had demanded and got pay increases, workers at parastatals such as Malawi Railways, Air Malawi, the National Bank of Malawi and the Reserve Bank of Malawi decided to flex their muscles. Strikes spread to the rural areas as workers on the tea and tobacco estates in Thyolo and Mulanje in southern Malawi, on the sugar plantations of Lonrho's Dwangwa Sugar Company in the central region and on the rubber and coffee plantations in the northern region joined the action – an ominous development from the MCP government's point of view, as tea, tobacco and sugar exports were Malawi's major foreign currency earners.

Indeed, these strikes and demonstrations marked a rite of passage for the country. At last the people had found their voices and one could sense that a major psychological barrier had been swept away. In fact, the crack had widened in the granite edifice of the Malawian regime and the process of change now seemed almost irreversible.

International pressure and human rights: foreign aid and donor conditionality

Until as recently as 1989, Western donor governments were comfortable with Banda's strict, paternalist, Protestant style, his cultural conservatism and his friendliness towards the West – when it still counted. Because of his pro-Western policies, Banda's regime got off rather lightly. But in the post-cold-war era, Malawi came under growing pressure from donor countries to follow the path of multi-party democracy. Old allies were now turning on the country; in fact, Malawi was in danger – because of the geo-political changes in the southern African region – of losing the traditional support of South Africa. And Western donor countries, in particular, now wanted to link aid to political reform.[10]

The release of a number of political prisoners temporarily staved off the loss of aid. But by the end of November 1991, European Community (EC) development ministers agreed to set strict political and human rights conditions for aid recipients. Then, in March 1992, there was a British-initiated EC *démarche* to Malawi, which made it clear that the EC countries disapproved of Malawi's record of poor governance, including human rights violations. Subsequently, Britain informed Malawi that it expected greater political freedom and respect for human rights, after having earlier halved its aid to US$8.6 million for 1992. And Scandinavian aid donors also started applying pressure to secure the release of political prisoners.[11]

The crunch came when the Malawian government asked the Paris meeting of donor nations – presided over by the World Bank and comprising Britain, the United States, Germany, France, Denmark, Portugal, Japan and various other multilateral agencies – for nearly US$800 million in balance-of-payments support. Malawi had recently introduced some important economic policies, such as allowing freer access to foreign exchange (except for luxury items), overhauling the monetary and tax system and improving control over parastatals. External debt service had also been showing a decline. The balance of payments had been projected to strengthen substantially, reflecting a reduction in the current account deficit. The government could therefore argue with donors that while its politics might not be a cause for joy to outsiders, they had to acknowledge that the country's economic performance had significantly improved after more than two years of strict austerity measures.

But, despite Malawi's obvious economic successes, it would have been a mistake to think of it as economically secure. Its foreign debt stood at about US$1.5 billion – and every year it required more than the country's entire export earnings to service. That was why it would not have been able to resist the pressure being applied by the international donor community to improve its human rights record. However, Malawi has a relatively small, modern economic sector and only a tiny political elite, so it would have been easier than in some other countries to keep going without foreign aid, as long as the Army and police remained loyal.

The Paris donor meeting concluded by suspending all new aid, except for drought and refugee relief, expressing deep concern about the lack of progress in the area of basic freedoms and human rights and linking new aid to 'good governance'. It was added that donors did not wish to impose 'any specific system of government'; but, clearly, they were seeking 'tangible and irreversible evidence of a basic transformation' in the way Malawi approached these matters, so that there was a fundamental shift in the way human rights in Malawi were viewed. Nevertheless, despite the refusal of donors to come up with the US$74 million Malawi wanted for 1992 and 1993 for new, non-humanitarian projects, other projects valued at around US$200 million already under way or in the pipeline were given the go-ahead. But what hurt Malawi badly was the fact that donors only pledged US$170 million of the estimated US$270 million needed for drought relief and programmes to help more than one million refugees from neighbouring Mozambique. This humanitarian assistance was not conditional on human rights improvements. It was primarily aid for structural adjustment and for infrastructural projects that was to be frozen.

Announcing these measures, the donor nations emphasised that they were putting Malawi 'under surveillance' for a period that might last six months, or until 'substantive progress' had been made towards improving the regime's human rights record, before any reassessment of foreign aid could be undertaken.[12] Thus, the already strained Malawian economy was facing additional problems as much-needed foreign aid was frozen and the poverty-stricken peasant population became restive.

The aftermath of the Blantyre and Lilongwe riots

Whatever Malawi's short-term response would have been to donor pressures and international calls for the implementation of a democratic process, there could have been no doubt that it would eventually have to fall into line with the rest of the emerging democracies in Africa – Banda's belligerence notwithstanding. Initially, though, Banda showed no greater willingness to respond to these pressures. A renewed police crackdown flew in the face of donor demands for reform.

With Banda becoming increasingly isolated from day-to-day state affairs, and with access to him effectively blocked by Tembo and Kadzamira, it is not surprising that the President remained unaware of the magnitude and significance of the mounting pressure for democratic change. In fact, he was unlikely to make any significant move as his leadership was faltering. At the same time, an internal opposition to the government was beginning, slowly and carefully and at extreme risk to take root, preparing itself for inevitable change. As elsewhere in Africa, ordinary Malawians had begun the process of rolling back the state that had brutalised and exploited them for almost three decades. Starved of open political activity under the rule of Banda, Malawians were either aghast at the sudden outpouring of criticism or galvanised into action.

What was now at issue was not *whether* Malawi would change, but when. The government was unable to suppress criticism totally, as it had been able to do in the past, or to ward off international pressure. Its security forces were, for once, powerless to prevent public manifestations of anti-government feeling. A more ominous turn of events was the fact that the traditional rivalry between the Army and police was becoming a major factor in the political equation, with the previously aloof Army showing signs of being ready to prevent the police from launching a full-scale crackdown on opponents of the regime.

Banda, like so many other African leaders, had failed to manage political reform and was about to pay the price for it. In reaction to the May 1992 disturbances, his only policy response was to dissolve parliament and hold new elections on 26 and 27 June 1992. Described as 'an exercise in self-deception' and 'a farce', the elections were for 91 of the 141 seats in the rubber-stamp parliament. Behind the scenes manipulation of can-didacies contributed to the lowest turnout in Malawian electoral history: around 40 per cent nationally, in the commercial centre of Blantyre a mere 20 per cent, and only 10 per cent in some other areas.[13] Clearly, the one-party elections were an exercise to try and persuade Malawians and the donor community that democracy was already in place and, at most, needed a little tinkering to make it work more smoothly. But the evidence of displeasure with the government, shown in the poor turnout, should have convinced Banda that reforms were necessary.

In addressing the party faithful from Dedza South constituency after the elections, Tembo implored people 'not to listen to calls for multi-partyism, which . . . [could] only bring [about] confusion'.[14] Other government func-tionaries regularly referred to the need 'to be vigilant against con-fusionists', 'to enlighten the people on the evils of [the] multi-party system of government', and 'to thwart the efforts of those who would like to see . . . Malawi plunge[d] into chaos through [the] alien politics of multi-partyism'; and then they proceeded to warn against 'misguided people [who] were trying to disrupt the prevailing peace in the country by propa-gating their ideologies of multi-partyism', that 'multi-party politics . . . only brought conflict, confusion, disunity, and chaos among [the] people' and that, therefore, there was 'no room for multi-party politics and its proponents [in Malawi]'.[15] At the 1992 MCP annual convention in Lilongwe from 27 September to 4 October, delegates again passed a reso-lution reaffirming 'their confidence in the one-party system and . . . declare[d] that Malawi . . . [would] continue to be a one-party state'.[16]

The emergence of internal pressure groups

The Livingstonia Synod of the Church of Central Africa Presbyterian (CCAP) decided on 25 August 1992 to set up a committee to campaign for a national referendum on multi-party politics. This initiative was intended to give new impetus to the opposition in the wake of the re-detention of Chakufwa Chihana. Opposition leaders were concerned that the MCP would be able to hold its annual convention at the end of September and claim that an organised opposition did not exist. Subsequently, the Christian Council of Malawi (CCM), representing seventeen Protestant churches, called in an open letter on the government to hold a referendum on a multi-party political system. In addition, several pro-democracy committees had been formed in all three regions and were circulating leaflets. Although the movement was shrouded in secrecy, it seemed to have been centred on two emerging groups: Chihana's Interim Committee for a Democratic Alliance (ICDA) and the United Democratic Party, which seemed to have become a generic term for any pro-democracy group.

With the announcement in September 1992 of the formation of the Alliance for Democracy (Aford), headed by a thirteen-member committee chaired by Chihana, the myth propagated by Banda that no internal opposition existed was finally removed. In response, Banda reluctantly appointed a so-called Presidential Committee on Dialogue (PCD), composed mainly of members of the National Executive Committee of the MCP and Cabinet Ministers, to discuss 'issues of national concern' with church leaders and other interested groups. According to a government spokesman, the PCD was mandated to meet all groups of people who had grievances to present to the government, including the newly formed pressure group – provided it had, paradoxically, 'no political designs'.[17]

Then, in a rather sudden change of course, Banda announced on 18 October that he had decided to call a national referendum on the question of whether people wanted to continue with the one-party system or preferred to introduce a multi-party system of government. He was convinced that Malawians wanted 'to vote for me and my party, the Malawi Congress Party, as the sole political party . . . [in Malawi] and to reject the introduction of other political parties'.[18] Nevertheless, the holding of a referendum appeared to have been a major concession to his opponents at home and to Western donor nations. For the first time, after nearly thirty years of one-party elections, Malawians now had the prospect of a genuine choice.

In the wake of these developments, a group of former politicians and civil servants of the Malawi government formed another pressure group, the United Democratic Front (UDF). Headed by Bakili Muluzi, a former

Secretary General of the MCP, the UDF was openly to mobilise support for a multi-party government by 'peaceful and lawful means'.[19] Both Aford and the UDF seemed to have similar agendas, although the UDF made it plain that it wanted nothing to do with the large and politically divided exiled community. Aford's position, on the other hand, was that exiles should be allowed to return and participate in the unfolding political process in Malawi. Despite these differences, however, it was unlikely – for practical reasons – that there would have been any hostile competition between the two groups before the referendum.[20]

Opposition pressure groups such as Aford, the UDF, Lesoma and the UFMD listed a number of demands in order 'to level the playing field' in the run-up to the referendum.[21] The PCD met with the Public Affairs Committee (PAC), comprising representatives from Aford, the UDF, church officials from various denominations (the Catholic Church, the Presbyterian Church, the Anglican Church, the Christian Council and the Ecumenical Council of Malawi), a delegation from the Malawi Law Society, the Muslim community and representatives from the Malawi Chamber of Commerce and Industry. This was a significant development in that it was the first time the Malawian government met its opponents in a face-to-face encounter to discuss political differences.

While the referendum announcement radically redefined the boundaries of politics in Malawi, it also seemed a complete *volte face* for Banda and the MCP after they unanimously decided at the 1992 MCP annual convention in Lilongwe that the MCP would remain 'the sole legal political party' in Malawi. Clearly, the referendum decision was a sign of growing desperation by the Malawian government, at a time when the donor aid freeze entered its sixth month and really started to bite. A referendum on reform may have seemed to be a nifty way out of the bind. While Banda's tactical switch left many of his lieutenants in the MCP gasping, the referendum turned out to be a big gamble that Banda was to lose on all counts: it would not bring him the foreign funds he needed, at least not immediately, and it was an exercise he was almost bound to lose. It appears, therefore, that the MCP's strategy – if it had one – was to sustain a climate of fear, harass the opposition and call a quick vote, hoping the majority rural population would vote to retain the one-party system.

Run-up to the referendum: the saga of the two ballot boxes

A five-person team of United Nations experts arrived in Malawi to advise the government on the modalities and logistics of conducting a referendum on multi-party democracy along internationally acceptable lines. It subsequently urged the government to scrap the referendum idea, to repeal Article 4 of the Malawi Constitution – which recognised the ruling MCP as the sole legal party – to unban all other political groups and to hold fresh elections under a revised constitution. However, the team also recommended that the Malawian government, should it proceed with the referendum on multi-party democracy, release all political prisoners and declare a general amnesty for exiles; draw up a new voters' register to allow political exiles to participate in the poll; provide free access to information; and allow freedom of the press for all participating groups.

Aford and the UDF agreed to work together for the referendum, and campaigned jointly. However, Aford expressed fears that the referendum would not be free or fair, because of the MCP government's unwillingness to respond to calls for it to restore all civil liberties and rights. And Aford feared the government would use its extensive security apparatus to prevent its opponents from campaigning, especially in the rural areas where the MCP controlled most aspects of daily life, including food distribution. Neither the UDF nor Aford were allowed to hold rallies to encourage people to vote in favour of a multi-party system. Although both Aford and the UDF had by then registered as associations (or 'pressure groups'), neither of their applications had been approved and members were arrested across the country for possessing or selling membership cards. The opposition newspapers – *The Malawi Democrat* (Aford) and *The UDF News* – were also banned.

In a New Year's Eve address to the nation, Dr Banda eventually set 15 March 1993 as the date for the referendum. Although he directed the Malawi Broadcasting Corporation (MBC) 'to report news and events on both sides of the referendum campaign', he also prohibited the corporation from allocating time for any groups to make partisan political broadcasts and to accept paid political advertisements. The ban on radio advertising hit the multi-party groups hard, because in a country where only 41.7 per cent of the population is literate, the radio was the only medium by which they could effectively communicate with the general population and present their case. This compelled Aford and the UDF to declare the referendum date 'unrealistic and unacceptable'; they were especially concerned at the short time available for campaigning and at restrictions imposed on the holding of rallies.

Subsequently, a twelve-member referendum commission was appointed to oversee the poll and to take overall charge of the administrative procedures for the referendum.[22] Although such a commission was one of the major opposition demands, Aford said it was disappointed in its composition, as it was clearly not 'neutral' and independent – indeed, stacked with MCP and government supporters. At the time only one member of the commission, the Reverend Dr Silas Nyirenda, who also chaired the PAC, was known to be a supporter of multi-partyism.[23]

In a UN report on the referendum, it was recommended that voting be conducted using a single ballot box on polling day, to improve the secrecy of the vote. The report further dwelt on technicalities related to the need for a rigorous voter registration campaign, the need to lower the voting age from twenty-one to eighteen years, for properly designed ballot boxes, for adequate protection against double voting, for polling to be undertaken on one day only, for the presence of independent observers and referendum agents from all sides and the need for ample lead-time to the referendum. But in response, Banda rejected the lowering of the age limit and the use of a single ballot box, in preference for the use of two, separate ballot boxes.[24] However, in a country with a record of extensive harassment of MCP government opponents, the lack of secrecy in voting procedures was prone to cause alarm among multi-party supporters.

Early in 1993, it already became apparent that pressure from the UN might lead to a postponement of the referendum, as the country's main opposition groups threatened to boycott the poll if the UN recommendations were not followed. The UN electoral assistance unit issued a report saying that the timing and the parameters for the referendum, as set out by the Malawian government, were not consistent with a free and fair electoral process. This was seen as a blow to Banda, who was attempting to legitimise the one-party state under the MCP by holding a snap referendum using the one-party electoral register. Banda had already suffered a moral and political defeat with his campaign rallies often drawing fewer than 1,000 people (and very seldom up to 5,000), as compared to those of the opposition which regularly attracted between 20,000 and 30,000 people.

Finally, Banda told an MCP rally in Mzuzu that he was postponing the referendum from 15 March to 14 June, on the recommendation of UN Secretary General Boutros Boutros-Ghali. Again the opposition, although welcoming the delay in the poll, expressed concern about a number of matters which could make the referendum less than free and fair. They then stated their bottom line for participation in the referendum: the use of a single ballot box, instead of separate boxes for 'yes' (one-party) and 'no' (multi-party) votes. Clearly, this was a voting procedure that was prone to irregularities and intimidation of the worst kind.

The issue of the 'two ballot boxes' came to a head around the middle of May – less than one month before the referendum – when the UN mediator, International Commission of Jurists Secretary General Adama Dieng, reached agreement with the Malawian government and the opposition on new proposals involving a system of two ballot papers used successfully in the Eritrean elections. One of two ballot papers (one representing the hurricane lamp of the Aford/UDF opposition 'pressure groups', and the other the black cockerel of the ruling MCP) would be selected by voters behind a screen and placed in an envelope, which would then be dropped into a single ballot box in public view. Banda formally announced the government's acceptance of the new voting system on 18 May, saying he felt the agreed-on procedures would make the referendum free and fair. But this climbdown was due primarily to financial constraints and international pressure, rather than opposition protestations.

Prior to the referendum, observers agreed that support for the ruling MCP was dwindling in the urban areas: naturally, the more sophisticated and literate sections of the Malawian electorate, able to draw information from a flowering of small independent newspapers, were to be found there. However, the airwaves of the MBC – the main source of information in the rural areas, where literacy levels are much lower – remained closed to the multi-party supporters. And in the rural areas other than in the north, conservatism and lack of information (and, alleged the opposition, the fact that drought relief was being distributed as gifts from the ruling party) had helped to maintain support for the one-party system.

Thus, while the urban and semi-urban areas appeared overwhelmingly in favour of multi-party democracy, it was a demographic fact that more than four out of five Malawians live in the rural areas. It was there that the referendum was to be decided. But even there, indications were that the MCP had, functionally, almost evaporated and the network of party channels had, for all intents and purposes, collapsed. The Malawian government's refusal to release Chihana in time to campaign in the run-up to the referendum was a recognition of his enormous stature as a rallying point and catalyst for the opposition, and a manifestation of the MCP's nervousness and lack of confidence in its own appeal and impact on the electorate.

THE JUNE 1993 REFERENDUM AND ITS AFTERMATH

The opposition alliance of the United Democratic Front (UDF) and the Alliance for Democracy (Aford) won the 14 June 1993 referendum with an almost landslide 63.5 per cent majority vote and immediately demanded that Dr Banda step aside for a coalition government of national unity to prepare for multi-party elections before the end of the year. According to the national referendum commission, a total of 3,153,448 people cast their ballots out of an electorate of some 4.7 million – a 67 per cent voter turnout; high by African, and certainly by world, standards.

However, the vote was very irregular and regionally based: the northern and southern regions provided an overwhelming vote for multi-party politics – up to 85 per cent. Malawi's largest city, Blantyre, was 86 per cent in favour of change. But, while the alliance swept the northern and southern regions, in an almost complete reversal of the national trend, the ruling MCP got about 63 per cent of the vote in the central region – the area where Banda and most of his ministers have their power bases. Final results gave those in favour of multi-party politics 1,993,996 votes and those for the continuation of one-party rule 1,088,473 votes – there were 70,979 spoilt votes, a mere 2.25 per cent of the total votes cast.[25]

The results of the referendum proved Banda to be tragically out of touch with the general mood of the electorate, as the MCP had won majority support in only eight of the twenty-four districts of Malawi. And this in spite of the fact that the UN monitoring team observed that the run-up to the polling day was marred by the intimidation of pressure groups by the infamous paramilitary Malawi Young Pioneers (MYP). International observers concluded that because it was the supporters of the multi-party option who were hampered by misconduct, their victory was valid – even though it would have been wrong to call the referendum 'free and fair'.

In his first public response to the referendum results, Banda declared that the win of the multi-party supporters:

> does not mean that the Malawi Congress Party ceases to exist. Neither does it mean that the multi-party advocates have been elected to replace . . . the present government. . . . The referendum was clearly about . . . [choosing a system] of national politics and people have voted for the option of political pluralism . . . they want other political parties to be formed . . . to compete with the Malawi Congress Party.[26]

He therefore saw no need to resign to make way for a transitional government, although he accepted the results and said that he would respect the people's verdict by setting up machinery to implement changes, starting with the legalisation of other political parties, a general review of the Constitution and other laws on the statute book, followed by general elections within a year.

Transitional arrangements and the interregnum: from President to Presidential Council

One of the most serious threats to the transition process in Malawi now lay in dissension among the opposition groups, notably the UDF and Aford. Given the voting pattern in the referendum, if opposition votes were split between two or more parties, there was a good chance of the MCP winning an election by the plurality margin unless, of course, the vote it garnered during the referendum was a consequence of fear and intimidation. And this suggested that, in the absence of clearly distinguishable and substantive opposition party platforms and programmes, the euphoria could well peter out into a compromise of the elites, which would leave the interests of the masses unaddressed.

However, after the referendum Malawi's governance had become remarkably transparent and for the first time journalists were reporting on issues that in the past were considered taboo. More than twenty independent newspapers, all of which were often very critical of the government and of Banda in particular, had mushroomed in the new climate of relative tolerance. The judicial system, which had lost credibility because of interventions by Banda and some of his colleagues in the Cabinet, also had some of its stature restored.

Opposition parties remained convinced, however, that the MCP would continue to obstruct the preparations for multi-party elections: they feared that the transition process would be swamped by the unwieldy structures and procedures set up by the MCP government. The main forum for negotiation was the regular meetings between the PCD and the PAC; however, the transitional National Consultative Council (NCC) was held up as the 'supreme body', and its decisions were to be followed by parliament. Three sub-committees were formed: one on new electoral laws and procedures, a second on constituency boundaries and a third on reviewing the Constitution and drafting a new one before elections. In essence, this was a diluted version of the interim government that the opposition had demanded previously. And the transitional National Executive Council (NEC), which oversaw the security services, the central bank and other key institutions, was in effect a type of 'shadow cabinet'.

Although progress towards democracy in Malawi was slow, because most of the country's legislation had been specifically designed for a one-party state, a political metamorphosis was clearly taking place. Thus, Malawi's largely rubber-stamp legislature convened in November 1993 to amend the Constitution and remove other legal underpinnings of decades of one-man rule by Dr Banda. Simultaneously, it was announced that an electoral commission – on which all parties contesting the elections would be represented – was to oversee Malawi's first multi-party elections on 17 May 1994. The NCC also agreed to increase the number of seats in the Malawian parliament to more accurately reflect population densities. And in a further development, the NCC agreed to separate parliamentary and presidential elections, and explained that 'the president may not necessarily come from the party with the largest block of seats in parliament, but would be a popularly elected president'. Results of the elections would be announced on 19 May and the new President sworn in on 21 May.

The MCP's annual convention was held in Lilongwe from 3 October 1993. Most commentators expected it to be a rather sober affair, with delegates tackling hard issues concerning the party's future. Although it was to unveil a new manifesto, it was expected to endorse Banda as its presidential candidate for the May 1994 presidential elections. On the opening day of the convention, however, it was announced that Banda would no longer open the proceedings as had been scheduled, because doctors had instructed him to rest. Only the following day it was divulged that Banda had been admitted to a clinic in Johannesburg on 2 October, for what was described as a 'routine check-up'. It was later confirmed that the President had suffered a 'minor brain haemorrhage', and that he was in a satisfactory condition after undergoing neurosurgery to remove excess fluid from his brain. The invincibility myth surrounding the President's health had finally been shattered.

Initially, the opposition parties were greatly heartened by Banda's apparent exit from the political scene. However, they were slow to capitalise on the uncertainty, and their indecision diminished their standing. To be sure, Banda's sudden illness sent waves of apprehension through political circles over who would run the country if his condition should worsen. A feeling seemed to emerge that Malawi 'could easily [be] plunge[d] into chaos if there continued to be no clear successor to [the] President . . . in his party'. And despite the fact that the NCC had been pressurising Banda to appoint an MCP Secretary General, he had always resisted the idea of nominating an heir-apparent.

On the final day of the MCP convention, however, in an unprecedented, almost nonsensical, move it was announced that Banda had appointed to the secretary generalship Gwanda Chakuamba-Phiri, who had once been one of Banda's staunch allies but had fallen into disfavour and had been jailed for more than ten years for sedition. The news of Chakuamba-Phiri's elevation was greeted with 'astonishment': he is considered a ruthless, but shrewd and intelligent political operator. Ominously, it also appeared to signal a return to a hardline position by the MCP. But his quick return to the MCP was seen by many Malawians as a move of political expediency unlikely to raise his, or the party's, public popularity.

Then, in another surprise move, it was announced on 14 October that, in accordance with Article 13 of the Constitution, a three-man Presidential Council had been set up to rule Malawi on behalf of President Banda, for as long as he '[was] unable to perform the functions of his office'. A spokesman for the Office of the President and Cabinet (OPC) said that the Council would be chaired by Gwanda Chakuamba-Phiri, and that the other two members were to be John Tembo and Minister of Transport, Robson Chirwa. Banda returned to Malawi on 24 October 1993: speculation concerning the leadership continued but the issue of succession became purely academic when it was announced on 7 December that the President was fit to resume his duties and the Presidential Council, which had ruled Malawi since early October, had been dissolved. Not having much of a choice, by virtue of his being Life President of the party, the MCP also indicated that it would field Dr Banda as its presidential candidate.

SQUARING UP FOR MULTI-PARTY ELECTIONS

Almost immediately after the June 1993 referendum, the MCP launched an offensive to win the hearts and minds of the people. Haunted by its defeat at the polls, it went on the campaign trail, trying to improve its image and regain legitimacy. Although few expected the ruling MCP to have anything other than a rough ride towards general elections, it had nevertheless initiated a concerted recruitment drive.

The Malawi Congress Party: rejuvenating a troglodyte?

Taking advantage of Banda's poor health, his lieutenants in the Presidential Council did what Banda had been loath to do for nearly three decades: recruit new blood and not worry about succession. During the last three months of 1993, the Cabinet was reshuffled as many times, with Banda relinquishing his last two key ministerial portfolios, that of agriculture and defence, two of five he had held since the 'Cabinet crisis' of October 1964.

Secretary General of the MCP, Gwanda Chakuamba-Phiri, consolidated his position and his seemingly unchallenged assumption of the leadership of the MCP suggested that, should President Banda eventually be forced to withdraw gradually from public life owing to ill-health, he would be at the party's helm. But, ironically, Chakuamba-Phiri was not more popular than Tembo and no more likely to lead the MCP back to power. Opposition parties regarded the Cabinet reshuffles as a political gimmick, an exercise in musical chairs, to spruce up the MCP's image. However, it is clear that the MCP wanted to go into elections not only as the ruling party, but also to gain credit for reforms being rushed through parliament.

Nevertheless, attempts at giving the ruling MCP a facelift were unlikely to rescue it from defeat in the general elections. The party's half-hearted attempts at political liberalisation meant only that people felt more free to express their grievances against the Banda regime and its baggage of three decades of authoritarian one-party rule and human rights abuses. The MCP's best hope, therefore, was to continue efforts to divide the opposition, then perhaps to negotiate its way into a post-election coalition with Aford or, perhaps, even the UDF – many of whose more prominent members are former MCP stalwarts. While MCP strategists might have harboured thoughts of emulating President Daniel arap Moi's much-disputed election victory in Kenya against a split opposition in December 1992, there were closer parallels with Zambia, where the dominant factor in the October 1991 elections in that country had been the unpopularity of the incumbent party and long-serving president representing the tradition of the one-party state.

In the run-up to multi-party elections, Banda and the MCP combined procrastination with an overtly regionalist and tribalist campaign against the opposition, which had strong northern (Aford) and southern (UDF) support but was proven weaker in the central region, home of the Chewa people where the MCP still enjoyed majority support. This strategy portrayed the opposition parties as merely representing non-Chewa, such as the Tonga, Tumbuka, Ngoni, Yao and Sena. The MCP government's sudden softening of attitude, announcing a general amnesty for exiles and inviting them to return home, was therefore clearly based on the hope that returned exiled politicians would encourage further fragmentation in the opposition, clearing the way for a Kenyan-style victory for the MCP government at the scheduled May 1994 poll.

A fragmented opposition: looming danger of the Kenyan scenario

The June 1993 referendum result opened a fierce battle among the various opposition parties. Despite protestations of a common goal and platform during the referendum campaign, both the UDF and Aford treated the exercise as a chance to carve out individual support bases across the country and were often hardly on speaking terms. While still more circumspect in their public pronouncements, they could privately barely disguise their dislike of each other. There was, therefore, always the risk that if prevailing signs of disunity in opposition ranks became concrete divisions, multi-party supporters could well become losers in the May 1994 general elections, despite having emerged as victors in the opening June 1993 referendum skirmish – won by a comfortable 63.5 per cent majority vote.

Meanwhile, the opposition also faced a raft of internal problems. The UDF, the wealthiest and best-organised party, had become the main target for MCP efforts to win back defectors. Aford, however, remained organisationally weak and politically unfocused. Underlying the rivalry between opposition groups were issues related to resolving incipient tribalism and regionalism, the need to hammer out party programmes addressing substantive political and socio-economic issues beyond a mere anti-Banda stance and the imperative of overriding the tendency to exploit the cult of personalities.

An unfortunate detracting issue among the opposition concerned the suspicion of exiles, and the desire by some to marginalise them. The main danger facing the opposition was that squabbling between the different groups could enable Banda to exploit splits and use the sort of divide-and-rule tactics he had used so effectively against opponents in the past. Meanwhile, exiled political parties that had taken advantage of Banda's amnesty to return to the country were finding it hard to garner support inside Malawi. They were seen as 'spoilers' by Aford and the UDF, who had pioneered the pro-democracy movement inside the country. Both these mainstream groups made attempts, therefore, to exclude or marginalise returned exiles from the centre stage of politics.

Indeed, it was imperative that opposition groups began to consult, debate, formulate and mobilise support for political agendas and platforms relating to long-term issues confronting the country.[27] In Malawian politics, a meaningful political platform could not avoid addressing and taking an unequivocal stand on the following issues:[28] the development strategy to be pursued, particularly as far as increased diversification and strengthening of the economy are concerned; redressing the gross economic and social inequities in land, income, employment opportunities, access to infrastructure, health and social services; the disadvantaged position and status of women in society, also as far as income, employment opportunities, and access to education are concerned; and the potentially explosive tendencies of tribalism and regionalism.[29] The latter issue can only be diffused by simultaneously recognising such regional/tribal proclivities and by accommodating them constructively; and by ensuring that political groupings are based on substantive platforms addressing the foregoing issues rather than being based on personalities or tribal/regional cliques.

THE MAY 1994 ELECTIONS: A WATERSHED IN MALAWIAN POLITICS

In the run-up to the elections, both the United Nations' Joint International Observer Group (JIOG) and the Independent Electoral Commission reported campaign violence and widespread intimidation, bribery and misuse of official positions. They named the ruling MCP as the main violator, pointing specifically to MCP functionaries – ministers, members of parliament and chiefs and village headmen – who misused their official positions to induce the electorate to participate in pro-MCP activities – sometimes by making use of the intimidatory tactics employed by dancers in the secret Nyau-Nyau initiation ceremonies – and to interfere with the registration process by the confiscation, theft or purchase of voter registration cards.

On the multi-party campaign trail

By the end of April 1994 it became clear that Malawi's first presidential elections under a multi-party system would be a four-way contest. The slate of candidates was headed by the incumbent nonagenarian President Kamuzu Banda of the Malawi Congress Party (MCP). His three challengers were Bakili Muluzi of the United Democratic Front (UDF) – forming a loose alliance, known as the Common Electoral Group (CEG), with Kanyama Chiume's Congress for the Second Republic (CSR), Harry Bwanausi's Malawi Democratic Union (MDU), George Kanyanya's United Front for Multi-Party Democracy (UFMD) and Tim Mangwazu's Malawi National Democratic Party (MNDP) who withdrew from the presidential race in favour of Muluzi[30] – Chakufwa Chihana of the Alliance for Democracy (Aford) and Kamlepu Kalua of the Malawi Democratic Party (MDP).

In contrast, the first multi-party parliamentary elections were contested by eight parties. The ruling MCP and the UDF opted to put up candidates for each of the 177 constituencies: a new delimitation awarded thirty-three to the sparsely populated northern region (one million), and sixty-eight and seventy-six each to the more densely populated central (3.7 million) and southern (4.8 million) regions. Besides the thirty-three constituencies in its northern stronghold, Aford contested an additional 129 seats in the two other regions. The smaller parties put up candidates in some constituencies, varying between thirty-two for the UFMD and two for the MDU, with thirteen independents.[31] But clearly, by making more than three-quarters of the constituencies three-way contests, Aford and the UDF's inability to reach an election agreement raised the spectre of a Kenyan-type scenario for Malawi's first post-independence, multi-party elections.

Chihana ignored public calls for his party to work with the UDF to topple the Banda regime, because he was convinced that he could win on his own: he argued that Aford was a strong enough party and had a clean image not in any way tainted by past 'blunders'. But he clearly had difficulty in translating this image into popular support and his refusal to work with other parties was weakening his challenge; many, even in his own party, saw him as simply manoeuvring for personal power. Aford's northern support base drew on that region's intellectual and dissenting tradition, in contrast to the south's commercial tradition; and Chihana's reluctance to address social and economic issues made it difficult to broaden that base – nationally, Aford seldom kept its head above a financial and organisational mire.[32] In contrast, the UDF promised to curtail government expenditure, to increase social spending and provide for free and universal primary education.

Neither the UDF nor Aford had any quarrel with the economic liberalisation that the MCP regime, pushed by aid donors, had pursued during the previous two years: privatisation, tariff cuts, lifting of exchange controls, a currency floating at a lower exchange rate – a typical IMF package. However, none of these specifics was discussed on the campaign trail, despite labour unrest prompted by price rises and by the threat to jobs as the private and public sectors slimmed. Although populist in tone, the UDF was undoubtedly the party of the disaffected business classes: medium-scale industrialists and merchants, entrepreneurs of all races excluded from the ruling MCP elite.

The fact that the UDF leadership is composed of some former MCP officials was seized upon by Aford. And the acrimonious opposition wrangling and mudslinging played right into the hands of the press. After the June 1993 referendum, there was an even greater proliferation of partisan newspapers – owned directly or indirectly by political parties or politicians – which invariably forsook all journalistic ethic and survived on libel, scandal and defamation.[33] Politicians have shown remarkable patience with the newspaper fraternity and their shoot-from-the-hip, factless journalism; but many Malawian journalists are embarrassed by the ethical and professional void in the media.[34]

The bickering between the UDF and Aford offered a welcome respite to the MCP, which was once the sole target of the opposition. Although in its campaign the Banda government maintained that the peace and stability that it had nurtured in Malawi would be jeopardised by a change in government, the MCP had done little to convince voters that it was not the same party which oversaw three decades of human rights abuses in Malawi.[35] Perhaps the best illustration of how difficult it was for the MCP to repackage itself was the fact that an ailing, feeble and senile Dr Banda remained the party's figurehead. At the same time, rallying behind Banda fitted in well with the MCP's apparent election strategy of fortifying its proven power base in the central region while the opposition split the vote in the rest of the country.[36] Part of this strategy was to try and ensure that the opposition would self-destruct.

Throughout the election campaign, politicians emphasised the dangers of tribalism, pointing to countries such as Rwanda, where an estimated one million people have died. The thrust of the opposition's campaign was that it was time for change, that the MCP government had failed to deliver the goods and that the country needed a new lease of life. But, essentially, the election debate was a tussle between the UDF, accusing the Banda government of squandering funds on unnecessary projects, and the MCP, emphasising its achievements. Human rights were not an issue, perhaps largely because of the prominence they enjoyed in the referendum on multi-partyism. The campaign turned out to be disappointing, mainly because the contestants failed to address serious issues and seemed rather short on constructive ideas. This caused the editor of the *Financial Post* to describe the debate in the run-up to elections as 'sadly lacking in substance'.[37]

Another potential problem in the run-up to the 17 May presidential and parliamentary elections was the possibility of voter apathy. Malawians, energised by the concrete prospect of voting a dictator out of power in the referendum on multi-party politics, showed less enthusiasm for an apparently unfocused opposition. The Independent Electoral Commission even moved the voter registration deadline forward two weeks to 26 March in order to allow more Malawians the opportunity to participate in the elections. However, the registration process was disappointing: a rather low figure of some 3.8 million, far short of the number who registered for the June 1993 referendum – about 4.7 million. This was despite predictions that a flood of voters would register after the minimum voting age was lowered from twenty-one to eighteen years. By April, however, it was estimated that a 'respectable' 80 per cent of those eligible to vote had indeed registered. The largely illiterate electorate was somehow wary of registering; they were seemingly confused by the proliferation of political parties which had no clear ideological differences.

As the election drew closer, it became clear that only the margin of a UDF victory was in doubt. Aford had failed – because of regional divisions, lack of resources and an inexperienced leadership – to translate its clean image to popular support in the southern and central regions. But the UDF exploited its populous base in the south, where the majority of the nation's 9.5 million people live, to emerge as the dominant political force. The MCP, however, was still a force to contend with, despite its having lost the referendum on multi-party politics; it still controlled the bureaucracy and commanded old allies through patronage.

In the final analysis, the MCP proved resilient and remained more disciplined than its rivals. On the all-party National Consultative Council (NCC), charged with overseeing the transition to democracy, the MCP followed a dual strategy of prevarication on sensitive issues and giving enough rope for opposition parties to hang each other with. The second strategy left the opposition bickering over the new constitution, which the NCC was trying to draft and get approved by parliament before the elections. Finally on 16 May, the day before the polls, the Malawian parliament met in emergency session to complete the formality of rubber-stamping a new constitution – a provisional document, subject to amendments within the next year – and effectively ending thirty years of one-party rule. In addition officially to permitting opposition parties, the Constitution abolished scores of repressive laws, including those allowing for detention without trial.

Multi-party elections and coalition: wooing the reluctant bride

The curtains were finally drawn on the ruling MCP when the UDF won both the presidential and parliamentary elections on 17 May 1994. But the results revealed the inherent tribal/ethnic and regional tendencies underlying Malawian politics. In nearly all constituencies the trend was that in a region where a presidential candidate had secured a majority vote that party's parliamentary candidates also won. The Commonwealth Election Monitoring Group declared the polls 'free and fair', but Malawi had split along potentially dangerous regional lines.

For the presidency, Bakili Muluzi drew 1,404,754 votes (47.16 per cent); Dr Kamuzu Banda came second with 996,363 votes (33.45 per cent); while Chakufwa Chihana finished a distant third with 552,862 votes, and Kamlepu Kalua mustered a paltry 15,624 votes. The UDF won the populous south, with support from Lilongwe in the centre; Aford swept the north and made some inroads in the northern parts of the central region; and the MCP support held up in rural central Malawi. However, with eighty-four seats out of a total of 177, the UDF finished five seats short of an overall majority; the MCP got fifty-five seats and Aford secured thirty-six, while two constituencies (Nsanje North and Nsanje Southwest) had to face election re-runs because of voting irregularities.[38]

It was perhaps predictable that none of the parties secured an outright victory. However, some significant trends did manifest themselves, leading to the emergence of regional power bases; besides being a serious source of concern, this made coalition inevitable. Although the opposition's much vaunted 'transparency' in government was likely to suffer, main policy platforms were unlikely to change notwithstanding the inevitable manoeuvring. But, to the benefit of all Malawians, power would at least be more diffused than in the past.

With Dr Banda out of the way, Muluzi was at pains to tell Malawians he wanted peace, not confrontation:

> As Malawians we have to work together. To me, what is important is the country – not the UDF or Aford, not Muluzi or Chihana. The UDF government is not a government of vengeance but of reconciliation. It is not a government of one region but of the entire nation. . . . This is a time for reconciliation, not retribution.[39]

Furthermore, he emphasised that his government's priorities were poverty alleviation and food security; in addition, all efforts would have to be made to sustain the democratisation process and safeguard human rights.

Immediately after the elections, Muluzi also indicated that he would prefer coalition to minority government – but he ruled out cooperation with the MCP. However, Chihana continued stubbornly to insist that he would make no deals with parties that he regarded as not *au fait*, rather theatrically lumping the UDF together with the MCP. The quality of democracy, he argued, lay as much in opposition as in government. Not surprisingly, negotiations broke down within a week when the UDF failed to meet Aford's rather unrealistic demands: an 'executive' vice presidency and either the foreign or home ministry for Chihana; seven other ministerial portfolios, including justice, works and supplies, and agriculture; and a 43 per cent quota of deputy ministers and diplomatic and parastatal staff.

Inflexibility on both sides (the UDF's stance that any deal be made public and Aford's insistence that it remained secret) effectively scuppered talks on coalition. Chihana seemed to be at best reluctant to join what he himself called 'a party of recycled MCP politicians'. The essentially regionally based voting pattern and the UDF's lack of an outright majority – although being the largest party in parliament – raised the spectre of a new political instability. A UDF–Aford coalition would have given the new government complete control of the legislature and drawn a firm and clear line between the MCP and its political foes, a development that might have been good for democracy from the start. Thus, not for the first time in Africa, Malawi has shown that democracy can cure some ills but may worsen others.

The exclusion of Aford from the government – and therefore the entire northern region, albeit by their own intransigence – spelt trouble for Malawi, given the legacy of discrimination against and historical exclusion of the north from the country's economic and political mainstream. Common sense demanded coalition rule: an arrangement that was bound to help Malawi along the rough road from dictatorship to a more democratic society, and a deal that could have tempered the glaring regional divisions that the election has so clearly exposed.

Then, in an improbable union – some would say an 'unholy alliance' –
that shocked most Aford supporters, Chihana joined forces with the MCP
(often described by him as 'that party of death and darkness') and signed a
'memorandum of understanding', pledging the two parties to work together
in parliament. Chihana declared that the pact was not meant to derail the
democratisation process, but to make sure the country was not divided
along regional lines.[40] The memorandum alleged that the UDF government
did not appreciate the regional trends as manifested in the voting patterns of the
general election – a coded complaint that Muluzi declined to agree to a
'government of national unity' comprising all parties – and promised opposition unity in the interest of 'national security'. Thus, Aford and the MCP
agreed to work together inside and outside parliament on matters of 'national
importance'.

The pact was a bitter pill to swallow for many Aford members, who saw
themselves as the true champions of democracy in Malawi and the natural
enemies of the MCP. Veteran northern politician, Machipisa Munthali, who
spent twenty-seven years in detention under the MCP government, publicly
expressed disgust with the alliance;[41] and the Reverend Peter Kaleso, who
led Aford's delegation in coalition talks with the government, defected to
the UDF. Dr Mapopa Chipeta, one of the brightest young politicians in
Aford, also fell out with Chihana over the issue but remained loyal to the
party. However, the MCP was buoyant because for it the pact has proved to
be an escape route from political marginalisation.[42]

Having failed to secure a coalition government, Muluzi pressed ahead
with a minority government in spite of the prospect of facing formidable
resistance from a unified opposition front in parliament. Indeed, the MCP–
Aford alliance quickly capitalised on their new-found strength by electing
an Aford member as Speaker of Parliament, while sharing the spoils for the
two deputy speakers. They also voted themselves into control of some key
parliamentary committees, including one which is to draft standing orders
on parliamentary procedures.

But clearly, Muluzi had to continue trying to bring Aford into the new
government for two reasons: first, the UDF's minority position in parliament could damage its legislative programme; and second, failure to make
Aford part of government could further alienate northern sentiment. In an
attempt to win goodwill in Aford-held constituencies, Muluzi toured the
Northern Region and promised more resources to improve educational,
health-care and communications infrastructure in this generally under-
developed area. Throughout the country, he promised that the new government will provide housing and pay monthly allowances to chiefs and

village headmen – a move particularly aimed at penetrating the traditional authorities previously loyal to the MCP.

Then, in another surprise move, it was announced on 26 September that the Constitution would be amended to make provision for a second Vice President and that Chakufwa Chihana would take up the post, in addition to that of Minister of Irrigation and Water Development. Five other Aford colleagues were also included in the Cabinet. Chihana's growing unpopularity and defections of key Aford members must have placed a great deal of pressure on him to enter into another round of talks on coalition with Muluzi's UDF. But while some observers say that Chihana has now salvaged his image, others accuse him of being a 'political prostitute'.[43] Nevertheless, the ruling UDF in coalition with Aford now have 121 seats in parliament, leaving the MCP as the only effective opposition with fifty-six seats.

Interface between the socio-economic environment and politics

It is clear that the cooption of Aford into a governing coalition was a shrewd move by Muluzi to strengthen national unity in the wake of the May elections. Besides the practical advantage of assuring the government of a comfortable, working majority in parliament, it could also reassure potential aid donors, worried about the risks of instability in the new democratic climate. Britain has already indicated that further development aid will depend on the new government's determination to tighten controls in public spending, crack down on corruption, ensure respect for human rights, and introduce a liberalisation of markets and other initiatives which are regarded as crucial for all developing countries.

Alarm bells are already ringing: for most Malawians, the outcome of multi-party politics has fallen woefully short of expectations. Five months after the election, the new government had made little progress in tackling the appalling economic inheritance – which has been worsened by what the World Bank regards as 'major over-expenditure' by the MCP government in its final months, underpinned by 'substantial' borrowing from domestic banks. This left the incoming administration with a budget deficit of about US$40 million and foreign debt of some US$1.9 billion. While seeking financial support and wooing foreign investors during his recent trip to the United States and Britain, Muluzi has had to bring home to donors the fact that Malawi's economy is in absolute dire straits.

But the restoration of aid promised by donors on condition of the successful completion of the democratisation process has yet to materialise in any significant way. And Malawi's economic woes are compounded by the self-devaluation of the *kwacha* by a staggering 29 per cent, blamed on inflation (averaging 23.5 per cent in 1993), foreign exchange hoarding and resultant shortages and the general dearth in foreign aid. Added to this, the IMF is likely to put pressure on the new government to raise interest rates, further stifling investment and constraining economic growth. With inflation at 36 per cent and a projected negative economic growth rate of 9 per cent for 1994, there seems to be a government consensus for a tougher fiscal and public spending regime in the revised budget for 1994/1995.[44]

Almost endemic poverty and rising unemployment are seen as political time-bombs ready to explode in the face of the new government. About six million of the country's 9.5 million people live below the poverty datum line, while fewer than one million of a potential 4.5 million work-force are gainfully employed. The common feature of the Malawi poor is their inability, according to a recent government report, to meet their minimum nutritional requirements and essential non-food needs, equivalent to only US$40 per capita per annum. Indeed, the unemployment situation is extremely acute and has reached record levels. With a per capita GDP of about US$210, Malawi needs to create 400 new jobs every day if it is to stabilise this unemployment problem. Those who do find employment, do so in low-productivity jobs in small-scale agriculture and in informal micro-enterprises. This is compounded by the fact that the formal sector absorbs less than 10 per cent of newcomers to the labour force each year. And Malawi's social indicators reveal even starker features of an embattled society: low life expectancy (forty-eight years) and adult literacy levels (41.9 per cent); while the population growth rate is a high 3 per cent per annum, one in every four children dies before reaching the age of five, and 50 per cent of children under that age suffer from chronic malnutrition.[45]

This shocking socio-economic situation has unleashed unprecedented urban crime. With much of the state's repressive apparatus dismantled, and against the background of a generally deteriorating security situation, there has been a marked increase in, especially, crimes of violence. Rival versions blame common criminals, rogue elements in the Army and police, or ex-Malawi Young Pioneers. But certainly, this is not the Malawi most Malawians know.

The Muluzi government's economic policy emphasises private sector investment through the promotion rather than regulation of private business and the stimulation of healthy competition. This includes the removal of disincentives that stifle business growth, such as excessive taxes and other regulatory constraints. However, it is incumbent on the new power-brokers to create an enabling environment for private sector investment by both local and foreign investors and to encourage diversification in the economy in order to achieve growth and a competitive advantage in regional and international markets.[46] Agricultural production accounts for 90 per cent of exports and the growth of the economy will hinge on the diversification of this sector, which is dominated by tobacco, tea and sugar.

As part of its poverty alleviation programme, the government has stated that it intends to encourage small-scale agro-industries and raise crop prices. Agriculture, the mainstay of the country's economy (43 per cent of GDP), provides employment and subsistence for a majority of Malawi's population (some 85 per cent), but this narrow resource base makes the economy more vulnerable to world commodity market prices and other external shocks. Drought and resultant crop failures have already led to famine and close to three million people are threatened by starvation in many parts of the country, while water shortages regularly occur.

In the drought of the early 1980s, Malawi was the one central and southern African state that did not need to import food. Today soil erosion is aggravated by the search for fuel-wood and enhanced by the competition for land between millions of smallholders and the big tobacco, tea, sugar, coffee and rubber estates. Smallholders are now even cultivating the mountain slopes, exacerbating deforestation. All this impacts on the country's only natural asset: its soil. Industrial wages in Malawi are generally low, and therefore it is a disincentive for rural–urban migration; thus there is less rural–urban drift in Malawi than in neighbouring countries. This makes it even more imperative for the new government to address the land issue with urgency.

CONCLUSION

Dr Banda transformed a small part of south-eastern Africa into a personal fiefdom that symbolised some of the worst excesses of post-colonial governance in Africa. For over a quarter of a century, the country was under his authoritarian rule. The former Life President's influence was present in virtually all aspects of life – social, economic and political – and in the rural areas the name of the nonagenarian *Ngwazi* had even become synonymous with government. His departure from the scene is more than the demise of just another African dictator in the wake of multi-party democracy that has swept across the continent. It marks the end of the most extraordinary of all the men who have ruled African countries in the first three decades of their independence.

But the result of Banda's despotism is that Malawi now lacks a strong civil society and a tradition of competitive politics, the two cornerstones of political democracy. It will take some time, therefore, for most ordinary

Malawians to come to grips with the significant social and political changes that the rest of the 1990s will usher in. The state's strict censorship of the press did not allow most ordinary people fully to grasp Malawi's political and economic situation; nor had it exposed them to changes sweeping across much of Africa today. This situation of limbo will not be altered without a massive public re-education programme.

In the short term, Muluzi's popularity will benefit from a 'liberation dividend' as he dismantles the apparatus of the old one-party state: he immediately closed three of the most notorious prisons (Mikuyu, Nsalika and Nsanje), commuted all outstanding death sentences to life imprisonment and released all remaining political prisoners. But the new President's honeymoon will be short. He will quickly be judged on his ability to create a new, more open style of government at the same time as laying the foundations for a more modern and less feudal economy. Although Muluzi's election victory was more regional than national, he was elected because Malawians expect him to address their chronic poverty and the legacy of state repression.

The process – of creating a new political ethos – cannot be successfully carried out unless Muluzi and his new UDF–Aford government confront the past and critically examine the history of state-directed violations to draw lessons from it for the construction of a viable democracy. A constitutional awareness campaign – for Malawians to debate the new Constitution and suggest changes – is essential to empower the people and give them a sense of ownership in the new order. Such popular participation will enhance a democratic culture and unite the nation behind the Muluzi government as it tackles the multitude of challenges facing it, including MCP domination of public institutions.[47] Otherwise, disillusionment will soon set in and foil the fragile attempt at creating an open society after so many years of authoritarianism.

Indeed, ridding Malawi of Dr Banda seems to have been the easy part; but now comes the difficult part – to erase the stains of the past, press on towards a new era of social justice, peace and prosperity in the Second Republic and yield the fruits of independence promised but not delivered to a restive electorate that naively believes that the new-found democracy is a magic wand which can produce miracles. Behind all the political euphoria lurks the fact that the UDF–Aford government will have to face the daunting task of not only jump-starting but also reinvigorating and resuscitating the economy which has been ravaged by the last two years of drought – a situation compounded by the continued presence of Mozambican refugees (although by the end of September 1994 reduced to an estimated 120,000 – from a one-time high of 1.1 million – through voluntary repatriation, in anticipation of a peaceful outcome of the October 1994 elections in that neighbouring country)[48] and the general economic mismanagement by an inefficient previous regime.

To be sure, Muluzi has pressing problems on his in-tray and he will have to deliver: pledging consensus-style government, free-market capitalism and a crackdown on all human rights abuses, he campaigned on a ticket of democracy, freedom and justice; poverty alleviation and the provision of social services – such as adequate health-care facilities; free and universal primary education within three years, through a crash programme of building new schools and training teachers; and an elimination of structural weaknesses in the economy. The latter include a too-narrow export base, stagnant smallholder agriculture, heavy import dependence and an inefficient public capacity for planning and resource management. However, he faces an uphill battle to rid the bloated civil and diplomatic service of personnel who were employed through graft and nepotism, apart from fulfilling the legitimate aspirations of the electorate. But UDF power-brokers have proved themselves to be tactful politicians and master strategists, eager to forge national unity by using political realism and compassion to patch up societal fragmentation fuelled by differing political leanings. Muluzi has, therefore, implored the civil service to adopt a new culture and role in a plural society and to be professional and non-partisan, ready to serve the government of the day.

But the real test for the Muluzi presidency will be how fast he can move on job creation and poverty alleviation. The economy is on the verge of collapse[49] and needs massive infusions of foreign aid and investment to rebuild the country – some of it already promised by the United States, Britain, the Nordic countries and Japan. Although hard-pressed to raise the necessary capital resources, Muluzi's drive for more foreign aid and investment will depend very much on his ability to convince the international donor community that 'good governance' is at last being practised in Malawi. An enabling environment through a generous investment policy should be created to attract foreign capital into the country.

Malawi cannot forever depend on foreign aid and will not be able to survive on handouts alone, thanks mainly to the widespread political changes that brought both Muluzi and South Africa's President Nelson Mandela to power. South Africa now seems to be the darling of the international donor community, not Malawi. But it should be remembered that there is a symbiotic relationship between economics and politics. Already democracy is under threat in neighbouring Zambia because of the general socio-economic paralysis in that country. The political futures of Angola and Mozambique are even more uncertain.

If the process of democratisation in Malawi is to be strengthened, it is imperative that the Malawian economy – which is in its most desperate state ever – be resuscitated, otherwise a backlash (and possibly a reversal of the democratisation process) is almost inevitable. Malawians feel that a multi-party system is in place, with a democratically elected government and President; and, very unrealistically, they want to see the benefits now! – new jobs, transformed education, improved housing, new hospitals and clinics, increased disposable income. Economic growth and sustained development is, therefore, of the essence in order to support a new-found and fledgling democratic system in Malawi and prevent a tragic relapse into despotism and authoritarianism. Democracy has to be carefully nurtured and democratic values cannot be inculcated in society overnight. A relatively sound economy seems to be an essential ingredient for the ultimate success of a democratic order.

NOTES

1 Two and a half decades ago, Roger Tangri said that 'of all the countries of East and Central Africa, Malawi . . . [has] the least documented record of its history . . . both for the pre-colonial as well as for the colonial . . . [period]': Roger Tangri, *African Reaction and Resistance to the Early Colonial Situation in Malawi, 1891–1915* (Salisbury, Central Africa Historical Association, 1968), p. 1. This is also true for the post-independence period and, therefore, this paper is based mainly on *Agence France-Presse* news reports, newspaper reports, articles in periodicals, and *Summary of World Broadcasts* verbatim reports. For a fairly detailed historical review of Malawi during the pre-colonial and colonial periods, see Bridglal Pachai, *Malawi: The History of the Nation* (London, Longman, 1973).

2 See Denis Venter, 'The Crisis Model as an Analytical Construct: Political Development and Change in Colonial Malawi', *Politeia*, Vol. 8, No. 2, 1989, pp. 18–47, especially pp. 20–21, and 38–39.

3 See Rakiya Omaar, 'Double Standards in British Human Rights Policy', *Southern Africa Political and Economic Monthly*, Vol. 5, No. 1, October 1991, pp. 14–17, especially p. 15.

4 See, for example, Adewale Maja-Pearce, 'The Press in Central and Southern Africa: Zimbabwe, Malawi, Zambia, Botswana, Namibia' [reprinted from *Index on Censorship*, Vol. 21, No. 4, April 1992], pp. 13–14; *Academic Freedom and Human Rights Abuses in Africa: A Report* (New York, Washington and London, Africa Watch, April 1991), pp. 35–40; and Richard Carver, 'Malawi: Severe Repression and Tight Control over Political Life', *Southern Africa Political and Economic Monthly*, Vol. 5, No. 7, April 1992, pp. 35–36.
Banda is now well into his nineties. Whatever his real age is – an educated guess would be between ninety-three and ninety-five – discussion of it was a political offence in Malawi until very recently and therefore strictly forbidden, as it apparently suggested mortality and the possibility of his physical and political demise. For this reason Banda had always refused to groom a successor, thus totally ignoring the power vacuum that would be left upon his

death. His attitude seemed to echo the words of French King Louis XIV: 'Après moi, le déluge'. But in the end Banda had to accept both his mortality and the fact that 'the people' would choose his successor.

5 In a face-to-face meeting, John Tembo does not come across as ruthless but rather as gentle, soft-spoken, considerate and modest. However, for years stories of his harsh manipulation of power filtered out of the country, and the fears and rumours about his dealings continue to persist: interview by the author with the former Minister of State John Tembo, on 13 March 1991 in Blantyre.

6 See Guy Mhone, 'The Political Economy of Malawi: An Overview', in Guy Mhone (ed.), *Malawi at the Crossroads: The Post-Colonial Political Economy* (Harare, SAPES Books, 1992), pp. 1–33, especially pp. 4–8.

7 See Archbishop James Chiona *et al.*, 'Catholic Bishops: "The Truth Shall Set You Free"', *Southern Africa Political and Economic Monthly*, Vol. 5, No. 8, May 1992, pp. 20–22.

8 See Chakufwa Chihana, 'Malawi: Prospects for Democracy', *Southern Africa Political and Economic Monthly*, Vol. 5, No. 8, May 1992, pp. 18–19, especially p. 18.

9 Interview by the author with retired General Melvin Khanga, on 8 May 1993 in Ntcheu – Khanga has always been highly critical of the increasing influence of John Tembo and Cecilia Kadzamira, and during the 1983 government crisis told Dr Banda that he would oppose his handing power temporarily to Tembo. Early in 1992, Banda again asked Khanga to support Tembo in taking over the government, but the army chief said that support would have to be the collective decision of the entire military council – clearly not on the cards, as the Army 'cordially loathed' Tembo. Although generally popular, Khanga fell out with some middle-ranking officers, because he urged restraint when they wanted to topple the government during the May 1992 disturbances.

10 See Tendai Dumbutshena, 'Malawi: The End of a Dictatorship', *Southern Africa Political and Economic Monthly*, Vol. 6, No. 9, June 1993, p. 4.

11 Norway, for example, decided to terminate development aid to Malawi owing to the MCP government's human rights abuses. As a result, it withdrew support for a US$22 million project to develop the telecommunications network in Malawi. This decision marked a tougher line of action towards recipients of Norwegian development aid: *Saturday Star*, Johannesburg, 25 September 1992.

12 As early as July 1992 it became clear, however, that attempts by donor governments to pressurise Malawi over its human rights record were strangely at odds with decisions by the World Bank and the International Monetary Fund. In fact, on 23 June, the World Bank approved its largest loan ever to Malawi: US$120 million in combined balance-of-payments support and emergency drought relief. It brought total lending to Malawi since the Paris meeting to US$199 million. The World Bank basically argued that the economy of a country should not be left to deteriorate to such a level that it would be almost impossible to resuscitate it when the need eventually arose.

13 See *Saturday Star*, Johannesburg, 27 June 1992; and *Financial Times*, London, 13 July 1992.

14 Quoted in *Summary of World Broadcasts*, 30 June 1992, p. ME/1420 B/3.

15 Quoted in the *Daily Times*, Blantyre, 3, 4 and 24 August, and 2 September 1992.

16 Quoted in the *Daily Times*, Blantyre, 6 October 1992.

17 See *ibid.*

18 Quoted in *Summary of World Broadcasts*, 20 October 1992, p. ME/ 1516 ii and 21 October 1992, p. ME/1517 B/3.

19 Interview by the author with President Bakili Muluzi, at the time a businessman and National Chairman of the United Democratic Front (UDF), on 7 May 1993 in Blantyre – a wide-ranging discussion, during which policies and strategies for the referendum were broached.

20 Interview by the author with Augustine Mnthambala, National Vice Chairman of the Alliance for Democracy (Aford), on 10 May 1993 in Lilongwe.

21 See Denis Venter, 'Malawi's Referendum on Multi-Party Politics: Banda's Battle of Hastings?', *International Update*, No. 1, 1993, pp. 1–2.

22 Interview by the author with Professor Brown Chimphamba, Chairman of the National Referendum Commission, on 4 May 1993 in Lilongwe – Chimphamba seemed to be thoroughly frustrated by the role that the Commission had to play as an honest broker between the PCD and PAC, without real power to stamp its authority on proceedings; also by the fact that its brief, to report directly to the President, impinged on its independent action and ability to resolve conflicting standpoints between the government and opposition. In fact, he regarded the Commission as very much a lame duck.

23 Interview by the author with the Reverend Dr Silas Nyirenda, member of the National Referendum Commission, on 3 May 1993 in Lilongwe – since the initial composition of the Commission, he had fallen into disfavour with the opposition and had been replaced as chairman of the PAC.

24 Interview by the author with MacDonald Banda, Secretary of the National Referendum Commission, and at the time Secretary to the President and Cabinet, on 3 May 1993 in Lilongwe – even at this very late stage, barely six weeks before the referendum, Banda was adamant that the two ballot box system was the correct way of handling the referendum poll and did not foresee, at the time, any compromise on this issue with opposition groups (as represented by the PAC).

25 See *Summary of World Broadcasts*, 17 June 1993, p. ME/1717 ii.

26 Quoted in *Summary of World Broadcasts*, 19 June 1993, p. ME/1719 B/1.

27 See Guy Mhone, 'Malawi: Now That the People Have Spoken – What Next?', *Southern Africa Political and Economic Monthly*, Vol. 6, No. 9, June 1993, p. 39.

28 *Ibid.*

29 See *ibid.*, pp. 35–37.

30 Interviews by the author with Tim Mangwazu, Minister of Housing, and President of the Malawi National Democratic Party (MNDP), on 8 February and 28 September 1994 in Pretoria and Lilongwe, respectively – in private conversations, the author advised Mangwazu that a relatively new party – as the MNDP, in fact, was at the time – had very little chance of making an impact in the scheduled May 1994 elections, especially if it had not secured sufficient funding and generally lacked the necessary organisational infrastructure.

31 See *Agence France-Presse*, 12 February, and 25 and 27 March 1994; and *Summary of World Broadcasts*, 5 April 1994, p. AL/1963 A/4.

32 Interview by the author with Professor Kings Phiri, Department of History, Chancellor College, University of Malawi, on 3 October 1994 in Zomba – he

was of the opinion that Chakufwa Chihana made two blunders at a rally in Zomba prior to the May 1994 elections, which cost him dearly in his effort to garner support in the Southern Region. Before the rally, Chihana was introduced to chiefs and headmen from the Zomba region but he failed to accord them privileged seating positions – a serious protocol lapse, perhaps due to the lack of organisational experience among his campaign staff. However, this was taken as an affront to the traditional leadership of the area.

During the course of the rally, he also introduced five members of his party to the crowd, praising them for building Aford and bringing it to the level where it was at the time. The reaction of the crowd was: 'Aha! All people from the Northern Region!' They, therefore, failed to identify with Aford and in the process the party's support in the Southern Region almost evaporated.

33 A perceptive foreign newsman rather poetically observed that most newspapers in Malawi 'find far more satisfaction in using their pages as a rough canvas for raging brush strokes of rancid insult and wild propaganda, signing their vitriol "a reliable source". It's a media free-for-all of surreal proportions': Bruce Cohen in 'Malawi's Magic Carpet Ride to Democracy', *The Weekly Mail and Guardian* (Johannesburg), 26 August to 1 September 1994. Janet Karim of *The Independent*, almost angrily, lamented that '[people] feel let down by such a squabbling media. I hope that all these party papers will go away and leave the news business to us professionals. . . . [And] I hope that we [in Malawi] have reached new maturity where the government can handle an independent, inquiring and critical press': quoted in Andrew Meldrum, 'Malawi: New Actors, Same Play?', *Africa Report*, Vol. 39, No. 4, July/August 1994, p. 54.

34 Interview by the author with Dr Ken Lipenga, Editor-in-Chief of *The Nation*, on 3 October 1994 in Blantyre – he fully supported the view that the Malawian press should adopt a more professional approach, and predicted that a number of the smaller tabloid newspapers will eventually disappear from the scene.

35 Interview by the author with Jake Muwamba, former Malawian Ambassador to the United Nations and Washington, High Commissioner to Ottawa, and now Consultant in Public Relations and Marketing and Member of the Commission Investigating the 'Mwanza Murders', on 4 October in Blantyre – a jovial and relaxed person, Muwamba was scathing on the former MCP regime's record, holding top figures in the Banda administration responsible for gross human rights violations.

36 Interview by the author with Gwanda Chakuamba-Phiri, Vice President of the Malawi Congress Party (MCP), and former Chairman of the Presidential Council and Secretary General of the MCP, on 4 October 1994 in Blantyre – Chakuamba-Phiri was almost arrogantly confident about the MCP's potential to return to government in the not too distant future. He, nevertheless, emphasised the 'important role a strong opposition party like the MCP can play in the new Malawi' – what a turn-around!

37 *The Star* (Johannesburg), 17 May 1994.

38 *Summary of World Broadcasts*, 24 May 1994, p. AL/2005 A/7 and 26 May 1994, p. AL/2006 A/7. In by-elections on 28 June, the MCP won the Nsanje North constituency and the UDF secured the Nsanje Southwest constituency. This brought the final results to UDF (85), MCP (56), and Aford (36): *Agence France-Presse*, 29 June 1994.

39 *Weekend Star* (Johannesburg), 21–22 May 1994.

40 Northerners, although professing to be apolitical, tended to rationalise the Aford–MCP pact in a rather strange way. However, Professor Kings Phiri of the Department of History at the University of Malawi, The Rev. Minjaso Kansilanga of the Church of Central Africa Presbyterian and the Public Affairs Committee, and even Dr Mapopa Chipeta (Aford), newly appointed Minister of Agriculture in the Muluzi government, refuted the contention of earlier interviewees – The Rev. Chande Mhone, Regional Director (Central and South), and The Rev. Jeff Brown Soko, Regional Director (North), Foundation for Integrity of Creation, Justice and Peace, on 29 September 1994 in Lilongwe – that people from the northern and central regions have greater affinities and, therefore, the arrangement between Aford and the MCP makes sense. Quite the opposite!

There is, indeed, a long history of co-operation between the people of the north and the south, dating back as far as the colonial period: for example, their working together in the so-called 'Native Associations' in the 1920s and 1930s, especially in the field of education and in matters pertaining to the colonial civil service. Owing to the fact that a lot of northerners worked and lived in the south (they share a patriarchal system of social organisation, and there are even some language affinities), there has been a great deal of intermarriage between people of the two regions.

41 Interview by the author with Machipisa Munthali (known as the 'Nelson Mandela of Malawi', for having spent twenty-seven years in detention), Alliance for Democracy (Aford) Executive Committee Member, on 27 September 1994 in Lilongwe – he expressed grave doubts about Chihana's leadership of Aford. Chihana had not called an executive committee meeting since the elections and his pact with the MCP was never discussed at party level. He seemed to handle important decisions very much on his own and his dictatorial attitude was beginning to antagonise high-ranking members of the party.

Having now joined the governing coalition, Chihana will be pushing his coalition partners hard to also bring the MCP into a 'government of national unity'. This stance is inexplicable in the light of his previous vehement opposition to the MCP and the Banda regime. His seemingly unprincipled conduct and his tendency to change course suddenly is fast eroding his credibility, even among some of his staunchest supporters. Munthali feels that a younger, more dynamic leader could reactivate Aford to become a real factor in the next election in 1999.

42 Interview by the author with Dr Mapopa Chipeta (Aford), Minister of Agriculture and Livestock Development, on 30 September 1994 in Lilongwe – as the MCP was engaged in a struggle for political survival after the May elections, a possible UDF–MCP alliance had to be forestalled. Aford, therefore, had to make a rather difficult decision to enter into some kind of arrangement with the MCP.

However, the continued exclusion of the MCP from government is posing a serious problem. Aford argues that it could have a moderating influence on the former governing party if it was tied into a 'government of national unity'. Indeed, Aford regards this as of cardinal importance in facilitating national reconciliation. The economic imperative has now forced Aford's hand to join the UDF in a coalition government, but it still wants to play a bridging role *vis-à-vis* the MCP.

43 Interviews by the author with The Rev. Minjaso Kansilanga, Secretary General of the Church of Central Africa Presbyterian (CCAP) and a Member of the Public Affairs Committee (PAC), on 30 September 1994 in Lilongwe; and with Jake Muwamba, former Malawian Ambassador to the United Nations and Washington, High Commissioner to Ottawa, and now Consultant in Public Relations and Marketing and Member of the Commission Investigating the 'Mwanza Murders', on October 4 in Blantyre – both were of the opinion that Chihana had now completely discredited himself by his vacillation and unprincipled conduct. In the process, his image might have been irretrievably damaged.

44 Interview by the author with Arif Zulfiqar, Resident Representative of the World Bank Mission to Malawi, on 29 September 1994 in Lilongwe – he is of the opinion that Press Holdings, which controls one-third of Malawi's GDP, should at least be partially unbundled. Its monopoly position, through its distribution network of seventeen affiliate companies, constitutes a significant structural weakness in the economy and is stifling initiative and keeps small entrepreneurs from entering the market.

The freezing of donor aid to Malawi in 1992 was probably the first and only example where donor countries intervened in the political affairs of a sovereign state (barring pressure that had previously been put on Kenya). This has affected a psychological change in the attitude of donors in that they now try to interfere in the day-to-day running of the government of Malawi, making it known that they disapprove of the regular visits government ministers and their entourages make abroad. These signals are being taken seriously by government and its sensitivity points towards the overdependence of Malawi on foreign aid, now worsened by the prevailing drought, a general economic decline and, until recently, the political uncertainty of the government not having a workable majority (on 24 September 1994 Aford joined the governing coalition). The Minister of Finance, Aleke Banda, has now promised to curb government spending and has made principal secretaries in all government departments personally responsible for overspending.

45 Interview by the author with El-Mostafa Benlamlih, Deputy Resident Representative of the United Nations Development Programme (UNDP) in Malawi, on 28 September 1994 in Lilongwe – he emphasised the need for Malawi to move away from its overdependence on agriculture, especially the production of tobacco and maize.

46 Interviews by the author with Arif Zulfiqar, Resident Representative of the World Bank Mission to Malawi, on 29 September 1994 in Lilongwe; with John Carter, Group Chief Executive, Press Corporation Ltd, on 30 September 1994 in Lilongwe; and with Pangani Thipa, Deputy Executive Director, Malawi Chamber of Commerce and Industry, on October 4 in Blantyre – all three stressed the importance of creating a favourable investment climate, especially in view of Malawi's almost desperate economic situation. Although foreign aid might provide some assistance in the short term, structural weaknesses in the economy had to be addressed in order to achieve sustained growth and development over the medium to longer term.

47 The dissolution of the boards of all parastatals released the grip on the public sector of John Tembo, who chaired Air Malawi, the Malawi Housing Corporation, the Malawi Development Corporation, the Council of the University of

Malawi and many other institutions. However, his influence may still be felt in the private sector, through his chairmanship of Press Corporation Limited. In 1993, this corporate giant (with holdings in agribusiness, manufacturing, distribution, service industries, and banking) recorded a colossal turnover of some US$400 million and profits of around a quarter of gross domestic product (GDP).

The Press group is wholly owned by Press Trust, nominally set up 'for the benefit of the Malawian people' and administered by Dr Banda, John Tembo and Louis Chimango. This concentration of economic power perfectly reflects the old concentration of political power, with its system of patronage and sycophancy. It is, therefore, not surprising that worries remain about the monopolistic tendencies of Press Corporation, and it clearly faces an uncertain future in the new order.

48   Interview by the author with Heikki Keto, Deputy Representative of the United Nations High Commissioner for Refugees (UNHCR) in Malawi, on 28 September 1994 in Lilongwe – at the height of the civil war in Mozambique, the number of refugees from that country in Malawi reached some 1.1 million. Today, about 175,000 refugees remain after more than 800,000 have voluntarily returned to Mozambique and some 104,000 (up to the end of September 1994) were assisted in being repatriated. Of the twelve affected districts in Malawi, there officially remain refugees only in the Nsanje district and even this figure might be inflated because many Malawians are in a position fraudulently to obtain food packages distributed by the UNHCR.

49   The inflationary impact of the *kwacha* flotation against foreign currencies – a decision taken by the previous regime – is now hitting most people hard. This causes President Muluzi to refer continuously to 'belt-tightening' and 'responsible wage bargaining' and he repeatedly stresses the need for foreign investment. The *kwacha* has continued to depreciate to an all-time low against the US dollar by the beginning of October 1994. Although the initial change of course in foreign exchange policy was intended to stimulate exports, the balance-of-payments situation and the economy generally, it is unlikely to be particularly effective in doing so during 1994 because of supply-side problems in the economy and weak international demand for the country's export commodities.

*   The author wishes to thank Madeline Lass, for the efficient and thorough work she has done in editing the final draft of this chapter.

BIBLIOGRAPHY

Academic Freedom and Human Rights Abuses in Africa: A Report, New York, Washington and London: Africa Watch, April 1991.

Agence France-Presse, 12 February, 25 and 27 March 1994; and 29 June 1994.

Richard Carver, 'Malawi: Severe Repression and Tight Control over Political Life', *Southern Africa Political and Economic Monthly*, Vol. 5, No. 7, April 1992.

Chakufwa Chihana, 'Malawi: Prospects for Democracy', *Southern Africa Political and Economic Monthly*, Vol. 5, No. 8, May 1992.

Archbishop James Chiona *et al.*, 'Catholic Bishops: "The Truth Shall Set You Free"', *Southern Africa Political and Economic Monthly*, Vol. 5, No. 8, May 1992.

Bruce Cohen, 'Malawi's Magic Carpet Ride to Democracy', *The Weekly Mail and Guardian*, Johannesburg, 26 August to 1 September 1994.

Daily Times, Blantyre, 3, 4, 24 August, 2 September and 6 October 1992.

Tendai Dumbutshena, 'Malawi: The End of a Dictatorship', *Southern Africa Political and Economic Monthly*, Vol. 6, No. 9, June 1993.

Financial Times, London, 13 July 1992.

Adewale Maja-Pearce, 'The Press in Central and Southern Africa: Zimbabwe, Malawi, Zambia, Botswana, Namibia' (reprinted from *Index on Censorship*, Vol. 21, No. 4, April 1992).

Andrew Meldrum, 'Malawi: New Actors, Same Play?', *Africa Report*, Vol. 39, No. 4, July/August 1994.

Guy Mhone, 'Malawi: Now That the People Have Spoken – What Next?', *Southern Africa Political and Economic Monthly*, Vol. 6, No. 9, June 1993.

Guy Mhone, 'The Political Economy of Malawi: An Overview', Guy Mhone (ed.), *Malawi at the Crossroads: The Post-Colonial Political Economy*, Harare: SAPES Books, 1992.

Rakiya Omaar, 'Double Standards in British Human Rights Policy', *Southern Africa Political and Economic Monthly*, Vol. 5, No. 1, October 1991.

Bridglal Pachai, *Malawi: The History of the Nation*, London, Longman, 1973.

Saturday Star, Johannesburg, 27 June and 25 September 1992.

Summary of World Broadcasts, 30 June and 20 and 21 October 1992; 17 and 19 June 1993; and 5 April, and 24 and 26 May 1994.

Roger Tangri, *African Reaction and Resistance to the Early Colonial Situation in Malawi, 1891–1915*, Salisbury: Central Africa Historical Association, 1968.

The Star, Johannesburg, 17 May 1994.

Denis Venter, 'Malawi's Referendum on Multi-Party Politics: Banda's Battle of Hastings?', *International Update*, No. 1, 1993.

Denis Venter, 'The Crisis Model as an Analytical Construct: Political Development and Change in Colonial Malawi', *Politeia*, Vol. 8, No. 2, 1989.

Weekend Star, Johannesburg, 21–22 May 1994.

9 Zambia: Kaunda and Chiluba

Enduring patterns of political culture

Jan Kees van Donge

Democratisation in Zambia can be considered a success story. A mass-based popular movement brought sufficient pressure to bear to abolish the one-party state, and the subsequent multi-party elections on 31 October 1991 led to a peaceful change of government. The situation in Zambia offers a perspective on African politics after democratisation: a new political configuration has emerged after twenty-seven years' rule by the United National Independence Party (UNIP) under the leadership of Kenneth Kaunda. The expression 'new political configuration' may be misleading, however. Another political party is in power – the Movement for Multi-party Democracy (MMD) – under another president – Frederick Chiluba – but major aspects of Zambian politics have not changed. Democratisation was supposed to lead to a parliamentary system of government, but power is still concentrated in the presidency. Legally, Zambia is a multi-party state, but in fact it is ruled by one party. MMD dominates in all regions of the country, except for Eastern Province. Before the introduction of a one-party state, UNIP dominated in all regions, except Southern Province. There are numerous opposition parties, but they are fragmented and ineffective. As a consequence, three years on, it is within the ruling party, rather than between contending parties, that political competition is to be found.

The continuities between UNIP and MMD had already been commented upon before the elections, and this has remained a major topic in political discussion. Chilufya Kapwepwe, a member of parliament for MMD, said shortly after the election: 'After six weeks in power, the leaders of the MMD appear to be no different from the fallen government of Kenneth Kaunda'. Edward Shamwana, one of the founders of MMD, commented in March 1992: 'There is no visible change in style in government since MMD is in power'. These comments are striking as they were made by people whose opposition to Kaunda and UNIP dates from long before the formation of MMD. Chilufya Kapwepwe is the daughter of Simon Kapwepwe who was Kaunda's childhood friend and close political companion. From the time he broke away from UNIP in the early 1970s until his death, however, he was Kaunda's implacable enemy. Kapwepwe was detained for long periods. Shamwana was sentenced to death – a sentence later commuted to life imprisonment – because of an attempt to topple Kaunda in 1980.

Apparently, there are strong enduring patterns in Zambian political behaviour – an enduring political culture – and it seems appropriate to view the reintroduction of multi-partyism from this perspective.[1] The analysis presented here takes issue with the political discourse normally associated with democratisation movements. Such discourse tends to be monocausal and ahistorical: no attention is paid to the effects of pressures in society, as distinct from the objectives of a few actors, in the creation of one-partyism and presidentialism. The dominant ruler is seen as the prime mover in political life since independence.

Economic decline is then also seen as directly related to the lack of democracy due to presidentialism and the one-party system. A politically privileged group has monopolised economic life and destroyed it.[2] The continuities after the abolition of one-partyism might be explained in similar ahistorical terms, but the argument put forward here is that one-partyism and presidentialism arose as responses to tangible political pressures. These forces remain unaltered after a change of government.

An analysis, in terms of political culture, which searches for deeply embedded tendencies towards action should not itself be static. The structures of a political culture are constructed by actors and can therefore also be changed by actors' social practices. There are distinct differences as well as similarities between the Kaunda and Chiluba periods. Zambia is now a much more open society where criticism is much more tolerated. Kaunda could present himself as above all parties and did not deign to debate with those who criticised him. At most, he answered critics, but Chiluba has to face their challenges in press conferences and on TV. Such changes may be seen as embedded in the emergence of new professional groups in Zambia which define themselves much more independently of the state and politics. Politicians in Zambia can nowadays easily proliferate outside the party structure dominated by the President. In fact, all political parties have to cope with intense internal competition for leadership. This is partly a result of multi-partyism, but it is also a manifestation of a struggle between generations. Old names which have been around in Zambian politics since independence continue to remain important in all parties, and political strife within parties is regularly expressed in terms of a generation struggle.

This contribution, therefore, will analyse the Zambian democratisation process and its aftermath in order to disentangle enduring patterns of political behaviour and significant changes in Zambian political life. For that purpose it is appropriate first to characterise the Zambian political process during the Kaunda years.

THE KAUNDA PERIOD

This necessarily sketchy account aims to elucidate the paradoxical nature of Zambian political life in the Kaunda period. On the one hand, political power was centred in the President, while at the same time it was diffused among many offices. Kaunda relied on repression; but opposition was often tolerated within the party as well as from non-governmental platforms, and he coopted it as much as possible. One-partyism never succeeded in regimenting Zambian political life. Kaunda and his government were accused of mismanagement of the economy, but there were always enquiries into, and court cases about, mismanagement and corruption. A unidimensional view does not do justice to this period.

The most striking aspect of Kaunda's rule was his attempt to make his party a maximum coalition.[3] UNIP emerged in 1958 as a breakaway party from the African National Congress (ANC), and it is typical that they called themselves the UNITED National Independence Party. The party won the independence elections in all regions, except for Southern Province which remained loyal to the ANC under the leadership of Harry Nkumbula. Kaunda proclaimed the one-party state as his ideal in the period from independence until 1972, but he wanted to establish it through the ballot box. From the late 1960s, however, he was confronted with fragmentation of his support. First the United Party (UP) under the leadership of Nalumino Mundia broke away but subsequently merged with the ANC, partly to protect itself against repression. In 1971, Kapwepwe formed his United Progressive Party (UPP). At this point, Kaunda started to rely heavily on suppression. He resorted to mass detentions which – again paradoxically – hit especially UNIP's leadership in the mining towns on the Copperbelt. The party seemed to turn against itself.[4] At the same time, he made overtures to the ANC, and the intention of proclaiming a one-party state was announced jointly in Choma, in the heart of Southern Province. It was enacted after a commission of enquiry under the chairmanship of Mainza Chona toured the whole nation to hear views. After one-partyism was established, Kaunda continued to woo Kapwepwe back into the UNIP fold. He seemed to be successful in 1978, but Kapwepwe insisted on the unacceptable step of challenging Kaunda for the party leadership. He succeeded in coopting Nalumino Mundia, who had been detained twice by Kaunda, the second time after the introduction of the one-party state which

Mundia had refused to accept. Mundia rose later, however, to the position of Prime Minister in the one-party state.

Kaunda extended the top leadership continuously. He enlarged the Cabinet by introducing Cabinet Ministers for each province in 1968. After the introduction of the one-party state, he duplicated the ministerial structure with sectoral and provincial members of UNIP's Central Committee. He also surrounded himself more and more with special advisers, each having sectoral responsibilities. The Army leadership was increasingly involved in government and the heads of the parastatal sector played a similar role in his entourage. Again, cooptation was the major political strategy to which he resorted. The enlargement of this elite group which surrounded him made the power structure in the country opaque, except for the fact that Kaunda was at the centre.

The second aspect of Kaunda's rule was, therefore, the firmly entrenched presidential system. He never abolished the state of emergency which was promulgated during the rising of the Lumpa sect in 1964.[5] During the whole of his rule, parliament remained at best a platform to let off steam and at worst, an inert mass.[6] Presidential rule had been the most contentious issue during the hearings of the Chona Commission to establish a one-party state. The Commission produced a green paper; the government responded with a white paper. None of the recommendations in the green paper to limit presidential power – notably a limitation of terms in office – was taken up by the government.[7]

Kaunda's presidential powers were vast. The most extreme of these was his power to detain without trial, but the most crucial was his prerogative in appointments. Top officials were sacked and appointed at will during the Kaunda period, and official reasons were not given. Few among the elite went permanently into oblivion; many made remarkable comebacks. The effects of this were shattering to the people involved when sacked, but great loyalty was rekindled in the event of a politician returning to power.

A third major aspect of the Kaunda period was the persistence of opposition. This was mainly along regional lines in the first decade after independence. It reached its height at the UNIP national conference of 1967, where Kaunda actually resigned for one night. The main issue was whether regions which were party strongholds should have more influence than others in the selection of the national leadership or whether the leadership of the country should be regionally balanced. From then until the end of his rule, Kaunda applied the latter option.

Sectionalism in Zambia is mostly expressed in terms of the language groups which are dominant in particular provinces. The most significant divisions are between Bemba speakers in Northern Province, Luapula

Province and in the urban areas of the Copperbelt; Chinyanja speakers in Eastern Province and in the capital Lusaka; Lozi speakers in Western Province; Tonga speakers in Southern Province. The breakaway parties UP and UPP were strongly associated with particular regional and ethnic groups, the Lozis in Western Province and the Bemba speakers in Northern Zambia and on the Copperbelt, respectively. Such sectionalism can probably best be interpreted as resulting from intra-elite struggles. It was a crucial background factor in the events leading up to the formation of a one-party state.[8] After one-partyism regulated political competition, tribalism was not a major political force in Zambian politics any more. It remained as a subdued factor.

Other opposition forces became much more vocal, however.[9] First there was opposition among intellectuals. The University of Zambia (UNZA) experienced dramatic closures in 1971 and 1976. The issues involved were then tied to the struggles in Southern Africa. Later, university closures became a common occurrence, with bread-and-butter issues at the centre of the debate. Protest against party dominance was, however, always an element in the politics surrounding UNZA. During the 1980s, intellectuals in both the Law Association of Zambia and the Economics Club voiced opposition. These forums also provided platforms for businessmen – very many of whom had previously held prominent government posts – to vent critical views.

Much more dramatic, however, was the urban rioting in protest at rising food prices. These clashes were very serious; for example, those in 1987 caused fifteen deaths. Important sections of the urban Zambian population – especially the mineworkers – were organised in trade unions. Kaunda contained their power until the early 1980s through such measures as cooptation of trade union leaders and government controls over unions, but these strategies failed after 1980, and Kaunda was confronted with a militant trade union movement.

Lastly, there were several coup attempts. The most important one (1980) was foiled at the last minute, although the role played in it by the Army was probably minimal. Two prominent figures in the Zambian elite, Edward Shamwana and Valentine Musakanya, tried to seize power with the help of a group of Zairian mercenaries. Christon Mwamba Tembo's attempt in 1989 was, judging from the court hearings, more inspired by fantasy than anything else. The last coup attempt, by Mwamba Luchembe, was the most puzzling of them all. It seemed that he acted on his own and walked into the Zambian broadcasting studios to announce to the background of soft rumba music that the armed forces had taken over. This led to mass jubilation in the streets, but this manifestation was severely repressed. There has been speculation about wider involvement in Luchembe's attempt, but it is unlikely that it was different in character from the other attempts: key figures in the army command were not involved, and there seems little reason to believe that substantial parts of the armed forces were a focus for protest.[10]

An appreciation of the declining economic fortunes of Zambia is essential to any understanding of the fervour and persistence of this opposition. Zambia depends for its foreign exchange and government income on the copper mines. Thus, the disastrous decline – especially since the mid-1970s – of copper prices seriously impaired the underlying strength of the economy.[11] This could have been foreseen. It is generally overlooked that Kapwepwe as Minister of Finance in 1968, and again when he broke away in 1971, was extremely concerned about the lack of attention to the fragile base of copper income. A political style which depends upon cooptation on as broad a front as possible cannot cope with decline in resources to distribute. It was not surprising that political protest became most fierce in urban streets where unemployment became increasingly rampant, and rises in food prices, demanded by Zambia's creditors, were a threat to people's very existence.

Mismanagement of the economy was rife. Government exposures of malpractices did not re-establish that government's legitimacy. For example, Francis Nkhoma, an ex-governor of the Bank of Zambia, did not make any denials at his trial, but claimed that what he had done was normal practice for a governor. Nkhoma's appointment as central bank governor was a surprise as he had been employed by Barclays Bank and had resisted high office in government. He was expected, therefore, to be more immune to malpractices. It seemed, however, that whoever was appointed governor of the bank was deemed to line his pockets. Nkhoma's successor was a Canadian.

As in many other African countries, private wealth contrasted more and more sharply with public squalor. Such wealth was often associated with politics. The moral stature of politics was therefore severely undermined towards the end of the Kaunda period.

THE RETURN OF MULTI-PARTYISM IN ZAMBIA

The call for multi-partyism should be seen not as a sudden break with the past, but rather as a logical expression of opposition which had always been there.[12] Two trade unionists called for a referendum on the one-party state in February 1990 because the apathy in party elections was a sign that enthusiasm for one-partyism had eroded to an unacceptable degree. In the next few months, the university was closed; and there were many deaths during protests against rising food prices and in the wake of Luchembe's aborted army coup. Kaunda's consent in April 1990 to the demand for a referendum can therefore also be seen as an attempt to regain legitimacy.

He was, however, confronted with a maximum coalition, the same political device to which he had always resorted. The Movement for Multi-party Democracy (MMD) was formed at a meeting at Lusaka's Garden Hotel in May 1990. Two prominent ex-UNIP politicians were leading this movement: Arthur Wina, the boy wonder Minister of Finance in the independence Cabinet was the leader and the ex-minister of Foreign Affairs, Vernon Mwaanga, his deputy. The original leadership of MMD was dominated by people from one part of the country: Lozis from Western Province. In the course of time, however, MMD attracted a variety of people from other walks of life and from all of Zambia's provinces.

MMD attracted a big following among the elite. Some prominent UNIP politicians joined, the most notable being two from North-western Province: Humphrey Mulemba, a UNIP member of parliament and ex-secretary general of the party, and Ludwig Sondashi, a high-ranking party bureaucrat who was also an MP. Mulemba, the ex-chief of the single party, declared he had always been against the one-party state. The politicians who crossed over from UNIP were all graduates. Professionals who had already voiced opposition soon became members of the new party. Two Northerners, Ephraim Chibwe and Emmanuel Kasonde, had spoken out against the political system in forums like the Economics Club and the Law Association of Zambia. They had been prominent in the financial system of the country, and after that they went into private business.[13] Prominent lawyers were particularly vocal in MMD. Roger Chongwe, originating from Eastern Province, had already used legal professional organisations as a platform to attack the one-party state before the formation of MMD. Others were Levy Mwanawasa, who came from Central Region, and the ex-detainee Shamwana, from Central Province. Shamwana was one of those, detained because of alleged involvement in coups, who had been released by Kaunda. MPs from Southern Province – which was an opposition area before one-partyism – virtually all defected to the new movement. Mwamba Luchembe, a Northerner and Christon Tembo, an Easterner, joined MMD. Godfrey Miyanda, an ex-Army general (Southern/Eastern) who had been detained in connection with the 1980 coup, also joined.

MMD was not merely an elite movement, however. Enormous crowds were mobilised for meetings and demonstrations. More importantly, trade union leaders were prominent in the movement: they included the President of the Zambian Congress of Trade Unions (ZCTU), Frederick Chiluba, a Luapulan, and his deputy, Newstead Zimba, from the East. They represented a long-standing opposition to Kaunda and UNIP. In the early 1980s they had been detained and, unlike many other trade union leaders, had refused to be coopted by Kaunda. Important pressure towards the introduction of multi-partyism came also from the churches, who were outside MMD. The Catholic bishops issued an episcopal letter in which they argued that a referendum on the one-party state was unnecessary, and thus a waste of money, as the outcome was clear.

Kaunda wanted to delay the referendum for administrative reasons. In the months between April and September 1990 the call for an immediate referendum on the one-party state became louder and louder, and later the demands were to move to multi-partyism without a referendum. Kaunda gave in to the opposition at UNIP's national council meeting in September 1990. He agreed that the referendum was superfluous. The outcome was clear beforehand, and it would be a waste of money for a country desperately short on essentials like medicine and schoolbooks to organise one.

Kaunda promised multi-party elections, but a new constitution would have to be drawn up to organise these. He announced, therefore, a Commission of Enquiry into the reintroduction of multi-partyism. The composition of this Commission was broad and included representatives of opposition groups. The Commission was carefully balanced regionally. Virtually none of those chosen were prominent in MMD, however. The chairman and vice chairman had been professors at UNZA: Patrick Mvunga, a lawyer originating from Eastern Province and Muyunda Mwanalushi, a psychologist from Western Province. The Commission included, for example, the chairman of the Law Association of Zambia, Julius Sakala, an Easterner; and a Roman Catholic Bishop, Tresford Mpundu, from the North. The trade union movement was represented by Herbert Bweupe, vice chairman of ZCTU, originating from Luapula, and Samuel Lungu, vice secretary general of ZCTU, from the East. Two representatives from MMD were invited, both Lozis from Western Province: Arthur Wina, the veteran ex-UNIP politician and Akashambatwa Mbikusita-Lewanika, a young economist.

Kaunda's strategy was thus to forge a national consensus on political reform through a broadly composed commission. But this was thwarted by MMD. They boycotted the Commission on the grounds that they were not consulted on its formation. It is significant that the trade unionists who joined the Commission lost their posts in the ZCTU elections which were held shortly afterwards. Chiluba and Zimba, both MMD leaders, were then re-elected unopposed. Throughout the period up to the election in October 1991, MMD opted for a strategy of maximising demands and refused encapsulation by Kaunda in a national forum. MMD did submit evidence to the Commission in the end. The reason may be that the hearings of the Commission proved to be popular. MMD's position was that a UNIP government was partisan and could therefore not properly conduct multi-party elections. The first priority was to install a bipartisan interim government. The state of emergency which had been in force in Zambia since independence had to be withdrawn immediately. Elections should be held under international supervision. A new constitution should abolish the presidential system and reintroduce parliamentary sovereignty.

Some constitutional changes had already been introduced before the Commission reported. On 30 November 1990 parliament voted unanimously for a constitutional amendment which made the introduction of multi-partyism possible. This was ratified by Kaunda in December, and MMD registered immediately as a political party on 4 January 1991. MMD held a national convention at the beginning of March to elect an executive. Thus, despite denying the legitimacy of political change initiated by a UNIP government, MMD used the opportunities which the changes in the law gave them. They also took part in a commission drawing constituency boundaries and a commission to look at the divestiture of party assets from the state.

The Mvunga Commission reported at the end of April 1991, and a government white paper on constitutional reform was published in June. The proposal was strongly inspired by the American Constitution and the doctrine of separation of powers. Executive power would be in the hands of the President; the legislature would consist of two chambers and have a limited power of veto over the budget. A constitutional court should have the power to check unconstitutional usurpation of powers and infringements of human rights. This was unacceptable to MMD who argued that the proposed constitution vested too much power in the President. Such a president could continue to maintain a state of emergency, detain political opponents and use his powers for political appointments. MMD proposed simply to reintroduce the Zambian Westminster-style Constitution of 1964, arguing that the government should emerge from a parliamentary majority and not from the powers of an elected president with executive powers. UNIP reacted by saying that they had always been accused of imitating Eastern Europe and that now there were protests when they took the United States as a model.

All along, MMD had maintained their demands for an interim government to prepare for elections and constitutional change; for repeal of the state of emergency; and for international supervision of elections. They proposed an interim government consisting of the chairman of the Supreme Court, the Speaker of Parliament and the chairman of the Electoral Commission. Kaunda and UNIP maintained that the present parliament was legitimately elected, had a mandate until 1993 and that therefore the power to change the Constitution was in their hands. Similarly, the powers under the state of emergency had been conferred on the President by the parliament. They further maintained that the present Constitution did not allow for the possibility of an interim government, and that, as there was no breakdown of law and order in the country, there was no reason to abrogate national sovereignty. They agreed that election observers would be welcome, but that outsiders should not organise the election.

The process of political reform was deadlocked. Kaunda proposed talks with MMD which seemed to be in disarray. One spokesman, Levy Mwanawasa, said that MMD would boycott the coming elections, but this was denied by MMD foreman Arthur Wina. MMD came under intense pressure from groups which had advocated multi-partyism, such as the Law Association of Zambia and church leaders, to resume the dialogue. In a surprising move, as he had recently again closed the university, Kaunda asked student leaders to mediate. Their mediation was successful, and Chiluba, by now President of MMD, met Kaunda. They were photographed shaking hands.

A slightly amended constitution was rushed through parliament. The state of emergency was not repealed however, and the Zambian government itself organised the elections announced by Kaunda for 31 October 1991. Kaunda and Chiluba once more shared a common platform when they participated in a massively attended church service to pray for peaceful elections, but there were no references to politics on this occasion.

The elections resulted in an overwhelming victory for Chiluba and MMD which won 125 of the 150 parliamentary seats. Only a quarter of the voters (24.21 per cent) voted for Kaunda, and Eastern Province was the only part of the country in which UNIP held on to huge support.[14] Turnout at these polls was low (45 per cent). The turnout figure is always to an extent arbitrary where population registration is less than perfect, but the low turnout may also reflect the more general popular mood as the process of democratisation wore on.[15] Once Kaunda had promised multi-party elections, the great intensity of desire for these elections started to abate.

WHY THIS OUTCOME?

Three questions spring to mind given this outcome. Why did UNIP lose? Why did MMD win? Why was the reintroduction of multi-partyism successful?

Kaunda campaigned hard during the whole period, using his language of love, peace and reconciliation. He invited trade union leaders for talks to tell him 'where we have gone wrong'. He called on ex-detainees like Shamwana and Tembo to return to UNIP as they had had such a good understanding with Kaunda in the past. His old tactics of forming unlikely alliances with adversaries did not succeed, however: there were no notable defections from MMD, but many from UNIP. Kaunda's attempt to encapsulate MMD by portraying the reintroduction of multi-partyism as a joint exercise was resisted all along by the new party.

Christianity is deeply engrained in Zambia, and Kaunda tried hard to establish his Christian credentials and to get the churches on his side. Christianity had always played a major part in his appeal to consensus underlying his strategy of the broad coalition. The twenty-fifth anniversary of the formation of the United Church of Zambia, into which many Protestant churches had merged, provided therefore an ideal forum in which he deplored the fact that both the Roman Catholics and the Hindus were still outside this ecumenical body. The logic of this statement may escape outsiders, but it is typical of Kaunda's political style to embrace as wide a spectrum as possible. He failed, however, to mobilise support on a platform of church unity. A prayer meeting of fundamentalist churches at State House led to divisions among these churches. Kaunda used a visit of the Anglican Bishop of Botswana as a forum to attack the church leaders who, he said, were carrying out a hate campaign against him. Kaunda charged that they had even gone so far as to accuse him of the death of the Archbishop of Kasama, Elias Mutale, who had died in a road accident. He succeeded, at best, in neutralising church opposition. A meeting with church leaders in November 1990 ended in a neutral communique containing many pious words.

The churches did not identify with particular parties after multi-partyism was reintroduced. They became active in monitoring groups and mediated in the deadlock before the elections. It is typical that the women's wing of the Zambian Christian Council organised an ecumenical church service in Lusaka's Anglican Cathedral, attended by Chiluba and Kaunda, where egoism among politicians was the main theme of the sermons.

The chiefs, salaried officials and therefore dependent upon government, were Kaunda's other main targets in the campaign. UNIP had coopted paramount chiefs, like the Litunga of Barotseland and Chitimukolo of the Bemba onto the Central Committee. Chiefs from Lundazi, a UNIP stronghold, assured Kaunda of their support, but stressed their neutrality in political conflicts as they were above the parties. On the question of electoral support, chiefs resorted mostly to a balancing act as they were also under pressure from MMD. Chiluba said unambiguously that the chiefs would lose their positions if they could not be neutral. A chief in Northwestern Province was pressurised into withdrawing as a UNIP parliamentary candidate. The Bemba paramount chief Chitimukulo was stoned when campaigning for UNIP and withdrew from the Central Committee just before the elections.

Most important, however, was the fact that no other UNIP politicians besides Kaunda were campaigning with any impact. There were recommendations to reinvigorate internal democracy in UNIP, but, at the crucial Mulungushi UNIP national convention before the elections, UNIP appeared still to be synonymous with Kaunda. Enoch Kavindele, a member of UNIP's Central Committee, had decided to challenge Kaunda for the leadership. The party was doomed, according to him, if it did not rejuvenate itself. He went out of his way to pay respect to Kaunda and asked him to accept a position in the background as anchor of the nation. Kavindele portrayed himself openly as a successful businessman and said that, while the country had needed political heroes in the past, it needed economic heroes now. He met with great obstruction. He could not register at the appointed time as a candidate because the chairman of UNIP's electoral commission had gone to Kasama. In the meantime, the radio broadcast UNIP commercials supporting Kaunda as candidate – commercials which were only withdrawn when Kavindele threatened to go to court. He alleged that the composition of delegations to the national convention was manipulated in Kaunda's favour. At the convention he was ostracised, and he withdrew his candidature.

UNIP espoused very few issues. The only exception was their insistence on the job losses and hardships which would result from MMD's stress on private enterprise. They fought essentially a negative campaign, discrediting the MMD leadership. Just before the elections, in advertisements under the heading 'UNIP, the voice of love and peace', UNIP released accusations against MMD leaders of involvement in drug dealing. They played the tribal card and accused MMD of being Bemba-dominated. In fact, the overrepresentation of Bemba speakers in MMD's leadership was a logical consequence of the rejection of tribal balancing. In the campaign, only strength among the grassroots and skill in mobilising votes counted. Kaunda was therefore UNIP's only asset and stressed increasingly his integrity as compared with that of MMD's leadership. He had, however, to a great extent lost his moral appeal, not least because of his dynastic tendencies. Two of his sons were big in UNIP politics; he himself appeared with a daughter – who had no political position – at UNIP's national council in October 1990. The trial of his son Kambarage on the charge of murdering a girlfriend was the most damaging factor, however. Kambarage stood trial on a murder charge, but, wearing in court a UNIP campaign badge and making V-signs, he portrayed the trial as political.

In the course of the campaign, MMD became more and more identified with Chiluba. Chiluba was not one of the trade unionists who had made the initial call for a referendum, neither was he on the first executive formed at the founding of MMD. Indeed, before MMD's first national convention, Arthur Wina had to deny rumours that Chiluba had been expelled at the last meeting of the interim executive. None the less, Chiluba emerged as the overwhelming victor at the convention elections with 683 votes as compared with 208 for Arthur Wina, 186 for Humphrey Mulemba and 24 for Edward Shamwana. This was a clear sign that MMD could not do without Chiluba's popularity if it wanted to win elections. His popularity stemmed in the first place from the fact that, unlike the others, he had never accepted high office under Kaunda, and, again unlike the others, he was not an intellectual. He had risen in the trade union movement through grassroots organising.

Chiluba immediately faced accusations of tribalism. Rex Mashumbamba, an MMD official in North-western Province, caught the mood: Western, North-western, Eastern, Central and Southern Province were disappointed. In other words, the Copperbelt and the two northern provinces – the Bemba speakers – were dominating MMD. The call for regional balancing was soon heard: if two provinces which had 1.3 million inhabitants got eighteen seats on the MMD executive and another province with one million inhabitants got only two seats, then these elections could not be fair. In the aftermath of the MMD convention elections, Kaunda concentrated his campaign in Western Province and North-western Province, the respective home areas of Wina and Mulemba – the losers in the contest for the top post. Throughout the whole campaign, UNIP compared their regional balancing with the domination of the Bemba in MMD. The MMD coalition held, however. Wina and Chiluba campaigned together in Western Province, a fact which is remarkable as there is long-standing antagonism to the Bemba there.

Chiluba became increasingly the personification of MMD. Programmatic issues hardly played a role, except with respect to constitutional matters. MMD's programme claimed that the deplorable state of the economy was the result of mismanagement by commandist, interventionist political authority. It offered little, however, on how the economy could be revived. Vinars Kumba, a journalist with the *Sunday Times of Zambia*, commented: 'How can a political party want to reduce income tax and raise government salaries; how can one increase prices paid to farmers and reduce the price of maize meal'. There was, nevertheless, a widespread, almost eschatological, expectation that multi-partyism would cure Zambia's economic ills. This arose not because of concrete policy measures, but because of a resurgence of belief in integrity in politics personified by Chiluba. Chiluba occupied the moral high ground in Zambian politics as he had never in the past been tempted by political office, which was associated with economic failure. This personal popularity of Chiluba meant he also had the possibility of keeping the coalition together. If fellow politicians wanted to do without him, they could not.

A final factor accounting for Chiluba's success was the failure of other opposition parties to attract a sufficient following to split the vote. Many parties were formed along a colourful spectrum: for example, the Theoretical Spiritual Political Party (TSPP) or the Christian Alliance for the Kingdom of Africa (CHAKA). The most serious among them seemed to be the National Alliance for Democracy (NADA) and the Movement for Democratic Process (MDP). The leader of the latter, Chama Chakomboka, almost managed to become a presidential candidate. He raised the deposit, but he could only muster twenty people to support his candidature instead of the required 200. Thus, parties other than MMD and UNIP were insignificant in the parliamentary elections.

The successful outcome of the reintroduction of multi-partyism cannot be explained, however, by the competition between the two parties alone: wider forces in society have to be taken into the reckoning. The account presented here has stressed the continuity of political protest in Zambia: MMD brought together various strands of protest which had been present in the Zambian political system for a long time. Of course, factors outside Zambian society played a role as well. International institutions legitimised MMD: Arthur Wina was received by the World Bank and IMF as the representative of MMD. The vocal role of the Catholic Church can only be seen in the context of its international character which confers on that church a voice of greater standing than that of a local church. There were many observers and monitors: the Carter Centre's presence, in particular, was a boost for the opposition to UNIP.[16] Kaunda and UNIP would undoubtedly have had to face the displeasure of the international community if they had thwarted the process; as Zambia is so dependent upon foreign aid there could have been serious repercussions.

Yet, these influences cannot be seen as decisive. Zambians actively reacted to these outside influences as is evident in the organisation of monitoring groups. The first monitoring group to be formed was the Zambian Independent Monitoring Team (ZIMT) under the leadership of David Phiri and supported by the British government. Phiri's impartiality was called into question as he had occupied important positions since independence in the parastatals and the diplomatic service, but, above all, because he played golf with Kaunda. Phiri defended himself by saying that he had been playing golf since the late 1950s and had not played golf with the President for three months. More important were the accusations that the monitoring group used materials printed by the government, and that members of 'repressive organs' were in the team. The churches then took the initiative of establishing their own monitoring organisation: the Zambian Elections Monitoring Coordinating Committee (ZEMCC) under the leadership of The Reverend John Mambo of the Church of God. This was supported by the Law Association of Zambia, the Press Association of Zambia and a new pressure group, the Women's Lobby Group. It did its work in close association with the Carter Centre and other outside monitors.

The resistance to one-partyism was also supported by important groups within the state. During the campaign, MMD opened a string of court cases, most of which they won. The judiciary ignored any possible claim of political allegiance and thus played a crucial role in legitimising resistance against political domination by UNIP. UNIP and Kaunda accused the judiciary of being partisan, but they countered this even to the extent of charging Kambarage Kaunda's lawyer with contempt of court when he suggested that they had made a deal with MMD. The police were accused of being partisan by both sides. For example, MMD demanded at one point that the Electoral Commission, and not the police, should issue permits for political rallies. There is, however, no clear evidence that the police were a tool in the hands of the government of the day.

An incident in February 1991 illustrates better than any other the role of the police. MMD had announced a big rally near Luburma market in Lusaka. This was a highly significant place as Kapwepwe, the leader of UPP, had been beaten up there by UNIP youth in 1971. UNIP youth announced that it was not possible to organise the rally there as there would be football matches from dawn to dusk on that day between teams of UNIP youth. MMD persisted in its intentions, and on the eve of the event clashes broke out between UNIP youth and MMD youth who had started slashing the grass. On the day itself, UNIP youth erected barricades and fighting erupted, leading the police to intervene. UNIP youth reacted by marching to State House where the demonstration was again forcibly broken up by the police. The police acted thus independent of party pressure. In fact, it was unthinkable in the whole post-independence period that the police would confront UNIP's youth brigade. It is even more significant that they did so in front of State House. It should also be noted that the press in this instance castigated not only UNIP but also MMD, as they had provoked the events.

The armed forces remained neutral by consent of both parties, but there were accusations by both sides of interference with this neutrality. MMD claimed that Kaunda had moved troops and weapons to Malawi; Kaunda claimed that MMD was plotting an armed revolt with the support of army officers and connections of the Angolan leader Jonas Savimbi in case of defeat. It was typical, however, that Christon Tembo, a hot-headed ex-detainee coup plotter, was disowned by Chiluba when he stated that 'our boys' in the barracks would react if the election result were unacceptable to MMD.

It would be wrong, however, to have the impression that the whole process of change was carried by professional groups who created clean politics. Politics in Zambia retained also a 'street fighter' side during the whole process of change. Much informal pressure on ordinary people may not even have come out in the open. UNIP leaders often resorted to intimidating language, arguing that MMD supporters should be banned from buses, markets, government housing, etc. If prominent politicians used such language, it was generally successfully challenged in the courts. People were manhandled for reasons like shouting 'Satan' when Kaunda talked about God, love and peace or for wearing the wrong T-shirt. MMD followers rioted and looted in Choma when an MMD meeting held in October 1990 was declared illegal as it was – supposedly – taking place in a state-owned building. MMD supporters went on the rampage against UNIP officials who attended the burial in May 1991 of Joseph Simakuni, a trade union leader. Kaunda was pelted with oranges, beer cans and stones when he attended a football match. The same happened to MMD foreman Roger Chongwe when he addressed an election rally in Chaisa in Lusaka. The violent side of Zambian politics was always near the surface; and it was an aspect of both parties' campaign. It did not derail the process of change, but it was a threat.

PRESIDENT CHILUBA'S STRUGGLE FOR POWER

Chiluba's victory is undoubtedly rooted in a massive democratic movement, but his democratic credentials have been persistently questioned since he came to power. The most persistent accusation has been that too much power is concentrated in him. Chiluba mixes a great penchant for power and vanity with modesty: he jokes about his size, saying that Zambia is lucky to have only a small man as president; but his official portrait was his greatest priority after his electoral victory. While refusing to be called 'Excellency' (according to him, a title for ambassadors), renouncing the chancellorship of the University of Zambia and opening parliament in an ordinary suit, he none the less made it clear that Zambia has only one president and that that president is in State House. He insisted that Kaunda retire from politics before the state could give him a pension and fought consistently any influence which Kaunda might have had after his defeat. Chiluba's political discourse, like Kaunda's, is intensely religious: both portray themselves as humble servants of God's will. There were, however, no more joint prayer meetings with Kaunda. Museveni invited both for such a prayer meeting in Uganda. Kaunda accepted the invitation, but Chiluba was engaged elsewhere. The transfer of power in Zambia has been peaceful, but Kaunda's magnanimity may have been overstated. Modesty and intransigence remain mixed in his personality, traits which he shares with Chiluba. Kaunda declared a seven days' fast to meditate on the defeat. He refused, however, to declare the elections free and fair. According to Kaunda, the defeat was caused not by massive popular will, but by the low turnout of women. He predicted in his retirement speech to UNIP that the party would be in power again before the next general election in 1996. An infuriated Chiluba – with justification – branded this remark as unconstitutional.

The antagonism between Kaunda and Chiluba did not, however, imply a radically different style of government. Chiluba maintained the presidential system, despite the fact that MMD had campaigned for a return to parliamentary government on the Westminster model. The constitution which brought MMD to power was a presidential one which had been only marginally amended. Chiluba had previously called it 'a recipe for dictatorship'. The issue of constitutional reform has been mooted several times, but it was only in early 1993 that a commission was appointed to draw up a new constitution. This was generously funded by the American government and outside pressure in this matter seems likely. In the meantime, Chiluba appoints and dismisses, at will, heads of parastatals and surrounds himself more and more with special advisers. The Army's budget is still the prerogative of the President and the Minister of Defence. He has maintained the security apparatus of Kaunda and even resorted to declaring a state of emergency for some time, an act which he considered an inexcusable arrogation of power by Kaunda when the situation was reversed.

This concentration of power in his office is, as in Kaunda's day, combined with an attempt to form maximum coalitions. MMD was of course such a coalition from its inception. Contrary to stated intentions, he formed a large, tribally balanced Cabinet. He resorts to large meetings – dubbed *indabas* – on political violence, on the press or on the economic situation, where he tries to bring together as many parties as possible. On the one hand, this is a means of gaining legitimacy, but it also has the result of making the power structure opaque, as in Kaunda's day. The President is surrounded by large numbers of people, but power seems to be concentrated in a close network about which there is much speculation.[17]

This continuity in political strategy can be explained as the crafty moves of political actors, but there are strong pressures in Zambian politics to be reckoned with. Political fragmentation was a big problem for UNIP before the introduction of the one-party state. Kaunda contained it in that institution. The introduction of multi-party democracy has, however, led to its resurgence to an extreme degree.

First, such fragmentation is evident in the competition for electoral office. MMD is *de facto* the single party in many areas, and competition for office is concentrated therefore inside the party. Many people want to stand, and disappointed candidates often run as independents, thereby splitting the vote. These conflicts are not merely between individuals. Many involve candidates who are preferred by the leadership as against those with strong grassroots support. Deep rifts came into the open when it was proposed that candidates in the local government elections should have completed at least primary school. Some MMD notables, especially the chairman of MMD's electoral commission, Sikota Wina, protested strongly and insisted that an ability to read and write was enough. Roger Chongwe, the Minister of Legal Affairs, retorted that 'some Zambians who have been working in South Africa as a cook or in some other capacity should not be eligible'. Wina comes from Western Province where there was much labour migration to South Africa. Wina had also a long career as a UNIP politician, while Chongwe had no background in politics before MMD. The new measure would be unfavourable to old political stalwarts. MMD's youth movement even pleaded for Form II as a minimum qualification as that could lead to a change of the guard: 'We do not want merely the change of a UNIP T-shirt for another. New people should come in'.

Second, there is intense political opposition at central level. A group of intellectuals under the name of Caucus for National Unity (CNU) organised an evaluation of MMD's performance after half a year in office. Again the name refers to a broad coalition, although it was – certainly in the eyes of the MMD leadership – an opposition group. MMD national secretary, Godfrey Miyanda, compared what they did to publicly undressing one's own wife and asked them to follow internal procedures within MMD. Chiluba dismissed them as people who had not dared to speak out under Kaunda. The *Times of Zambia*, however, said that they were the Young Turks who formed MMD at the so-called Garden Party. They were mostly UNZA graduates and had been active in the Economics Club and the Law Association of Zambia. Chiluba told the Caucus to become a political party. They did so, thus leading to their dissolution. Two political parties were formed under the name and only one survived as a negligible entity in Zambian politics. Akashambatwa Lewanika, the most prominent MMD politician in the Caucus, remained in the party. Patrick Katyoka, who led the new party, has since rejoined MMD.

Nevertheless, the Caucus illustrates the continuity in Zambian political culture: their name reflected a broad political coalition. They were building upon a long-standing tradition of political protest by professional groups in Zambia. On the other hand, their existence may point to an important source of change. People with a past in the UNIP hierarchy were strikingly absent from this group. The members were usually from the younger age group, but even here continuity with the past slipped in. The major foreman of the Caucus was Akashambatwa Lewanika, the son of Godwin Lewanika, first chairman of the Northern Rhodesia Federation of Welfare Societies, first chairman of the ANC and Litunga (paramount chief) of Barotseland.

Akashambatwa Lewanika did not take part in the formation of the CNU party, but he resigned soon after as a minister in the Chiluba government. At the same time, Baldwin Nkumbula also resigned from the front bench. Baldwin is a son of Harry Nkumbula, the founder and leader of the ANC, the party from which UNIP split in 1958. These two names therefore reverberate with strong historical associations. They were not particularly explicit about their reasons, but their departure heralded the beginning of many resignations and sackings from the Cabinet. Central issues surrounding these were allegations of corruption, allegations of tribalism, and complaints about the authoritarian style of Chiluba's politics. Ephraim Chibwe was dismissed as Minister of Public Works in the wake of allegations of corruption. Stan Kristofoor, the Minister for Information, was sacked because he had told his secretary to work harder, otherwise people could say that Africans were lazy. This was considered to be a racist remark. These issues were part of rumblings of opposition in MMD, but these rumblings exploded in revolt when Chiluba dismissed four very prominent MMD politicians, Arthur Wina, Humphrey Mulemba, Guy Scott and Emmanuel Kasonde, from the Cabinet in April 1993. Initially they made humble comments, but afterwards they protested vehemently and demanded to know the reasons for their sacking.

This led to accusations about corruption connected with maize buying for drought relief in the case of Scott and Kasonde. Kasonde also became entangled in a fight for control of MMD in Northern Province with the Cabinet Minister there, Daniel Kapapa. The sacked ministers, with the exception of Guy Scott, then left MMD and formed a new party, the National Party (NP). Thirteen MPs left MMD in a confused scenario of expulsion and resignation. Among them were Akashambatwa Lewanika, his sister Inonge Lewanika, who was also on the front bench, and Chilufya Kapwepwe, the daughter of Simon Kapwepwe. Not all of them joined the NP. Guy Scott challenged his expulsion before the court and insisted that he wanted to reform MMD from within. Akashambatwa Lewanika attended the foundation meeting of the NP, but he and Chilufya Kapwepwe then denied having become members of it. MPs who had switched parties lost their seats in accordance with the terms of the Constitution. Four of them contested this in court as they wanted to continue as independents, but they were unsuccessful. Many of the rebels were therefore hesitant about joining parties other than MMD.

In the ensuing by-elections,[18] MMD lost where they were opposed by a name which strongly recalled past Zambian politics associated with regional power: Mulemba, Lewanika, Wina, Nkumbula were winners. The exception was the contest for Kasonde's seat in Northern Province where MMD won after a bitter fight. The NP has been called a party of future presidential contenders, and indeed many of their founders have a strong following. There is little indication yet that this personal popularity can mobilise broader coalitions since MMD won where the NP did not field such heavyweights. The latter invariably stood in their home areas, and it is therefore yet to be seen whether they can muster a following in other places.

That was not the end of the fragmentation of MMD. Roger Chongwe, a prominent lawyer, who had been moved to local government in the Cabinet reshuffle of April 1993, resigned in December. Early in 1994 more resignations followed: Vernon Mwaanga, the Minister of Foreign Affairs resigned; both Sikota Wina, MMD's leader in parliament and chairman of the elections committee, and his wife Princess Nakatindi resigned because of alleged drug trafficking. Again, the MMD leadership was divided on this issue. The return of Finance Minister Ronald Penza and Planning Minister Dean Mung'omba from Paris, carrying the message that donor countries demanded that something should be done about drug trafficking, had revived the allegations. Chiluba forbade MMD leaders to speak about the issue, but the pressure within the party on Wina and Princess Nakatindi to resign to clear the air became too great.

UNIP, the party which emerged as the main opposition party after the October 1991 elections has, however, been as hard hit by fragmentation as MMD. Kaunda resigned as party leader during a National Party convention in September 1992, which had been postponed several times. There was strong pressure in UNIP, organised within a group called Support UNIP Group (SUPG), to democratise the party thoroughly first before holding the convention. SUPG was allied to Enoch Kavindele who had challenged Kaunda for the presidential candidature in the run-up to the multi-party elections. The Secretary of the Youth Wing, Chibembe Nyalugwe, was a moving force in SUPG. Kavindele resigned from UNIP in May 1993, however, and formed the United Democratic Party (UDP). When the elections for UNIP party leader were held, the hand-picked successor, Kebby Musokotwane, won. The new leadership of UNIP was similar to that in the last days of UNIP dominance. There were strong complaints about intimidation in the election, especially of journalists. UNIP chose a tribally balanced leadership, despite the fact that their only stronghold is in Eastern Province. The Vice President, Patrick Mvunga, comes from there and all three candidates for the post were Easterners. That did not lead, however, to the emergence of UNIP as a united party. The party was racked by conflicts during the controversies surrounding the zero-option plan, which aimed to overthrow the MMD government by extra-parliamentary means: by instigating strikes, organising street sellers and other *lumpenproletariat* to disrupt public life and by infiltrating police, security and Army. Kaunda's son, Wezi, was most strongly associated with the plan. Musokotwane was under pressure from UNIP members, notably the wives of the detainees, to reveal the authors of the plan, but he refused. Chiluba's introduction of the state of emergency in response to the zero-option plan was controversial and unpopular.

There seemed to be an opening here for UNIP to regain popularity, but it was marred by the controversies about the quality of the leadership and the direction which the party should take. Musokotwane appeared to be associated with another strategy to revive UNIP. He backed a UNIP revival plan initiated by Lucy Sichone, a member of the Central Committee. This was a campaign of self-criticism starting from the assumption that UNIP had alienated itself from all sections of society, especially the poor. UNIP was equated with a party of exploiters, who should, according to Sichone, belong to MMD. The criticism of such a soft approach was persistent however, the return of a Kaunda was mentioned, and one result was the expulsion of Sichone from the party. Chibembe Nyalugwe, the Secretary General of UNIP youth, left as well amidst confusion as to whether he had resigned or was expelled. UNIP also lost Kennedy Shepande, one of the few young intellectuals in the leadership, and Mavis Muyunda who joined the NP via Kavindele's UDP.

The two main parties are subject to continuing fragmentation, a characteristic of the whole political scene. There are more than thirty other small parties in Zambia, but none of them has managed to make any impact. Frequently, mergers and other forms of cooperation are proposed, by both MMD and UNIP, but they come to nothing. On the contrary, virtually all these small parties are racked by leadership struggles. A BBC correspondent at the press *indaba* summed them up in a neat judgement: 'It is difficult to take them seriously. They are one-man affairs whose main activity is to spread wild rumours on corruption'. A personalised style of politics is of course not unusual in Africa, but a leader in such a situation must be able to gain a wide following. The leaders of these small parties do not succeed in doing so. Kavindele's UDP failed to make any headway outside North-western Province. He has since disbanded the party and joined MMD. The NP is different because it is not the party of one big man: it includes many prominent former MMD members. It is, however, the product of a fragmentation which fragmented immediately also: only some of those who were expelled or resigned from MMD joined. It has already been branded a tribal party because of the predominance of Lozi politicians.

CONCLUSION

This article is necessarily selective, and some topics mentioned deserve further analysis. In particular, sectionalism and accusations of sectionalism in Zambia should be studied in much more depth. Selectivity has not, however, filtered out evidence contrary to the main thesis proposed here on the nature of Zambian politics.

The reintroduction of multi-partyism represents not a definite break in Zambian political history, but rather the culmination of pressures from opposition forces which were always manifest in the one-party state.[19] The people involved in the movement often had an extensive political history within UNIP, and there is a recurrence in the younger generation of names which were previously important in politics: Lewanika, Nkumbula, Kapwepwe. It seems that dynastic tendencies are strong not only in the Kaunda family. Most important, however, are the continuities in the particular political style of Zambia, the ways in which political behaviour is structured.

The main thesis proposed here is that there are strong pressures in Zambian politics which lead to the continuity of a politics dominated by a maximum coalition and a presidential system. It may seem paradoxical that a strong tendency towards fragmentation – as documented above – is a pressure to form a maximum coalition. The names of fragmenting parties already indicate, however, the desire to form exactly such a coalition: Caucus for National Unity, United Democratic Party, National Party, etc. If there is an extreme tendency towards fragmentation, then one unit which can overcome fragmentation will be at an advantage. Political competition will concentrate within this unit, and ambitious people will be attracted into the organisation. The only way to defeat such a maximum coalition is to form a rival maximum coalition which, if successful, leads automatically to the defeat of the original one, as UNIP found out to their cost. As long as Chiluba is seen as the potential winner in the next elections, he will stand a chance of attracting support. Otherwise, he will face defections, just like UNIP; and the question is whether the expulsions and the resignations from the party are already a sign of this. The ability of the disaffected to form a rival maximum coalition will determine whether they will continue to attract support. The crucial battleground in forming such a coalition seems to be the moral integrity of the leader. Accusations of corruption, favouritism and lust for power, rather than policies, are dominant in political discourse. If a rival leader emerges who has greater moral credentials than the incumbent, he may be able to overcome the tendency towards fragmentation.

There is great pressure on a president to arrogate power if he faces unstable support. In a situation of extreme fragmentation – and we have not dealt with the many other frictions he has to face, e.g., trade unions versus the elite; women's lobbies – he will have to cast himself in the role of mediator in order to maintain the coalition. It is easier to share power if one can build upon a cohesive supporting group. In the absence of cohesive support, sharing power means quickly losing control. It is therefore not surprising that Chiluba has kept strict control over key institutions like security or the copper mines. If he delegated power over these key institutions, he would have no power left.

Cabinet government in a parliamentary system implies that power is much more dispersed than in a presidential system. An extreme tendency towards fragmentation of support in a political system creates a situation in which parliamentary Cabinet government becomes very difficult. A parliamentary system demands a minimum of stability to form coalitions, unless one allows the country to be run by the civil service. In the Zambian political culture, parliament also has to compete in the struggle to establish moral credentials, as is evident from the vocal opposition by individuals in parliament on such grounds: notably against Chiluba's reintroduction of the state of emergency. The moral status of parliament has not, however, been greatly enhanced since October 1991. It discredited itself notably when MPs considered Toyota Hi-Lux pick-ups not commensurate with their status and wanted top of the range Land Cruisers instead. Parliamentary debates hardly touch on policy.

This argument is no excuse for any degree of arrogation of power on the part of Zambian presidents. It merely suggests that explanations for the emergence of one-partyism and the presidential system cannot be reduced simply to power-hungry designs. In the Zambian context, they emerged also as responses to political fragmentation in which regional and tribal sentiments played a major role. The question remains whether a dominant party in a multi-party context can be successful in regulating such political competition. It is understandable in these circumstances that one focal point, for example, the presidential system, should emerge to transcend fragmentation.

NOTES

1   M.G. Schatzberg, 'Power, Legitimacy and Democratisation in Africa', *Africa*, 1993, (63,4), pp. 445–462, pleads also for more attention to be paid to political culture in the study of African politics. He uses the concept in a different sense than I do, however. Political culture in his analysis is akin to political thought, albeit that he advocates a much more informal approach and demands attention for the ways in which it is formulated and felt in the wider polity, rather than concentrating on policy documents emanating from the top. He stresses discourse analysis as the principal method of analysis. The relationship between discourse and behaviour is problematic, however: stated interpretations of the world have no necessary connection with behaviour. If politicians make frequent references to the family as a metaphor – as Schatzberg documents – then this does not imply any actual pattern of politics: Mobutu as well as Nyerere did so. Therefore the study of political culture can be more fruitful if it deduces the actual rules governing political action from political behaviour, as is done here. This approach should not be confused with institutional analysis. People can act very differently under similar political institutions. For example, the establishment of a one-party state does not necessarily lead to similar forms of political behaviour in different countries. See: Jan Kees van Donge, 'Tanzanian Political Culture and the Cabinet', *Journal of Modern African Studies*, 1986, (24,4), pp. 619–641.

2   K. Good, 'Debt and the One-party State in Zambia', *Journal of Modern African Studies*, 1989, (27,2), pp. 297–315 gives such an interpretation in academic terms.

3   This crucial observation on the nature of UNIP was made in M. Szeftel, 'Conflicts, Spoils and Class Formation in Zambia', Ph.D. thesis, University of Manchester, 1978.

4   I. Scott, 'Party Politics in Zambia; A Study of the Organization of U.N.I.P.', Ph.D. thesis, University of Toronto, 1976.

5   A.D. Roberts, 'The Lumpa Church of Alice Lenshina', in R. Rotberg and A.A. Mazrui (eds), *Protest and Power in Black Africa* (New York: Oxford University Press, 1970), pp. 531–571.

6   W. Tordoff, 'Residual Legislatures in Tanzania and Zambia', *The Journal of Commonwealth and Comparative Politics*, 1977, (15,3), pp. 184–213; and C. Gertzel, 'Dissent and Authority in the Zambian One-party State 1973–80' in C. Gertzel (ed.), *The Dynamics of the One-party State in Zambia* (Manchester: Manchester University Press, 1984), pp. 79–115.

7   J. Pettman, *Zambia, Security and Conflict* (Lewis: Julian Friedman Publishers, 1974), pp. 235–241 summarises these events succinctly.

8   R. Molteno, 'Cleavage and Conflict in Zambian Politics: A Study in Sectionalism', in W. Tordoff (ed.), *Politics in Zambia* (Manchester: Manchester University Press, 1974), pp. 62–107.

9   C. Gertzel (op.cit.) documented carefully the continuing pluralistic nature of Zambian politics after the introduction of one-partyism. See also, G.F. Lungu, 'The Church, Labour and the Press in Zambia: The Role of Critical Observers in a One-party State', *African Affairs*, 1986, (85,340), pp. 385–410.

10   The 1980 coup was essentially an attempt by civilians to overthrow the government with the help of Zairian exiles. The plotters contacted officers of the

Zambian Army, but these did not support them. Several army officers were detained after the coup, but only one – the Air Force Major Anderson Mporokoso – was convicted in the ensuing trial. He was sentenced to ten years' imprisonment on the charge of concealing the plot and not for actual plotting. The 1989 coup attempt was a military affair and involved more senior officers. Christon Tembo, the main conspirator in 1989, was a Major General and had been Chief of Staff. His alleged co-conspirators were two Lieutenant Colonels and a Major. However, at the time of the alleged planning of the coup Tembo was ambassador to Germany and, from the details that emerged in the ensuing trial, his conspiracy appeared to have been heavily infiltrated by informers. Mwamba Luchembe was a Lieutenant. The official claim that he acted alone is questioned in S. Chan, *Kaunda and Southern Africa, Image and Reality in Foreign Policy* (London: The British Academic Press, 1992), pp. 177–178. The only concrete evidence for wider involvement is a protest by soldiers who were retrenched by the Army. They went to see Luchembe in the beginning of 1993 and brought him to the offices of the *Times of Zambia* to publicise their plight. He was, according to them, responsible for their involvement 'in this business'. They portrayed themselves merely as ordinary soldiers who had to follow orders.

11 This decline is documented in M.M. Burdette, *Zambia: Between Two Worlds*, (Boulder: Colorado, Westview, 1988), pp. 95–123.

12 The data presented in the following sections are all drawn from Zambia's two main newspapers: *Times of Zambia* and *Zambia Daily Mail*, unless otherwise stated. I am indebted to the *Zambia Nieuwsbrief*, a Dutch newsletter on Zambia, which provided me generously with cuttings in return for a three-monthly overview of political developments in Zambia.

13 The relationships between high office in government and business success in Zambia urgently need detailed study. C. Baylies and M. Szeftel, 'The Rise of a Zambian Capitalist Class in the 1970's', *Journal of Southern African Studies*, 1982, (8,2), pp. 184–213, made a forceful argument that politics in Zambia under the one-party state became more and more dominated by businessmen. *Africa Confidential* nowadays identifies virtually all Zambian politicians with business interests. We do not know, however, whether business success precedes success in politics or the other way round. Second, we do not know enough of the substance of these businesses. The concept of businessman needs to be defined. Baylies and Szeftel use it as a very wide category which may include a person whose bottle store is empty, whose lorries and buses are off the road, etc. Third, we do not know whether there is a business sector in Zambia which keeps aloof from politics: attention has been focused only on political interests in business. There is at present a dearth in the case material needed to answer such questions.

14 The newspapers did not publish a full overview of the election results. It is doubtful however whether this would have provided much more material for fruitful analysis. It could be that UNIP had suffered from the first-past-the-post system if there were substantial UNIP minorities elsewhere in the country. If one assumed that those who voted for Kaunda would also vote for UNIP in the parliamentary elections then UNIP would have gained thirty-six seats instead of twenty-five, but the balance of power would not have been thereby affected. UNIP's support seemed therefore to be eroded to an enormous extent outside

Eastern Province where they won all twenty-one seats. UNIP's four other seats were scattered in Northern, North-western and Western Province. It may be that local leadership was a factor there, but the election result does not suggest that local political leadership was important.

15   The turnout figures may deserve further analysis. C. Baylies and M. Szeftel, 'The Fall and Rise of Multi-party Politics in Zambia', *Review of African Political Economy*, 1992, (54), pp. 75–91, compare the turnout unfavourably with previous elections. They note, for example, a turnout of 66.7 per cent in 1968 under one-partyism. Such comparisons are only meaningful, however, if the number of registered voters is compared with the estimated potential number of voters based on census results, but Baylies and Szeftel do not do so. Turnout comparisons on a regional basis could also provide insights into possible regional variations in apathy: such insights could be enlightening given the influence of regional affiliation in African politics. According to E. Bjornlund, M. Bratton and C. Gibson, 'Observing Multi-party Elections in Africa: Lessons from Zambia', *African Affairs*, 1992, (91,364), pp. 405–431, voter registration was one of the more serious disputes between MMD and UNIP. Kaunda used the need for proper voter registration as a forceful argument to postpone the referendum which would then have been held after the rainy season, in the middle of 1991. Insistence on proper registration in the elections would similarly have meant their postponement until the middle of 1992. The last voter registration had taken place in 1987, although there had been a brief supplementary registration exercise in 1990 in the run-up to the referendum that never took place. There were thus large numbers of voters who had not registered, including those who had reached voting age in the interim and those who had not registered previously under the one-party state. There were those who had lost their voter's registration card and could therefore not vote, and those who had changed location but were registered to vote in their previous place of residence. In the end, there was an emergency voter registration but this lasted only a few days. People had to show a national registration card to obtain a voter's registration card. National registration cards are highly valued documents in Zambia and many people make great efforts to get one, but alas the procedure of registering citizens is highly inefficient and erratic. There were, therefore, probably many voters on the register who could not vote because they had died, lost their voter's registration card or had moved and could not travel back home. This could partly explain the low turnout. There may also have been many voters who wanted to register but did not have a national registration card. The actual turnout is therefore an imperfect measure of apathy.

16   See, E. Bjornlund, M. Bratton and C. Gibson, op.cit.

17   The columns of *Africa Confidential* abound with such speculation. For example, an article under the telling title 'Zambia, All Change, but No Change', *Africa Confidential*, 1992, (33,13), pp. 5–6 discusses an inner circle called the G-7 Group.

18   Before the formation of the NP, MMD had won all by-elections except one in Chadiza (Eastern Province), where Kaunda's son Panji won for UNIP. Nine seats were disputed on 11 November 1993 after the formation of the NP. The NP won four, MMD won four and UNIP won one in Eastern Province. MMD lost in Mongu (Western Province) on 28 January 1994, where Akashambatwa

Mbikusita-Lewanika held on to his seat for the NP. Turnout was very low in all by-elections, and it made no difference in this respect whether big names stood on an NP platform or not. For example, Humphrey Mulemba won overwhelmingly in Solwezi (2,037 for the NP against 560 for MMD) but only 3,037 out of the 22,032 registered voters cast their vote. Mbikusita-Lewanika gained 4,277 votes against MMD's Mundia Sikatana's 955 votes, but only 5,375 people voted out of the 29,000 registered.

19 Multi-partyism did not, however, lead to the re-emergence of the parties which had existed before one-partyism (ANC, UP, UPP), nor did references to their names recur in those of the new parties. There was a minor attempt to revive UPP. Government, however, refused registration of the party on the grounds that UPP was still a proscribed organisation (!). The founders were allowed to form a party under any other name except UP. UPP was associated with the Bemba, but the revivalists held their meeting in Southern Province (Choma). An editorial in the *Zambia Daily Mail* associated the party with similar attempts to revive the ANC there. The idea of reviving UPP petered out quickly however; and amidst the splits and rumours about splits in Southern Province, the acronym ANC is not mentioned.

10 Conclusion: assessing the prospects for the consolidation of democracy in Africa

Christopher Clapham and John A. Wiseman

In assessing the prospects for the consolidation of democracy in Africa, it is necessary to take an unromantic and pragmatic view as to what type of system might be consolidated, how widespead a phenomenon this might be, and the degree of 'permanence' which consolidation might imply. The idea that all or most African states will create perfectly functioning democracies which will survive indefinitely is too improbable to warrant serious consideration – however much one might wish it were otherwise. We suggest that a realistic notion of what type of democracy might be evolving in Africa has to be found much closer to the minimalist end of the spectrum than to the more ambitious maximalist end. This judgement is not intended to indicate what system African states 'ought' to have, but rather what it may be practicable to achieve. Such a minimalist system of democracy would involve public contestation for public power (almost inevitably between competing political parties), in which a universally enfranchised citizenry would make their choice through a regular electoral process which was free from serious malpractice. For such a system to operate in a meaningful fashion, it would be necessary to maintain the level of freedom of association and expression required to permit the unhindered formation, not only of alternative political parties but also of the other societal groups which constitute a civil society. An additional component of this system would be the operation of the rule of law, with a judiciary free from government control and able to check abuses and the use of arbitrary power from whatever source. In the real world, the operation of such a system will inevitably be flawed, and the best that can be expected empirically is a rather rough and ready version. To those who object that this would constitute a 'merely' procedural form of democracy, it may be pointed out that it would represent a marked improvement on the level of democracy that most African states have hitherto experienced.

The criteria by which the 'consolidation' of democracy is to be assessed are inherently judgemental, since a consolidated democracy must be one in which democratic practices are very widely expected to continue into the future, and this can never be extrapolated from the experience of the past. In July 1994, for example, a military *coup d'état* in The Gambia brought to an end exactly the type of rough and ready democracy described above which had existed in that country since independence in 1965, and which might well have been regarded as among the most firmly established in the continent. At the very least, however, consolidation must require the holding of a regular series of elections under democratic conditions, rather than simply the 'one-off' tests of electoral support which have taken place in the immediate pre-independence period, in selecting a civilian successor to a military regime or as a result of the upheavals in the early 1990s which set in train the most recent process of democratisation. And while a contested change of government cannot be taken as a condition for democratic consolidation, it certainly provides the clearest indicator that an electoral democracy is in place.

THE FAILURE OF THE ALTERNATIVES

There can be little doubt that non-democratic political systems in Africa have failed either to deliver their promised benefits of economic development and national unity or even to maintain in power the regimes that have espoused them. Whatever the arguments that have been made, notably in east and south-east Asia, for the authoritarian 'developmental state', these have manifestly failed to hold in Africa, where state control of the economy has been associated, not only with high levels of corruption but with the diversion of resources away from the more productive sectors and towards consumption-oriented groups dependent on access to state power. Far from generating national unity, unaccountable and authoritarian regimes have led at best to public alienation from the political process, and at worst, in a significant number of African states, to a level of brutality and repression which must be regarded as inexcusable by the most basic standards of humanity. Even the most intense repression has moreover proved counter-productive, even for the limited purpose of maintaining public order and keeping the regime in power. In the most extreme cases, such as Ethiopia, Liberia, Somalia or Uganda, it has led to popular reactions which in turn have exposed the fragility of the state itself.

This failure has been clearly recognised within Africa, and has prompted the emergence throughout the continent of movements calling for multi-party democratic systems of government. Rooted in the often bitter experience of many millions of Africans, these movements provide the most encouraging evidence for the creation of new structures and values on which any sustained process of re-democratisation must be built. External support for multi-party democracy, though undoubtedly significant in bringing pressure on recalcitrant incumbent regimes and helping to provide a favourable international setting for newly elected governments, is only and can only be a subordinate element in the process. None the less, even though the internal recognition of the need for change is an essential condition for democracy, its implementation and consolidation remain extremely difficult, especially at a time of economic crisis.

The key question is the extent to which the widespead movement in the direction of more democratic political systems should be seen as the beginning of a process of fundamental and positive change in the way in which a significant number of African states are governed. An examination of recent changes in Africa presents rather a mixed picture. Even if we exclude South Africa, we are still left with eleven states in which a peaceful change of government through the ballot box has taken place since 1990. In one of these, the small island state of Sao Tome and Principe, this has now happened twice: the defeated incumbent party in the 1991 election was able to win a majority of seats in the 1994 election. Until recently, the only peaceful changes of government through the ballot box in Africa in the post-independence period have occurred in Mauritius, in 1982 and 1983. While it may be tempting to search for parallels with the terminal colonial period, when competitive elections produced governments which, in most cases, subsequently abandoned democratic frameworks, it would be unwise to assume that the same process will inevitably be repeated. The collective learning experience, and the almost total undermining of the claims to legitimacy of authoritarian ideologies, have created a different situation from that which existed thirty or more years ago. Nevertheless, one has to recognise that there have been quite a number of cases where incumbent regimes have managed to retain power, following elections in which they profited to a varying degree from the considerable advantages of incumbency, or in which no meaningful electoral contest has taken place at all.

These variations in recent experience help to remind us that African states differ enormously in terms of almost all the indices that are likely to affect successful democratisation, and that generalisations will certainly prove unwarranted – especially when they are drawn disproportionately from those states which offer the most or the least hopeful prospects for democratic consolidation. But even if the answers differ, the questions that need to be asked of prospective African democracies are much the same. The remainder of this concluding chapter will therefore seek to map out the key questions that must be asked, and the range of answers that are available.

DEMOCRATISATION AND STATE INTEGRITY

The first question to be asked is whether democratisation is likely to involve any significant challenge to the integrity of African states or whether it can be accommodated within existing state frontiers and draw on at least the basic structure of existing state institutions. If not, then democratisation must be accompanied by a level of upheaval that must vastly complicate the process, and potentially lead to widespread state breakdown. The evidence to date suggests that the 'threat' presented by democracy to state integrity is considerably less than the artificiality of many African states might lead one to expect. Even in a state as ethnically varied as Nigeria, democratisation may plausibly be regarded as an integrating rather than a centrifugal force; in Zambia, whose boundaries most starkly demonstrate the arbitrary nature of colonial state formation, it has been possible to hold national elections, leading to a peaceful transfer of power, without raising any challenge to the integrity of the state.

It is likewise the case that fair and open multi-party elections have strengthened national identities within African states and enhanced their prospects of survival as viable territorial units. This could by no means be taken for granted, and is indeed in some respects surprising. Given the artificiality of most African states, as a result of their colonial formation, it might well be assumed that any shift to participant political systems could destroy the very basis of statehood, in the way that both the former Soviet Union and Yugoslavia have been split apart by the collapse of the communist regimes that previously held them together. Democratisation, on this view, could be expected to intensify internal ethnic, regional and religious divisions, and lead to a process of fragmentation even greater than that which has afflicted parts of Eastern Europe, ultimately calling into question the existence of the state as the basis for government in Africa.

In practice, however, a very plausible case can be made for precisely the opposite conclusion: that it is only through democratisation – even if this has to be imposed from outside – that African states can be rescued from the consequences of their own misgovernment. None of those African states that have collapsed into anarchy could remotely be described as democratic, and in most cases – such as Doe's Liberia or Siyad Barre's Somali Republic – political collapse can be directly related to the gross abuse of power. Conversely, even in a number of fairly surprising cases, democratisation has provided the means through which some form of national political community has been re-established. Although Zambia, for example, is one of the most evidently artificial African states, Chiluba's victory in 1991 was achieved with support from across the country. Abiola's evident (though aborted) victory in the 1993 elections in Nigeria marked the first occasion on which voting in that country has not turned on the mobilisation of regional and ethnic constituencies: indeed, it was probably the failure of the Nigerian electorate to vote along the expected ethnic lines that induced the military incumbent, Ibrahim Babangida, to cancel the election. In the aftermath of that decision, it is becoming all too clear that the military's disregard for popular opinion poses vastly greater dangers to Nigerian national unity than would have followed from a peaceful transfer of power. Peaceful and reasonably participant politics has been revived both in countries (like Benin) with a record of chronic instability and in ones (like Malawi and Cape Verde) with no history of multi-party politics at all.

Where democratisation *does* challenge state integrity, this can be related, as in Ethiopia, to an anomalous pattern of state formation, or to a recent experience of abuse of state power so intense as to destroy any residual commitment to the state as the framework for political action. In short, it is autocracy rather than ethnic variety that has posed the most important threat to the maintenance of African states. In those cases, such as Eritrea, where by the 1980s widespread support for continued unity with Ethiopia no longer existed, then democratisation may provide the mechanism for a relatively peaceful divorce; but there is as yet little evidence to suggest that 'Balkanisation' along the lines of the former Soviet Union and Yugoslavia is likely to occur.

THE EMERGENCE OF A 'CIVIL SOCIETY'

Even though there is widespread popular recognition of the value of multi-party democracy throughout almost all of Africa, the maintenance of social values and institutions that will help to provide a popular base for democratic government and opposition remains variable and uncertain. Recognition of this problem has led to attempts to apply to Africa the idea of a 'civil society', which has often been regarded as a key element in maintaining democratic government elsewhere. A functioning civil society rests on a set of widely shared values and institutions which help to limit and regulate both the intensity of competition between different groups within the society, and the exercise of power by the government. The process of democratic renewal in Africa has certainly been greatly assisted by the emergence to much greater political prominence of the institutions that are commonly taken to characterise a civil society, such as trade unions, professional associations and religious organisations. There are none the less very significant differences between African states in the extent to which a functioning civil society can be said to have been established, and these differences unsurprisingly correspond to a considerable degree to the level of democratisation. In many cases the weakness of civil society can be seen, in part at least, as an element of the legacy of authoritarian rule. As part of the attempt to curb alternative sources of power, many governments have quite deliberately sought to abolish or strictly control any societal grouping not directly associated with the regime. In some cases the degree of government control was far from complete; in Zambia, for example, the trade union movement was able to take an independent role which was crucial in the challenge to single-party rule. In many countries, churches and on occasion Islamic movements were able to retain a degree of autonomy which enabled them to take the lead in the democratisation process.

As these examples help to indicate, the emergence of civil societies correlates most closely with the strength of 'imported' institutions, which are associated with levels of education and economic development. Except in a small number of cases, it is difficult to draw any clear correlation between the structure of civil society and the structures and values of pre-colonial societies. Even where such societies had significant democratic elements, it has proved extremely difficult to incorporate these elements into a working modern democratic state, not least because the post-colonial state itself derives from very different origins, and embodies very different principles, than those which guided pre-colonial society. Though the ideas of 'modernisation' and 'development' which were so prevalent in the 1950s and 1960s have disappeared from the political vocabulary of Africa, some of the relationships which they postulated between forms of social change and the maintenance of effective political institutions may now be worth reconsidering.

THE EMERGENCE OF AN ALTERNATIVE POLITICAL LEADERSHIP

The demand for multi-party democracy in Africa has been marked, as elsewhere, by the emergence of individuals and groups who have challenged the monopolisation of power by established regimes. The maintenance of democracy likewise requires that competing leadership groups should be able to maintain themselves within a structure of ordered competition. There have however been important variations, both in the way in which such groups have emerged, and in the political demands which they have sought to articulate. These in turn have a considerable bearing on the prospects for democratic consolidation.

As with the emergence of civil society, the authoritarianism of the past has inhibited the development of an alternative political leadership which might have evolved in a more open political climate. The jailing, exile or even killing of those perceived by the regime as alternative leaders has effectively reduced the pool of individuals from which a new leadership might emerge. Furthermore, this past record of ill-treatment of political opponents provides a difficult background for the development of democratic tolerance. Few leaders can be expected to display the magnanimity of a Nelson Mandela, with his absence of rancour towards those who had imprisoned him for nearly three decades.

In some cases, 'new' leadership groups have not really been new at all, but have simply consisted in the re-emergence of individuals and political tendencies which have survived from earlier periods of political competition, and which have used the changed political climate as a means to promote dormant ambitions. These leaders have likewise tended to resuscitate dormant political organisations and networks. The presidential candidacy of Jaramogi Oginga Odinga in Kenya provides a classic example. In such cases, it is all too likely that the failed political divisions of the past will fail once more in the future, just as the attempted re-democratisation schemes launched by outgoing military regimes have invariably failed to lead to any stable democratic system.

At the other extreme, there have been states in which the new political leadership has emerged through insurgent warfare, in violent opposition to established state elites. Understandably, this has characteristically been the pattern in states where the abuse of state power has been most extreme and the opportunities for peaceful opposition have been most slight. Guerrilla insurgency may lead, as in Uganda, to the installation of a more effective and even accountable regime than its predecessor, though it may also lead, as in Liberia and Somalia, to the collapse of state institutions as a whole. In neither case, however, does it provide a propitious setting for the consolidation of multi-party democracy.

Experience suggests that democratic consolidation is most likely to take place when a new leadership emerges, seeking to organise politics in a different way from those adopted by discredited parties and leaders in the past, but within the context of non-violent opposition and the acceptance of basic state institutions.

ECONOMIC CRISIS AND POLITICAL CHANGE

Democratic renewal in Africa coincides, and is indeed closely associated, with economic crisis and the effective cooptation of economic decision-making by external financial institutions. The relationship between economic management and the structure of democratic competition is perhaps the most basic factor affecting the success of democratic consolidation.

At one level, this concerns the relationship between politicians and their domestic constituency. Given the abuse of the economic power of the state by non-democratic regimes in the past, it may forcefully be argued that democracy provides the only means through which to ensure that governments pursue economic policies which favour the interests of the mass of the population, and which in particular favour producer rather than consumer interests, and rural rather than urban ones. On the other hand, fragile governments may be all the more likely to resort to short-term and economically counterproductive measures in order to maintain the support of the particular economic constituencies on which they most depend. The creation of stable groups based on mass economic interests remains extremely problematical, in a continent in which clientelist modes of resource distribution and political support are often deeply entrenched. The mobilisation of rural interests is especially difficult.

At another level, the success of democratisation must depend on the overall process of economic development, and the ability of elected regimes to demonstrate their effectiveness to the electorate. This ability is likely to be threatened, both by the very limited control which these regimes actually have over the management of their own economies and by the low absolute level of available resources. Democratisation has historically proved more successful as a means of broadening political participation within expanding economies than as a means of reversing the decay of declining ones. Though the economic liberalism of the market bears an evident conceptual similarity to the political liberalism of multi-party politics, it cannot be assumed that the two will inevitably go together in practice. Indeed, the external imposition of economic management threatens to remove precisely that element of choice or freedom of action which democracy is intended to enhance.

DEMOCRACY AND GOVERNANCE

The consolidation of democracy in Africa also requires a demonstrable relationship between political accountability and the quality of government. Here, as with economic development, there is a potential clash between the principles of accountability which should, in the long term, create more effective systems of government geared to the public welfare and the short-term expedients, such as political patronage, to which elected regimes may be drawn. The assumption that democratic government will lead to measures that favour the long-term interests of the mass of the population is undermined by the continued electoral influence of political bosses whose interests lie in the control of state patronage. In some cases, most notoriously in Second Republic Nigeria, the transition to civilian rule has been followed by the massive misappropriation of funds by politicians anxious to reap the rewards of victory, and recoup the investments that they had made in order to get themselves elected. Public confidence in the democratic process is thereby eroded, and the claims of the military to represent a 'national' interest, in contrast to the self-serving actions of elected politicians, acquire at least an initial plausibility – though the military, in Nigeria as elsewhere, have rapidly proved to be every bit as rapacious as their civilian predecessors.

The relationship between democracy and that collection of practices which are generally taken to constitute 'good government' is complex. Democracy and human rights do indeed generally seem to go together; we are not aware of any case where democratically elected governments have been guilty of human rights violations on the scale found, for example, in states such as Ethiopia, Liberia, Somalia, Sudan or Zaire, let alone the systematic genocide of Rwanda; the worst excesses, including all those noted above, together with Bokassa's Central Africa and Amin's Uganda, have almost always been committed by regimes whose leaders originated in the military. The relationship between democracy and either efficiency or honesty in government is by no means so easily established.

THE EXTERNAL FACTOR

African regimes are likely to remain highly dependent on the outside world, not least for financial assistance. Even though external pressure was one factor promoting democratisation, however, it cannot be assumed that external powers will continue to support democratic consolidation. While foreign governments certainly gave an initial boost to the democratising process, and may assist subsequent consolidation by materially rewarding those states which have made significant progress in a democratic direction, we remain unconvinced that foreign pressure can do much more than this. For one thing, Western pressure for democratisation is likely to be ephemeral, and there are already plentiful indications that it is on the decline; it has proved vulnerable to the domestic political factors which have reduced the democratising drive of the United States, and to the *raisons d'état* which re-established the links between the Mitterrand regime in France and the Mobutu one in Zaire. For another, a democratic regime must axiomatically be accountable to its own people, and external dependence – especially over domestically unpopular economic policies – can only weaken it; nor can it be assumed that the domestic interests which elected governments seek to promote will coincide with those of outside powers. The limits of Western intervention have already been shown up by events in Somalia and Yugoslavia, and the overall conclusion must be that democratic governments in Africa will have to survive on their own.

CONCLUSION

Attempting to predict the likelihood of democratic consolidation in African states is indeed a 'journey without maps'. Historical comparisons with cases of democratisation in other parts of the world, for example Latin America or Southern Europe, offer little guidance because of the vast differences which exist between the historical experiences and the social and economic structures of those areas in comparison with Africa. Even within Africa, a comparative examination of developments to date in the direction of democratisation provides at least as many questions as answers. We think it unlikely that observers of African politics a few years ago would have predicted that Ahmed Kerekou of Benin would be the first leader of a mainland African state to be voted out of office in a democratic election, or that Mali and Malawi would provide such clear examples of peaceful change through the ballot box. The precise conjunction of circumstances which may arise in any particular state is almost impossible to predict, and there will doubtless be more surprises, both positive and negative, down the road.

However, in spite of these difficulties, it still seems reasonable to argue that African states are not all equally likely, or unlikely, to consolidate democratic political systems. Some characteristics of states and political systems are clearly more likely to contribute to democratic consolidation than are their opposites. The balance of probability can then be said to favour those states with more favourable characteristics and fewer unfavourable ones, though even so, it would be unwise to adopt any deterministic approach. These characteristics, it seems to us, are most conveniently summarised under the headings of economy, culture and leadership.

The capacity for economic growth and development, which must ultimately underpin the government of any state which depends on meeting the minimal expectations of its people, is not equally shared among African

states. This capacity is not simply a product of policy-making and administration – though really bad government can destroy an economy faster than
anything else – but also of the resource base available. In tandem with
economic growth, we should consider not just the distribution of benefits
but the perceptions of distribution, the latter notably involving the avoidance of conspicuous corruption. Democratic consolidation is more likely in
states which can achieve at least modest economic growth (and this does
not apply to all), and convince the population that this is not too unequally
shared. Some types of resource base, and notably those which convey large
sums by way of rent to whoever controls the national government, are
inherently vulnerable to inequality and corruption – a point which helps to
explain why no African oil-exporting state, from Algeria south to Angola
by way of Nigeria, Cameroon and Gabon, has yet achieved a successful
democratic transition.

African states likewise differ markedly in the extent to which their
peoples have become accustomed to associating peacefully together. In
some states, indigenous values or attitudes towards government arising
from well before the colonial era – 'governmentalities' as Bayart terms
them – may retain a profound influence over the possibilities for peaceful
political competition. States where a vibrant civil society exists, or can
fairly rapidly be developed, are more likely to be able to consolidate
democratic systems than ones where civil society is weak. The presence of
active churches and other institutions which help to provide a moral basis
for social and political life may be more important in this respect than
organisations that attract the support from a narrow professional elite
whose members aspire to political careers. Though ethnicity or 'tribalism'
is not, as we have already argued, the barrier to democracy that it is often
taken to be, there are none the less different patterns of identity in different
states which may be more or less conducive to electoral competition.
African states have, too, in the more than thirty years since independence,
built up different attitudes or traditions towards political life which may
help to guide their futures.

The role of individuals is none the less critical, and few if any African
states have passed the point at which societal and institutional pressures can
so guide the political system that leadership is reduced to a secondary
consideration. To take the examples of probably the two most important
states in the continent, the role of Mandela in the transition to democracy in
South Africa and the refusal of Babangida to carry through his own programme for a multi-party system in Nigeria have both had incalculable
effects, not just within their own states but through the regions within
which each of those states is the dominant power.

One further characteristic which is often overlooked is size. While there is no necessary link between democracy and a small population (Equatorial Guinea has one of the smallest populations in Africa, but has experienced nothing but brutal authoritarianism since independence), the evidence suggests that smallness helps. The past experience of Botswana, Mauritius and The Gambia (the 1994 *coup d'état* notwithstanding), or the more recent experience of democratic transition in Namibia, Cape Verde, Seychelles, and Sao Tome and Principe, none of which have a population of more than one and a half million, bear out this correlation.

None of these criteria enable us to draw any hard and fast conclusions; but rather than closing with mere vacuous generalisations, we find it more interesting to end with our own subjective assessments of the prospects for democratic consolidation in each of sub-Saharan Africa's forty-eight states, from the perspective of late 1994. However wildly inaccurate these asssessments may prove to be, they may help to show how the factors outlined above can be applied to individual states, and provide material for the amusement or derision (or just possibly the respect) of those who can look back on our judgement with the benefit of hindsight. To this end, we have allocated each state to one of four categories, according to whether we feel their prospects are good, fair, slight or more or less non-existent.

The states where we assess the prospects to be *good* are those where all or most of the positive characteristics identified above appear to exist, and where current problems and impediments seem to be soluble. These states are Botswana, Cape Verde, Mauritius, Namibia, Sao Tome and Principe, Senegal, Seychelles, South Africa and Zimbabwe. All of them have recently held reasonably fair multi-party elections and seem to be capable of maintaining the level of openness necessary for these to continue, though the extreme economic weakness of both Sao Tome and Cape Verde must count against them. It could seriously be argued that democracy has already been consolidated in Botswana and Mauritius.

The states where we assess the prospects to be *fair* exhibit many of the positive characteristics, but less convincingly so, and problems still exist. These states are Benin, Côte d'Ivoire, The Gambia (despite recent events), Ghana, Guinea-Bissau, Kenya, Lesotho, Madagascar, Malawi, Mali, Niger, Nigeria (again despite recent events), Swaziland, Tanzania and Zambia. Several of these have achieved the initial breakthrough of a peacefully contested change of government, and although many of them have problems either of leadership or of economic weakness, they all appear to have attained a level of self-identity which allows at least the possibility of stable democracy.

The states where we assess the prospects as *slight* exhibit some positive characteristics, but also have serious problems to overcome. These are Angola, Burkina Faso, Burundi, Cameroon, Central African Republic, Comoros, Congo, Djibouti, Eritrea, Ethiopia, Gabon, Guinea, Mauritania, Mozambique, Sierra Leone, Togo and Uganda. Few of these have yet achieved a peacefully contested change of government, and several of them have crippling economic weaknesses, uncertain national identities, high levels of militarisation and recent experience of civil war. While democratic consolidation cannot altogether be ruled out, we would not expect to find it in more than possibly one or two of these seventeen states.

There are seven states, finally, where prospects for democratic consolidation currently appear to us to be virtually *non-existent*, as the result of levels of government brutality and civil war which have destroyed or very seriously undermined the basis for statehood itself. These are Chad, Equatorial Guinea, Liberia, Rwanda, Somalia, Sudan and Zaire. Even in these cases, it may be noted that Liberia had an extraordinary (though highly inegalitarian) record of political stability for over a century until 1980; that Somali political culture in the 1960s was open and vibrant, though deeply fissured; and that Sudan has had a democratically elected government within the last decade. The foundations for democracy even in those states which once appeared to have reasonable prospects of it have none the less been shattered, and we would be extremely surprised (albeit agreeably so) if any of these were to emerge as consolidated democracies in the foreseeable future.

Though some readers may feel that we are being unduly optimistic in holding out even the prospect of democratic consolidation in so many African states, in some respects our conclusions are in fact more sombre than they may appear. The problem lies in the uncertainty of the prospects for stable and effective *non-democratic* states; and if authoritarianism fails to work, as it has evidently failed in so many African states over the past three decades, then the middle way between states which achieve at least some form of democracy on the one hand, and the traumatic experience of state collapse on the other, becomes frighteningly narrow.

Index